Max Schmeling: An Autobiography

Translated and Edited by
George B. von der Lippe, Ph.D.

Bonus Books, Inc.
Chicago, IL

02 01 00 99 98   5 4 3 2 1

Library of Congress Cataloging-in-Publication Data

Schmeling, Max, 1905–
   [Erinnerungen. English]
   Max Schmeling : an autobiography / translated by George B. von der Lippe.
     p.   cm.
   Includes index.
   ISBN 1-56625-108-7 (alk. paper)
   1. Schmeling, Max, 1905– . 2. Boxers (Sports)—Germany—Biography.
I. Title.
GV1132.S5A2913 1998
796.83′092—dc21
   [b]   98-24533
                                                         CIP

Bonus Books, Inc.
160 East Illinois Street
Chicago, Illinois 60611

Printed in the United States of America

Contents

Translator's Preface

When I happened upon Max Schmeling's autobiography a few years back in a small Heidelberg bookstore, I was looking for some enjoyable, recreational reading material with which to relax at the end of a workday. As a Germanist and boxing fan, I felt that I had made the perfect find. What I didn't realize at the time, however, was that once I had begun to read, I would never be able to put this book down until I had finished it. Max Schmeling's life story was simply one of the most compelling accounts that I had ever read. Notwithstanding his elegant prose, Max Schmeling tells of a life unparalleled in its depth and breadth of experience. He tells not only of a German life that spans this most tumultuous century in German history, but also of his incredible American odyssey during the twenties and thirties—a unique and enduring relationship to his American "second home." I knew immediately that this was a book that had to be brought to an American readership if at all possible.

I would like to make just a few notations for the benefit of the English-language reader, in order to establish a chronological context for Max Schmeling's life as lived and recounted. He was born on September 28, 1905, and his autobiography first appeared in German in 1977. The epilogue by Max Schmeling was written in 1998 especially for this English-language edition.

With respect to the translation, the English equivalent for any terms appearing in German generally follows immediately in brackets (e.g., *Rassenschande* [race crime]). Names and terms that might not be familiar to the reader appear with an asterisk (*), which indicates that there is additional information in the alphabetized glossary at the end of the text. Such names as appear multiple times may not be asterisked after their first two occurrences. Even a casual perusal of the glossary will serve to impress the reader with the sheer range and magnitude Max Schmeling's circle of friends and acquaintances in Berlin's "Golden Twenties"—a veritable "Who's Who" of the Weimar Republic's cultural elite, who were drawn first to the exotic presence of this world-class athlete but then more essentially to the enormously likeable, somewhat shy young man whose intellectual curiosity knew no bounds. At the same time, this list of names underscores just how many of the lives that comprised Max Schmeling's circle were disrupted or destroyed with the onset of the Third Reich. The reader will also note that many of those who were forced into exile found a new home in the USA, where they went on to further enrich the fabric of American cultural life.

The limited number of endnotes that appear within the text are to be found at the end of their respective chapters. Additionally, the glossary is followed by a complete record of Max Schmeling's career as a professional boxer.

Finally, I would like to express particular thanks to Sandra Braun of Ullstein Verlag in Berlin, without whose patience and untiring efforts this project might never have been completed.

GvdL

Fifty Years Later

Sometimes I see myself as a changing monument. Wherever I go, I'm met with a barrage of questions: What was your most important fight? What is your most vivid memory? Was it the fight with Sharkey, from whom you were the first non-American to win the heavyweight title? Or the victory over Joe Louis in 1936? Or the crushing defeat by him two years later? I'm usually at a loss for an answer, because I don't know myself. Sometimes I wonder whether it was any one fight at all, or whether it was more the larger fight as an experience of putting one's own existence on the line, of making life an adventure.

When I start this type of reflection, I'm not sure whether it is boxing to which I owe the greatest experiences of my life. Of course boxing was my world. I owe to it everything that I am. But wasn't it in the end perhaps only a means to break away from the crowd, to climb into the spotlight? When I think back, it is less the individual fights that emerge before my inner eye, but rather the satisfaction that from early on I was able to take my life into my own hands and make something of it.

I certainly do not intend to underrate the satisfaction that came from success and fame in the ring—police barracades, crowds of celebrating people, ticker-tape parades and motor escorts are overwhelming experiences for a man in his twenties. I had all that and greatly enjoyed it. But aside from that, it always meant a lot to me that I made my way in the social scene outside the ring, became friends with some prominent figures of that long-ago time. Actors from Fritz Kortner* and Emil Jannings* to Ernst Deutsch* and Marlene Dietrich,* to Gregory Peck and Douglas Fairbanks were part of that group. I met singers such as Michael Bohnen,* Heinrich Schlusnus,* or Richard Tauber* at the bars and cafes around the Kurfürstendamm* or on ocean voyages. And the artists of that time between the wars—from George Grosz* to Rudolf

Belling* and Renée Sintenis* to Ernesto de Fiori used me as a model for painting and sculpture. All that was something for a man who had grown up in Hamburg-Eilbek.

But the accomplishment that has drawn perhaps the least public attention was probably my greatest success: that, after my boxing career had ended and I had lost everything—when I stood before the unknown with a cardboard box in hand as the sixteen-year-old once had—I was able to start over. With that I proved to myself that I was more than just a successful prizefighter, and I think that is what makes me proudest.

A lot of the things that were once important to me have faded from memory: fireside meetings with Hitler at the Reich Chancellory or on outings to Tegernsee; Franklin D. Roosevelt's visit to my training camp and my correspondence with him; my clash with the Reich Ministry of Sports when they insisted that I drop my Jewish manager; the paratroop jump over Crete into defending English gunfire; the "stolen" victory against Sharkey that cost me the title; none of that bothers me anymore. It's all behind me now, like so much else.

Really, no single event comes to mind when I think back. Isn't it, after all, the decades with Anny that really mattered—no earth-shaking event, simply happiness. That was really it.

What about my life? Let's take a look back.

—1976

1
My Youth in Hamburg

I am fourteen years old and stand with my father at the window of our fifth-floor apartment on Hasselbrookstrasse. The street is gray and it's foggy outside. World War One had ended over a year ago, and there has been no color for five years. Diagonally across there are stairs leading down to a grocery store. A few worn signs indicate a cobbler's shop, the grocery store, and a pub. It's a district in which workers and lower middle class live.

My father has just asked me if I had given any thought to the future. School was behind me. I hadn't been a particularly gifted pupil, but there hadn't been any real problems except for singing. As compensation, however, I had been one of the best in school at sports. At fourteen no boy thinks a great deal about the future or a career. The war was just over, and returning soldiers filled the streets; no one had any great expectations at that time.

My father had gone to sea as a navigator for HAPAG.* Our family came from the village of Klein-Luckow in Uckermark.* At some point my father had brought us to Hamburg, so that he could be with his family whenever he returned from his travels. He envisioned for me a career calling for physical strength, as I was quite strong for my age. My mother, who had worked for the postal service during the war, had somehow always gotten extra food rations for me, my brother and little sister, even during the time known as Turnip Winter.[1] We were luckier than most.

Unscrupulous types sought to make a profit from the terrible need. I still remember the scandal surrounding a businessman whose potted meat had sold very quickly. It was soon discovered, however, that the meat consisted of rats, and he came close to being lynched by an angry mob. But instead he was tied to a wagon and paraded around the city amid shouts and curses before being thrown into the Alster River. He was then fished out and taken to the city hall. He was said later to have been found guilty and sentenced.

I had gone along with the parade and came home filled with the experience. But my telling of the story brought only punishment rather than the applause I had expected. For my father, participation in this type of mob activity was against his sense of order. Besides, there had been shooting in the inner city, and when the Hamburg Spartakists[2] had riddled the city hall with bullets, I had barely escaped by jumping into a building hallway.

A few weeks later there was a job opening at the ad placement agency William Wilkens. I had already worked there from time to time as a messenger, and now they were offering me an apprenticeship, which I accepted immediately. The entire enterprise consisted of Herr Wilkens, the clerk Herr Schramm, and an additional office worker, Fräulein Kühn. As an apprentice I was to handle petty cash and operate the machine that copied the bills and checks. Every day I went to the *Hamburg Correspondent* and the *Hamburg News* and brought them the stencil; then I delivered the copy back to our office. But my greatest moment came whenever Herr Wilkens allowed me to wash and polish his Isotta, a large car with chrome lamps and flashing spoked wheels.

Wilkens also encouraged my passion for sports, especially track and wrestling. I played goalie for the St. George Youth Soccer Team as well. I was regarded as having good hands and quick reflexes, and my idol was Heiner Stuhlfauth, the goalkeeper of the championship Nuremberg team. For a while I thought that I would become a pro soccer player.

Boxing, about which my world-travelling father had told me a great deal, played almost no role in the sports clubs of that time. In the old Reich boxing had been illegal; and although it was said that even the sons of the crown prince secretly boxed, it remained publicly limited to a very small circle up until the early postwar years. Even Otto Flint, the German heavyweight champion until 1920, had to fight mostly hidden from the eyes of the law. Boxing had really been reintroduced to Germany by a group of returning prisoners of war who had learned it from their English guards. A number of these German boxers were drawn to Walter Rothenburg, a versatile and gifted man who came across as a mix of army officer and captain of industry. Smart, energetic, and enterprising as he was, he became Germany's first boxing promoter, and I am thankful to him for part of my career and for his lasting friendship.

In any case, I was rather intrigued when one of the local movie theaters advertised a film about the world heavyweight championship fight between Jack Dempsey and Georges Carpentier. The film impressed me so much that I saw it practically every evening for a week, spending most of my apprentice's pay. At home, too, I couldn't restrain my enthusiasm, and my mother told me later that my boxing chatter started to get on everyone's nerves. Then, finally, I was able to convince my father to come along, and as the film ran I watched him, trying to determine what kind of impression the fight scenes were making on him. But his face showed nothing, even when Dempsey scored his spectacular knockout in the fourth round. On the way home I kept trying to infuse my father with some of my enthusiasm. But he just kept walking, saying nothing. Then, finally, he seemed to have guessed the reason for my excitement; stopping, he asked me with gentle amusement whether I was seriously thinking of boxing as a profession. For a moment I stared at him in surprise, because I really hadn't had that thought at all. I said nothing. But after a few steps my father held back, maybe fearing that he had hurt my feelings. Anyway, he then came right out and said, "I have nothing against it if you want to take boxing lessons."

A few days later I bought my first boxing gloves at a secondhand store. I still remember bringing home the worn and patched gloves and how I hung them over my bed like a sacred relic. Boxing's lure—dreams of epic battles—had captured me forever.

---

[1] A time of home-front privation during World War One known as the *Kohlrüben-winter* or "Turnip Winter."

[2] The Spartakists were members of the *Spartakusbund,* a radical arm of the Social Democrat Party (SPD) that developed during World War One under the leadership of Karl Liebknecht and Rosa Luxemburg; it became the German Communist Party (KPD) in 1918 and was put down during the bloody November Revolution of 1918-19.

2
The Decision to Box

My next big decision was made by boxing, and it determined the path that the rest of my life would take. My father was right: the office work at Wilkens soon bored me. When a job as a pipe fitter opened up at the construction firm Otto Meyer, I took it. But shortly after starting I injured my right hand and found myself, arm in sling, suddenly unemployed. I can still hear the words of my friend and co-worker Matthias Jung (who also dreamed of a boxing career) that we should head out for the Rhineland. Nothing would come of boxing here in Hamburg, but a number of boxing clubs had been started in the West under the English occupying forces,[1] and there we would have a chance to make something of ourselves.

    We soon talked ourselves into a Rhineland frenzy and decided to pack our bags and take off. But when the day of departure arrived, my friend lost his courage. My parents also tried to talk me out of my impetuous and seemingly immature decision; my father called it a foolish prank. But my impatience couldn't be contained. My desire to box had become all-consuming and even stronger than my sense of family. So I took off by myself.

    I felt sort of uneasy that evening as I boarded the train leaving from the Hamburg station. It was a so-called "wood-class" train, and my car was filled with the biting stench of the brown coal that was used to fuel the locomotives during that time of shortages. I vaguely remember a few of my fellow passengers, simple people who sat silently in the darkness, wrapped in their coats, trying to get some sleep. But I never closed my eyes, and I only remember that from time to time my heart beat wildly as the train rumbled along the departing tracks.

    With almost no money and knowing nobody I arrived in Düsseldorf. Here too the search for work was hard. The occupation of the Rhineland had only increased the general misery, and the first signs of inflation were already being felt.[2] Crowds of the unemployed formed in front of factory gates, a dark mass in cheap overalls. And I can still see the English sentries: apparently this was the officers' headquarters of the occupying army. For an unskilled apprentice it was an impossible undertaking to find a job.

So for several days I ran from office to office looking for a job: "Do you have *anything*?" Finally I was taken on by a glass factory where, to my amazement, I could begin immediately in the otherwise empty firm. When I came back from lunch there were a dozen workers blocking the entrance who threatened me and called me a strikebreaker. Helplessly, I tried to explain that I was no strikebreaker and had only been doing my job. But they seemed to feel that I was insulting them, because they then began to drag me towards the Rhine to throw me in.

Somehow I managed to break free and went into a fighting stance, yelling, "OK, go ahead and try," and they let me go. But they wanted to know where I was from, and even after I had explained to them that I was new to the city and had only been trying to find work, they still mistrusted me, and one of them accompanied me on the streetcar back to my furnished room in Grafenberg, just to check out my story.

But then I had some luck. Just a few days later I found work at a well-excavation firm, and I liked the outdoors work more than any I had done to that point. Most of all, I now had the time to devote to my sport. I joined a sports club in Benrath, where they practiced pyramids, lifted weights, and staged boxing matches. But this was a "strength sports" club, which really wasn't a good place for a novice boxer. Strength sports require short, bulky muscles, where a boxer should have long, flexible muscles requiring a different type of training. So I soon began to look around for a regular boxing club.

I was, therefore, quite pleased when my firm transferred me to Cologne-Mülheim, where there were two well-known boxing clubs that were already staging public boxing evenings. Both clubs later became famous—one was the Colonia-Cologne Club, and the other, which I joined, was the Mülheim Boxing Club. That was where I spent my free evenings. Nothing else mattered. I still remember going to the movies a couple of times—the first Charlie Chaplin film, as well as *The Cabinet of Dr. Caligari*.* I had saved my money to see them, but they really didn't mean much to me. Boxing was now my world.

The Catholic Rhineland mentality was really foreign to me. I came from the Protestant North, which was rather severe in its outlook and saw life as a struggle. Here, however, the people enjoyed life, happily partaking of its pleasures. This was particularly evident in the clergy. Back home at the St. George Sports Club it would have been unthinkable to see a clergyman sitting at ringside. But here, next to our practice rings, the cassocks often mingled with the other spectators, and not infrequently it was a priest who cheered the loudest.

❦

The old imperial ban on boxing had long since been forgotten. The clergy openly supported such activities as a positive alternative to more questionable doings. One of the priests who had befriended the young boxing enthusiasts told me that it had been, after all, St. Bernard who in 1201 had encouraged boxing matches in Tuscan Siena, in order to put an end to the knife fights that had plagued the area: the combatants would box instead. There was even some thought in church circles of making St. Bernard the patron saint of boxers.

At that time I started to learn something of the history of boxing; until then I had only known that it had originally come to Germany via English sailors. I now learned that at the beginning of the eighteenth century an English boxer named James Figg had started the first boxing school and after fifteen victories had declared himself the "pugilistic champion." These crude beginnings had been refined a half century later by an English nobleman, the Marquis of Queensbury. And a few years after that the rules were further modified by a Scotsman named John Scholte, in order to conform to his sense of fairness. That was when boxing gloves became mandatory and the three-minute round was introduced. At the same time illegal punches and maneuvers were established, and boxing was given a system.

The Mülheim Boxing Club didn't have a real trainer, but there was a member who had had a few professional bouts. He was the older brother of the future European champion Franz Dübbers, and it was from him that I got my beginner's course in real boxing. We all met several times a week, and Adolf Dübbers gave us instructions in footwork, body movement, defensive moves, and punching techniques—it was all a bit amateurish, but we were dead serious.

One evening he said to us, "You're all holding your hands wrong —you'll break them in a real match." Then he took two wooden slats and bound them to our wrists so that the lower arm and back of the hand made a straight line. Any bending of the wrist would now be painful. Explaining, he added, "The same way a bent stick gives way when thrust, you won't have any punching power if you bend your wrist." He also gave us hard rubber balls that we were to continually squeeze in our fists. "Your hands have to get hard, boys," he used to say, "and flexible at the same time"—all very modest lessons, but lessons which, I believe to this day, are indispensable knowledge for the boxer who takes his craft seriously. It was exactly these small, practical lessons that helped me so much, because up until then the Dempsey film and a page-worn book of instruction by Georges Carpentier had been my only teachers.

Then came my first important bout and, as luck would have it, my opponent was a thin blond boy named Louis. I was fighting him for the amateur championship of western Germany,[3] and I lost by a close margin.

The loss didn't depress me. After all, it was a championship fight at a time when my career had barely begun. I saw Willy Louis a few more times and fought him twice as a pro. Both times, in 1924 and early 1926, I scored emphatic first-round knockouts. Louis was an excellent technician, but he had no punching power and didn't take a punch very well. So he disappeared from the scene almost as fast as he had appeared, and I never heard of him again.

Despite my loss, I fought in 1924 for the Western Germany team at the German Championships in Chemnitz. In the light-heavyweight division I won all my qualifying fights up to the finals, where my opponent was the experienced Otto Nispel, who had already earned a certain measure of fame—a left-handed virtuoso who would later become one of the stars of the Berlin boxing club, "Heros." Like most boxers of his generation, Nispel had a rugged constitution and no fear of trading punches; the refined techniques of movement—lightning-quick ducking and side-stepping—were unknown. That all really didn't start until Dempsey.

I only have a vague recollection of how the fight went. In any case, a tie-breaking round at the end was supposed to decide the fight, but it too was even. After a second such round, Nispel was awarded the fight on points. But I must have made a passable impression on that October 10, 1924, because Arthur Bülow, the influential editor of *Boxsport,* said to some friends who had told him of me, "So that's your man! Cold-blooded, but no notion of boxing. He has to be totally retrained—learn to punch with a fluid motion. But there's potential. If he learns how to fight, he can be a world champion!"

Another encounter around this time was also pretty important. After a fight, Hugo Abels, a manager from Cologne, came up to me and said, "Listen, Schmeling! I was watching you. You still have a lot to learn, but you show talent. You should turn pro. I would manage you. You could make something of yourself." I still remember my reply: "Of course I want to turn pro, but I have the feeling that it's still too soon." I had turned nineteen by then. Abels answered simply, "My boy, you can't start too soon." He mentioned a few big names as examples, among them none other than my idol Jack Dempsey. He had begun at fifteen.

That was in July 1924. I went home, gave notice on my furnished room, and moved to Hugo Abels's place in Cologne. He had a large apartment on Heinsbergstrasse with a spare room where I took up residence. He owned a rolling-blinds-and-doors business and spent his days mostly at his office; he looked the part of a typical businessman.

Now I was a pro. I had no other profession. Boxing was now my life.

And with that, my daily routine took on a totally new rhythm. I would no longer take it easy on myself. Everything else became secondary to training. Gone were the long evenings with friends, gone was life by whim without order now that there were stricter rules than ever before. But I never felt these new restrictions to be a sacrifice. From the very start it was clear to me that achievement was built on discipline. No inventor, no businessperson, no important researcher reached their goal easily. Accomplishment in sports also demands the commitment of one's entire self: morally, intellectually, spiritually. Discipline over the body alone does not make a great athlete. The will to achieve the exceptional demands the ultimate concentration on one's goal.

People used to wonder why, before a big fight, or even after a long layoff, I never had to lose any great amount of weight. From the first bell of the first sparring round I fought, I was usually in shape. That is a matter of attitude and will. In my case, the price to be paid for the performance I wanted lay in an ever-present self-discipline: it was the drive to go to bed early, to avoid alcohol and cigarettes, to live life according to a strict diet—and not just with respect to food. To the young athletes who visit me from time to time, I always say, "Don't kid yourselves! The years between twenty and thirty don't belong to you. For half a dozen fights which will live on only in the memories of a few experts, you have to give up the best years of your life."

But a slight delay in reaction time, a letdown in exact timing, a deficient punch, or the famous "glass jaw" can cost one a career *despite* all the sacrifice. And even if all the right traits are there, it can still be that a boxer lacks what the Americans call "brains"—that which is valued more than any other physical advantage: ring intelligence. Without it a boxer will never make it to the top.

I experienced what it means to have all that—but I also know what it means to no longer have it. When I had to start from scratch again after the war and boxed with mixed success, many thought that the forty-year-old had lost his self-discipline. In fact, I still had it. What was lacking were the few hundredths of a second in reaction time, which couldn't be restored by any amount of effort, training, or self-denial. I alone and a few friends were the only ones who knew. My defeats were no surprise to me.

On August 2, 1924 I had my first pro fight. My opponent's name was Jean Czapp, a local boy from Düsseldorf. As I went into the ring, I felt the way I would usually feel just before a fight; first of all, I wasn't boxing for sports glory. I stood in my corner with the awareness that my very existence was being staked on whether I would win or lose. After six rounds of a scheduled eight-rounder I was awarded the victory by TKO. The win brought my first notoriety in the local papers. I cut out the articles and sent them to my parents.

From August to December 1924 I appeared no less than ten times in the ring. Among my opponents were two Americans, a Belgian, and a

Frenchman. Practically all of my fights were won in the early rounds, thanks to my hard right. Only once was I defeated—my victorious opponent was the Berliner Max Dieckmann, at that time the hardest puncher in the light-heavyweight division. The defeat had to happen in the Berlin Sports Palace. In the second round Dieckmann caught me on the ear with one of his notorious hooks, and it started to bleed immediately. Between rounds my corner tried unsuccessfully to stop the bleeding. Two rounds later, the referee stopped the fight.

After a string of wins in the next few months, the experts started to notice me. At the beginning of 1925 I was again in Berlin: "Mehling versus Schmeling" read the posters on the kiosks. After six rounds I was declared the winner on points, and Arthur Bülow praised me in his article, as did other Berlin journalists who had noticed my improvement since the amateur championships in Chemnitz.

Managers also started to become interested. A few wanted me to switch over to them, some making very attractive offers. Up until then I had been getting between 100 and 200 marks per fight. Now I suddenly had a telegram from Walter Rothenburg in front of me that offered a fight against the best-known Hamburg boxer: "Offering for the fight Schmeling versus Stein 800 marks." I said to Abels, "That can't be true! No one has that kind of money. It'll never happen!" And it never did. The fight never took place.

At the same time, the heavyweight champion Jack Dempsey came to Europe on his honeymoon. He had just married the film diva Estelle Taylor and showed up in Cologne with an impressive entourage—Jack Dempsey, my idol since I had seen him years before in Hamburg in the film of his fight against Carpentier. Dempsey had come to boxing at a time when technique and tactics were starting to replace pure punching; he combined excellent boxing skills with a tremendous punch, like some fighter from another galaxy. Not without good reason was he called the "man killer" by his countrymen.

The Luna Park in Cologne had a big day with Dempsey showing off his wares to thousands of spectators. I was one of three Cologne boxers who were chosen to box two exhibition rounds each with him. Since I was last, I watched him carefully and noticed that his punches were always delivered with the full power of his shoulders. Finally I climbed into the ring, excited but determined not to make a bad impression. Since I was a whole weight class under Dempsey, I wanted to make up for size with speed. Using this tactic, I actually managed to get a good punch past Dempsey's rather casual guard. Of course, the world champion wasn't fazed or hurt; but for a moment he looked surprised and even a little concerned. A cheer came from the crowd which was worth more to me than the 100 marks which I received for the brief appearance.

A lunch in Dempsey's honor was given the next day at the Dom Hotel. Instead of the incapacitated mayor Dr. Adenauer,* the vice-mayor, local politicians, sports figures and dignitaries came, about fifty people in all. When the lunch was over, Dempsey came up to me and said a few kind words, telling me that I was a future champion. I was very proud and thought of how my father had asked me after our movie outing whether I ever intended to compete at that level. A few years later in New York, after Dempsey and I had become friends, I reminded him of his earlier prophesy. He only laughed and said, "That's what I told all the young boxers I met back then."

Also in 1925 I had a total of ten mostly winning fights, eight of them against foreigners; boxing had definitely become international. But despite this success, I still thought about what I would do when a necessarily short boxing career was over. Originally I had thought of a retail business. But then one hot summer day I noticed how quickly ice-cream cones sold in hot, humid Cologne. So I went to Abels and suggested starting an ice-cream factory: "Hugo, you have an empty cellar downstairs. We could set up a machine down there and hire a girl to make ice cream." Abels let himself be talked into it, and I invested my entire savings in the enterprise, around 600 marks. The business started pretty well. We hired two men who pulled a colorful ice-cream wagon through the streets, and before long our sales were quite respectable. I saw myself as an entrepreneur.

At this time I received a letter from a Herr Sandwiener, whose wife was appearing in the Busch Circus in Mainz as "The World's Strongest Woman." Frau Sandwiener—in fact a colossal woman as she appeared in the spotlight to the roll of drums—bent rusty horseshoes straight, broke chains, and withstood the weight of cars driving over her: she was indeed very impressive. The couple had a son who, as one might expect, was very strong, and his parents wanted him trained as a boxer. So for a handsome salary and room and board at the circus, Herr Sandwiener offered me the job of teaching his offspring the rudiments of boxing.

I had enough time before my next fight, so I agreed. For four weeks I travelled the Rhine-Main area with the knife-throwers, magicians, and fire-eaters. Mornings I trained the boy, and in the afternoon I made myself useful. I helped the stable boy with the horses, hung decorations and posters, hosed down the elephants. On the last day of my wandering life with the jugglers, Luigi Toniselli, our young tightrope artist, fell from a bicycle during rehersal on the highwire. For a moment he lay motionless in the sand. But it was nothing serious, only a broken collarbone and a moment's unconsciousness.

⌒⌒⌒

But the brief scare was enough to make a lasting impression. For the first time I became aware of how "break-neck," in a literal sense, the life of the *artiste* can be. And yet it was just such a life that I had chosen. My future performances would also be in the spotlight. All of us who stood in the arena's spotlight were vagabonds. And each one of us risked the fatal plunge at any given moment. It is this constant risk which made the lifestyle of the boxer, like that of the *artiste,* so uncertain; but in the risk lay at the same time a great attraction, which, for me anyway, never let go. That is also the reason why I felt so comfortable in the circus world and have never forgotten the short interlude with "The World's Strongest Woman."

There was a surprise waiting for me when I returned to Cologne. For when I asked Abels about the sales figures for our cellar ice-cream factory, it turned out that there weren't any: pressed for money, Abels had liquidated our business. The machine and ice-cream wagon had been sold for a total of 250 marks. Abels had paid his debts with that, and my savings were gone. It would be a long time before I dared play the entrepreneur again.

From that time on, my relationship with Abels began to deteriorate. After his wife died a short time later, Abels wanted nothing more to do with boxing. Maybe he had also lost faith in my career. In any case, we went our separate ways.

So I was unexpectedly without a manager, and as I was sitting in the locker room one day before a match in Cologne, the door suddenly opened and a small, lively man was standing before me. "Who are you and what's your name?" he asked. Right away I told him my name. "I know that," he replied, "but who manages you? Who's your second?" I shrugged my shoulders: "I don't know. At the moment nobody." Without hesitation he said, "Look, I'll do it." When I entered the ring, he was waiting there with a helper to cool me off between rounds while he coached me. I won the fight by KO, and when I thanked him afterwards, he said, "You've got talent—we can make something of you."

That was my first encounter with Max Machon, a Berlin native who had started in horse racing and who had come to this boxing evening in Cologne with his protégé, Richard Naujoks, known by the sports writers as "King Richard." A short while later, Machon would become my manager, trainer, and closest friend.

But for the time being, I found a spot in the stable of Willi Fuchs, a well-known Cologne trainer who guided a few promising boxers. His premier fighter, who would take on any challengers, was Hein Domgörgen, the German middleweight champion. Pretty soon I noticed that Domgörgen, one of the most technically brilliant German fighters of that time, received all of

Fuchs's attention while I was pretty much ignored. I didn't want to be a third wheel. So one day it finally came to a confrontation with Fuchs, and I decided to leave Cologne. As my destination I chose Berlin.

[1]As one of the conditions of the Treaty of Versailles, German territory west of the Rhine was a demilitarized zone occupied by Allied forces (from 1919 until Hitler's defiance in March 1936).

[2] The legendary German inflation of the early twenties reached a point where a dollar had been worth 4.20 marks in 1914 and by November 1923 the exchange rate was 4.2 *trillion* marks to the dollar.

[3] "Western Germany" at this point is not to be confused with the designations East and West Germany after World War II.

❦

3

Rise in Berlin

Tired and aching from the ten-hour train ride, I arrived in Berlin on an early summer morning in 1926. Up on the luggage rack was the cardboard box holding everything I owned: a couple of shirts, a second pair of pants, a suit, and my boxing gloves. The train gradually reduced speed, the pine forests started to fade, and in the small villages that surround any large city I began to see a mix of brick houses, small factories, and barracks-like complexes. The single track that we had travelled since early dawn became many as we neared the city. Soon there emerged the first of the courts behind the buildings, blackened walls with worn ads, broken up by small garden plots with their weekend huts.[1] In the residence windows were geraniums and the occasional tomato plant. The great capital city presented itself to the traveller as do all such cities when seen from an approaching train—poor, gray, dirty. But it was the city in which I placed all my hopes. At Friedrichstrasse station I brought my box to the luggage check. It was 5:30 A.M. and the heart of the city was still dead. I had an appointment with Arthur Bülow at *Boxsport* magazine to get whatever information he could give me, but since his office didn't open until nine, I had over three hours to kill. So I wandered aimlessly around Friedrichstadt (which was then the real heart of the city), walked down Unter den Linden* to the Palace, up to Alexanderplatz, and then back to Friedrichstrasse station.

Slowly the city awakened. I encountered the milk wagons and paperboys. The first streetcars screeched into Königsplatz. From the subway trains came first a few and then increasingly more people, either ready for bed or starting their workday; everywhere—kiosks, stores, apartment buildings —were posters and signs. The city seemed to consist solely of theatre openings, sporting events, and other amusements. In a little pub, the stale smell of

~∽∼

last night still in the air, I ate a standing breakfast.[2] Even as I stood drinking
my coffee, overwhelmed by the awakening but still impressive capital city, I
was sure that I had made the right move. From my first time in Berlin, when I
had fought in the Sports Palace, I had known that a real career would only be
launched from this city. Success in Hamburg, Cologne, or Düsseldorf couldn't
bring a young man to the top. The jungle of screaming posters through which
I had been walking for the past two hours had convinced me that this was true
for any profession. Actors, directors, show-business people, artists, musicians:
they all had to make it in Berlin. That gave the city life, change, chaos—the atmosphere of a huge cultural train station. In Cologne they had often referred
to Berlin as a modern Whore of Babylon; but on this morning I began to realize that this was the city of gold for anyone who wanted to make it to the top.

The man behind the counter pulled me from my thoughts: "Hey,
young man, another coffee?" I gestured "no," still used to weak breakfast tea.
And while he mechanically wiped the counter, an attractive young woman
who had been eyeing me from the next table joined in. "It's on me—give him
another and put it on my check." She was blond, with a short pageboy cut and
a jaunty cap, wearing a violet-colored silk dress. She had a flowing boa on her
shoulders and was probably around twenty. She brought her cup over to my
table and started talking. Mute from shyness and only occasionally looking up,
I stood there sipping my coffee.

Except for the girl there was only one other patron in the cafe: a
young man of about thirty joined us, slightly drunk from the previous evening
and wearing a tuxedo. They seemed to know each other. He began to speak
of this and that, of lost chances and new opportunities. Just a few days ago he
had run into an old friend from the cavalry, now with great connections, and
everything was going to take off now; he only had to move on this one—people would see. I think he was mostly trying to convince himself. He then left,
and the girl soon left too.

"Two of my regulars," said the barman. "They come in every few days.
At one time he was somebody, but no more." Without passing judgment, he
told me that the man had been a cavalry officer from Saxony, ruined by the
war. Then the bartender brightened, "The little lady," he said, "sure, she
makes her living on her back right now. But she'll be somebody. She knows
what she wants! She won't be beaten! She's pulling herself together!" By way
of a summary observation he concluded, "An exemplary girl!"

Just before nine I found myself at the door of the *Boxsport* office on
Schiffbauerdamm. Bülow greeted me cordially. He remembered my appearances in Chemnitz and Berlin. I didn't say anything about having pulled up
stakes in Cologne and told him that I had only come to Berlin to see the fight between Paul Samson-Körner and Franz Diener. In fact I didn't even have the price

of a ticket. Bülow must have sensed that, because when I left he pressed twenty marks into my hand. "You can pay me back when you have it," he said at the door, and then shouted after me, "maybe you should just stay in Berlin. We've got good training facilities here. Think about it! The opportunities for a guy like yourself are better here than in Cologne." I promised to think it over.

The next day I left my little bed-and-breakfast and took the *S-Bahn* [streetcar] to Treptow. The ring for the championship match was in the middle of a bicycle-racing track known to Berliners as "Noodle Top." I had never attended a boxing match of this magnitude. Samson-Körner had spent a while in America and had even boxed the great Gene Tunney to a draw. He had picked up the American style: that is, no-nonsense and effective. The bull-like Franz Diener was still a relatively young up-and-comer. The fight went back and forth for the distance, and Diener's victory on points was controversial. But it was a great fight.

Still under the spell of the fight, I found myself once again in front of Bülow. But this time he wasn't alone; on the other side of the desk sat Max Machon, who had been so helpful in Cologne. They were speaking about the training camp that Machon had recently set up in Lanke bei Bernau (with financial input from Bülow) just outside of Berlin. Machon trained three top-notch fighters, and Bülow asked me if I'd like to join the stable, saying that Machon was a first-rate trainer and the conditions at the camp were ideal.

I gathered all my courage and confessed that I couldn't afford the stay in a training camp. So Bülow asked Machon if he would take me on and train me for fifty marks a month, which he would gladly put up. Machon agreed and took me out to the camp that very day. The training camp was located at an old resort. The owner, Heinz Modisch, was more a friend than a landlord. Here, only a half-hour from the great metropolis, there reigned a friendly country atmosphere that to this day I've never experienced anywhere else. We had our routine. In nice weather we trained outdoors in the courtyard behind the hotel. When it rained we moved into a nearby abandoned millhouse. On the weekend we would get a few visitors from Berlin who watched us, told us of the city, and played billiards with us.

One enthusiastic visitor was a young scamp who was somewhat small and thin for his age. The boy, who was the most avid fan of our sparring sessions, had been taken in by an uncle after his father's death in a bike-racing accident. He was nervously twisting his hat in his hands when Machon asked him his name. "Frömming," he said, "Hans Frömming." He later became the most famous trotting jockey in the world, known as "The Wizard of the Sulky."

Our training was hard and our pleasures harmless—maybe a stroll and then coffee in a cafe. More than that we neither had nor wanted. The days were all the same. We got up at 6:30, put on a heavy sweater over our sweatsuits and

⌒⌒⌒

began our run through the woods surrounding Berlin, a hilly landscape of pines and lakes. Following a distance run, we did 100-meter sprints, then ran hills, and then did calisthenics; it was an early form of interval training. Our distance run soon increased from fifteen to twenty kilometers. Back at camp, a massage followed, then came breakfast. The rest of the morning was taken up by instruction, where Machon often showed us fight films of famous boxers to demonstrate the fine points. Lunch came before noon so that we could sleep two hours before training in the ring.

From time to time Bülow came by to monitor our progress. He had previously criticized my left hand on several occasions, saying that any success that I'd had was due to my hard right. Now he was praising not only my increased mobility but also my improved left.

Just a few weeks later Bülow got me my first fight. On July 13, 1926 I knocked out August Vengehr in the first round. My entire purse came to eighty marks, which was less than I had gotten for my last fight in Cologne. But the victory and Bülow's astute management made me a contender. I wasn't yet twenty-one.

The boxing commission designated Max Dieckmann as my next opponent, to whom I had lost two years earlier and then boxed to a draw in a return bout. August 24 was to be the date. The bout took place in Berlin's Luna Park, located at the upper end of Kurfürstendamm.* It was an amusement park in the turn-of-the-century style. Shooting galleries, restaurants, carousels, and tents were crowded together, with a boathouse on the shore of Habensee. On this day the park was open only for boxing, and the spectators crowded around an open-air ring.

The four thousand fans expecting a dramatic confrontation hardly got their money's worth, because it was all over in thirty seconds. Thanks to my improved technique, I caught Dieckmann with a hard right flush on the chin before he had even thrown a punch. Soundlessly and with eyes wide open, he fell near his corner, and referee Paul Samson-Körner didn't even need to count ten. I say this without any conceit—that's just the way it happened.

That evening a small group of fifteen or twenty celebrated the victory. We met on the picture-book houseboat run by the gargantuan gourmet Paul Remde. Next to us was anchored the type of large float that you would see at the outdoor restaurants along the Wannsee. There were dancers from the amusement park and a magician performed some tricks. There were no speeches or champagne, but we probably had more fun in that small circle of friends than at all the grand banquets of later years.

When I opened the latest edition of *Boxsport* a few days later, I couldn't believe my eyes. It said in black and white: "Dieckmann defeated by a greater boxer—by a great boxer. German boxing has a new champion on which it can build, maybe a star in the boxing galaxy who has what it takes to surpass all those from the past and present."

For my victory over Dieckmann I got 1,500 marks. That was more than I had ever seen in one place. Now I could pay back Bülow's loan and declare my financial independence. Most of all, however, I was able to send more to my mother. She and my sister had followed me to Cologne shortly before my leaving for Berlin, and now they were alone again in a strange city.

At that time the title of German Champion meant something different than it does today. The newspapers began to publish photos of me, and for the first time there were now longer stories instead of just short notices. It was very strange to read my name with the addition "German Champion."

In the next ten months I had ten fights and won them all, eight by knockout. The tenth fight was for the European championship. Bülow had challenged the titleholder, the Belgian Fernand Delarge. The fight was to take place in mid-June at the Westfalen Hall in Dortmund.

In the meantime I was right at the light-heavyweight weight limit and had trouble making weight for the Delarge fight. Max Machon finally managed to get the surplus pounds off: he had me run hard for an hour, then bundled me in heavy wool blankets to sweat in bed. Of course I lost strength and some punching power by doing this, but I still won the fight against the Belgian European champion.

Delarge was a hard-punching combination fighter, but with the improvement of my boxing skills and increased movement I had him missing, followed by my heavy counterpunches. This strategy paid off. In the thirteenth round the title holder gave up with tears in his eyes. I was the first German boxer to win a European championship. "A new epoch has begun," read the newspapers.

After the victory over Delarge I travelled outside the country for the first time in my life. Machon had wanted to surprise me, and he did so at breakfast one morning with two tickets. "We are going to Paris and London," he said, and he further said that I had earned it and that it would be instructional for me to see the world championship fight in London between Tommy Milligan and Mickey Walker.

The omnipresent Bülow came along. In Paris I did the usual tourist tour from the Eifel Tower to the Pantheon. On Montmartre I saw the Sacre Coeur and Georges Carpentier, who was appearing at the Moulin Rouge with Mistinguette.* Seeing Carpentier in person was the high point of the trip. Backstage, Bülow and Machon introduced me as the new European champion,

∽∾∾

and it turned out that the great man had already read of the fight in the French press. "Delarge cried," said Carpentier over and over as he shook his head; he seemed unable to grasp this: "Cried!" We remained friends until his death.

In London as well, Bülow and Machon wanted to drag me on a sight-seeing tour, but my thoughts were only on the fight between Walker and Milligan. Milligan had predicted that he would beat his opponent and bring the title to England. But the unbelievably hard fight was to end in the ominous seventh round. The tough Scot fell victim to Walker's endless barrage of punches. By the sixth knockdown he was out for the referee's ten-count and longer.

Three experiences in particular made an impression on me. As I went through the turnstile of the London Olympia Hall, an usher tipped his hat and said respectfully, "Pass through, Mr. Dempsey." People had quite often commented on a striking resemblance between the American world champion and myself, the newcomer. Now for the first time I was being confused with him, and later Dempsey and I would play the trick of dressing alike to confuse people.

I saw then for the first time that while a boxing card in Germany was still being staged at amusement parks and bicycle tracks, in England it was a social occasion. Around the ring sat members of society, men in tails and tuxedos, women in fine clothing: politicians, industrialists, film stars, and aristocrats.

The most lasting impression of all, however, was the fight itself. On the evening of June 30, 1927 I grasped for the first time how much concentration, mercilessness, and toughness American boxers brought to their profession. The way Walker hammered down his challenger, the ditchdigger Milligan, remained an unforgetable lesson for me. Here it was demonstrated to me for the first time how unconditionally the boxer puts his existence on the line.

But one dark shadow fell over this happy time. It was the time of the large motorcycles, and everyone dreamed of owning a big Norton or Harley-Davidson. The machines represented not only the intoxication by speed that was so characteristic of the times; the feeling of unlimited freedom played a role as well. It was *the* luxury ride—a status symbol for the rich and famous. Even we, out in Lanke, were obsessed by the idea. So with the money I was now making I bought a big Harley-Davidson with a sidecar. By then I had brought my mother and fourteen-year-old sister from Cologne to Berlin. On the weekends when I didn't have to train, I invited them for a ride through the surrounding countryside.

On one such outing we came to a detour. In changing lanes I lost control when we went over some debris from the road construction. All three of

༄

us landed in a ditch. More laughing than shaken up, my mother and I got up —only Edith lay motionless by the side of the road. In the fall she had hit the back of her head on a curbstone. A few hours later she died without regaining consciousness.

It was my first experience of deep and jarring pain, which only deepened with the gnawing guilt and self-recrimination. For days I was in shock, more in need of consolation myself than in a position to console my mother, for I had loved Edith very much.

As circumstances would have it, I was supposed to fight the American Jack Taylor five days later in Hamburg. I asked Walter Rothenburg to reschedule the fight. But although everyone, including my opponent, showed understanding and sympathy, a four-day postponement was the best that could be done. So immediately after Edith's funeral I had to fight. I had no concentration, and every round was extremely hard. Yet somehow I managed to scrape by with a win on points.

In the following three months I fought three more times, winning each contest by knockout. Immediately after these victories I received a challenge from none other than Hein Domgörgen, whom I knew from our time together in Cologne under Willi Fuchs. Fuchs, still smarting from my departure, wanted to prove to himself that he had made the right decision *for* Domgörgen and *against* me. He was so sure that Domgörgen would outbox me that he insisted, against our objection, that the entire purse go to the winner.

Domgörgen really was a great boxer, a textbook technician who had made boxing into an art. As a middleweight he was a weight class below me, but he expected to outmaneuver me with his boxing skill. Being a champion, he had the right to box for a title above his weight class.

The eagerly-awaited fight was to take place in Leipzig. On the day of the fight a great migration came from all over into the city. But the fight preparations were not going that well for me. I was again having trouble making weight, but I could not under any circumstances come in overweight against the [German] middleweight champion. To avoid losing the title at the weighin I had to struggle to come in at the weight limit. It was a torture that drained my strength.

Domgörgen was in tremendous shape. With his rapier left jab, dancing and ducking, he was soon clearly ahead on points. Yet once again the seventh round was decisive. For a split second he dropped his guard. The referee didn't need to count this time either; he helped Hein's handlers drag the fallen boxer to his corner. Because Willi Fuchs had chosen to play winner-takes-all, Domgörgen didn't get a penny, while I received 20,000 marks.

∽∾∾

The press raved. For the first time I rated headlines. But that was nothing compared to the hoopla surrounding the title fight with the Italian Michele Bonaglia in early January at the Berlin Sports Palace.

Only two minutes into the first round I hit him so hard that he went down in his corner as if struck by a lightning bolt. The Sports Palace erupted; suddenly there was a churning mob of fans surrounding me. Those near the ring broke into the national anthem and eight thousand fans joined them. Hundreds stormed the ring as never before in the Sports Palace. I stood there dazed as the title belt went around my waist again.

[1] Then as today, the beloved *Schrebergarten* is to be found on the outskirts of any German metropolis; the garden plot with its weekend hut (some quite luxurious) has been the favorite weekend pastime for stressed-out Germans since the mid-nineteenth century (introduced by Dr. Daniel Gottlob Moritz Schreber).

[2] At the German *Stehcafe* [standing cafe] the quick meal is eaten while standing at small elevated tables.

4

In Society

A short time later I was invited to the Victoria Street apartment of Alfred Flechtheim.* Flechtheim was one of the great art collectors of the twenties and the founder of *Querschnitt,* a witty, cosmopolitan magazine that reported somewhat snobbily on the Russian Revolution and modert art, the aesthetics of the streamline and the naked body. The invitation was my debut in the social scene.

Flechtheim was a slight, animated man with the bookish look of the intellectuals of the day. He also reflected the times in his passionate devotion to the sporting scene. As the maid led me into the living room, he greeted me enthusiastically: "I'm pleased that you're here. I know you probably don't know me, but I've followed you for a considerable time." Then he told me that he had not only seen nearly all of my Berlin fights, but, together with the sculptor Rudolf Belling* and the conductor Leopold Stokowski, he had travelled to Leipzig to see the Domgörgen fight.

That invitation to Flechtheim's was soon followed by others. Hardly a week went by that I wasn't meeting new people and soon making new friends. I was now in society. And that Berlin society of the twenties consisted not so much of the rich and important, but rather of those whose names were on the tip of everyone's tongue. Even the evening at Flechtheim's introduced me to a lively mix from all spheres: artists and bankers, showgirls, actors, journalists and writers, racing drivers and scholars. On this first evening I was approached by Heinrich Mann*—the sophistocate with glass in hand and accompanied by a striking woman—who asked me about some detail of boxing technique. I believe that on that evening I also met Fritz Kortner,* a small stocky man of demonic vitality. In our conversation he revealed himself as an avid boxing fan, and later he would travel throughout Germany to see my fights. We remained friends until his death, to the extent that anyone could be his friend. Also there was Josef von Sternberg,* who would shortly achieve world renown with Marlene Dietrich,* and German-Italian sculptor Ernesto de Fiori, a darling of the Berlin salons.

I must have cut a pretty strange figure in this circle. I was acutely aware that this was a world unto itself. Most of the names meant nothing to me, and I knew little of the matters they discussed. During the first evening I mostly stood there smiling politely and, unless the talk was of boxing, saying nothing. But everyone was interested in me and pulled me into their conversations. They were people for whom there were no outsiders, because in their own way they were themselves all outsiders. They were "society," and that society wanted to include me.

It was an overwhelming and also slightly unsettling experience for a young man of twenty-two. I knew that they were inviting me as the boxer, not Max Schmeling from Hamburg; only later would I be more than that to them. First and foremost I was yet another exotic presence for them, a kind of mythical animal. But I somehow belonged because I too was now someone who was talked about.

I think I served a double function in this era that had just discovered sports. As a boxer I symbolized sports. The "natural" now reigned, and the fall of Wilhelminian conventions—the corset and high collar—had brought with it a rather eccentric cult of the body: a glorification of the human body from the cabaret revue to nudism. No self-respecting intellectual journal refused to print nude photos. The Haller Revue brought dozens of undressed girls to the stage. *Querschnitt* published pictures of naked boxers in poses reminiscent of classical and renaissance sculptures, and the 1925 UFA* film *Paths to Strength and Beauty* offered the cultural history of the naked body from the beginning of mankind to the present. Some of this was truly comical, but behind it there was a longing for freedom.

The pronouncement of Kasimir Edschmidt*: "The story of mankind is possible without Aeschylus and Dante, but not without sailing," sounds pretty ridiculous today, but at that time he expressed the sports mania of a generation whose artists once again, really for the first time since classical antiquity, made the human body in sport and competition the subject of their art. Liebermann* painted riders and polo players, Raoul Dufy horse races and regattas, Beckmann* the fury of the bicycle race, and Futurism mythologized the "heroes at the wheel."

The boxer was here again the ideal. Ernesto de Fiori, who had sculpted Hindenburg,* Marlene Dietrich, and [Elisabeth] Bergner,* was now working on a Jack Dempsey sculpture. One day at Flechtheim's place he came

⤮⤮⤮

up to me and asked if I would model for him. And I also became good friends with the great Renée Sintenis,* the regal woman with the unforgettable Indian face. She too sculpted me in a fighting pose, and during that time we often met at the cafes around the Kaiser-Wilhelm-Gedächtniskirche.[1]

But it wasn't just society that had been infected by boxing fever. The passion became almost a mass mania. The two biggest Berlin newspapers, *BZ am Mittag* and the *Morgenpost,* offered boxing instruction for individuals and groups. I think this was more than just a wave of sports enthusiasm. People felt that through boxing courses they were being trained for real life; whoever trained harder and boxed better would be better prepared for the challenges of real life. But when I think back, it really was rubbish. The *BZ* quoted former Heavyweight Champion Jim Corbett as saying that whoever boxed would also be a better person and, therefore, a better citizen.

I later read in some book about the twenties that I was the "show-piece of the soirees" at Alfred Flechtheim's. But I never felt that way, and I really don't think that was the case. Once when Victor Schwanneke asked me to sign his guest book, I composed a comical little two-liner, which, when I think about it today, shows how badly I wanted to fit in this new milieu: "Artists, take me to your heart / For boxing too can be an art."

Of course I was aware of my limited knowledge and how unprepared I was to make conversation in my new surroundings. But I don't think that I've ever tried to be anyone except who I am. Now I began to read the classics, to go to the theater and film premieres. I no longer just read the sports section, and I bought the books that were being discussed. I said to myself, "You're a man from a humble background, what you didn't learn in school you'll learn now. Catch up. You can get what you missed."

I also dressed for the times: I bought a tuxedo and tails, two articles of clothing that everyone wore, whether to a premiere or at ringside. George Grosz,* the wild scourge of the bourgeoisie, would appear in high collar and double-breasted suit, topped off by a bowler hat—this was the attire of the day for any artist who wanted to appear the gentleman. Only two exceptions come to mind. Bertolt Brecht,* who also sought to shock the upstanding *Bürger* [middle-class citizen], and another scurrilous literary type whose name I've forgotten, but who was such a devotee of the Paris scene that he would dress each morning according to the weather report for Paris.

One day I visited a Picasso exhibition at Flechtheim's gallery on Lützowplatz. The gallery owner led me through the exhibition and attempted to give me a sense of modern art. At the end of the tour he gave me a questioning look, to which I managed with some embarassment and hesitation, "No, Herr Flechtheim, I would never hang this type of picture on my walls, with that kind of head, a guitar, and everything else." Flechtheim only replied, "Max, collect ! Just collect! Then store them! You won't regret it." But I wasn't ready for that yet. Picasso's paintings didn't cost more than a few thousand marks at that time, which I could have easily afforded. Today they would be worth millions. But it's really a moot point; everything that I owned would be lost along with my house in Pomerania* anyway.

I couldn't make anything of George Grosz's art then either. Flechtheim wanted him to paint me. He probably believed that a Schmeling portrait by the famous-infamous artist would cause a sensation and sell for a great deal. What I had seen of George Grosz to that point I didn't much care for, and I could only imagine the monstrosity he would make of me.

Flechtheim let the matter drop. But a few weeks later I made my way to Nassauische Strasse and climbed the steps to Grosz's studio. I rang the bell and was greeted by a meticulously dressed gentleman asking me politely whom I wished to see. It was George Grosz, whose appearance did not at all correspond to the image I had expected—that of the bitter critic of war, the military, and the government.

Even at this first meeting George Grosz asked me if I would model for him. Apparently Flechtheim had already told him of his plans, and Grosz appeared to be interested. "I would like to paint your portrait not so much as Max Schmeling," he said to my surprise, "but rather as an archetype: the fighter. What I envision is a picture which shows you as a fighter or, more exactly, as the idea of the man in the ring. Therefore I would like to paint you in a fighting pose." After talking a little more, we agreed on a time for the first session.

Two days later I was at his studio with boxing trunks in hand. Grosz, this time in a wool jacket and cap, had already prepared the canvas and palette. Then he posed me in a fighting stance. When I had posed for an artist for the first time a few months before, it had made me very uncomfortable. But Grosz quickly pulled me into a discussion, partly about boxing and partly about art, that put me at ease.

"What makes a good boxer?" he asked after a few minutes of silent work. "Is power more important or speed?" I tried to explain to him that both are important. Above all, however, it's a matter of hard work. Most people think that the boxer is some bearlike strongman who climbs into the ring a couple times a year and beats up his opponent.

"But the physical part is only the beginning," I explained to him. "You know, Herr Grosz," I continued, "boxing is really a trade and the boxer is in a sense a craftsman. And like the craftsman, the boxer must develop his tools —the hands, legs, and eyes—and then keep them in top working order."

Outside it was a rainy early spring day. In the morning it had smelled like snow, but then it had only drizzled. A milky light came into the studio. For a while Grosz worked silently. I was considering whether I should continue the conversation when he suddenly asked me, "What is a combination puncher anyway? I recently heard the term somewhere, but no one could really say whether it was a compliment or criticism." Grosz looked up with surprise, but then seemed to nod in agreement when I said that I considered a series of ten or fifteen rapid-fire punches to be a waste of energy. He thought about it and appeared to grasp my point—a flurry of punches mostly missed the mark and only made a boxer arm-weary. He laughed at this as he gestured to my raised fists, which I had been holding up for a good two hours: "You've probably had enough for today?"

On the next day I was again in Grosz's studio, and the skies were even drearier than the previous day. For a while you could only hear the sound of his brush, which seemed to me strangely loud and scratchy. I started to worry a little, because the way Grosz attacked his canvas led me to believe that he was going to make me into one of those odd characters that I had seen at Flechtheim's.

Since he had asked me so much about my profession the day before, I gathered my courage and casually asked him, "Listen, Herr Grosz, why are all the people in your pictures thick-headed and bald with ugly scars and big guts? I never meet people who look that way, and you never meet anyone else."

Grosz laughed again. He worked on silently, seeming to reflect on the question. "It's like this," he finally said, "I'm no portrait painter in the traditional sense. I'm not at all interested in the real Frau Meier, the real business tycoon Müller, or the real butcher Lehmann. And don't misunderstand me—the real Max Schmeling doesn't interest me either." Then he added, as apology or clarification, "When I'm painting, that is!"

Then there was another of the thoughtful pauses that seemed to characterize Grosz's conversations. "What I try to capture is the *idea* of these people—the greed of Frau Meier, the arrogance of Herr Müller, the brutality of Herr Lehmann. I'm always more interested in the type than in the individual person." He smiled to himself, "So that's what I meant when I said to you that it wasn't Max Schmeling that I wanted to paint, but rather the boxer." Grosz continued to speak of his theory of painting. He touched on Picasso, Blue Rider* and the Expressionists,* although I have forgotten what he said.

At the next session Grosz came back to boxing, but, again, it was more as a psychologist than as a sports fan. He was interested in how the boxer feels when he has bloodied or knocked out an opponent—satisfaction, upset, hate? And how does the boxer feel on the receiving end of such punishment? Grosz wanted to know whether, as many thought, a hurt fighter went into a rage and became more dangerous than a thinking fighter.

"It occurs to me," he interrupted himself suddenly, "that boxers and painters both have to have a certain quality: both have to be able to size up the stranger facing them right away. What kind of a man is he, what's his life like, what's his character? I have to be able to come up with a picture, you have to come up with a fight strategy."

That was an interesting thought that had never occurred to me. In fact there were many opponents that I hadn't seen until the weighin, and then again at the start of the fight. Then I tried to study them closely, which gave me the reputation of being a slow starter. A boxing match is somewhat like a chess match—one must develop one's fight carefully, and that is only done through knowledge of the opponent. You have to study his movement and reactions, and everything depends on finding out his style and habits in the first few rounds. Only the intelligent boxer can make major adjustments in the course of the fight.

Grosz listened closely, finally putting down his brush and sitting on a stool near the window. I had the impression that the theory of boxing interested him more than an actual fight. Then he wanted to know how a boxer would judge the dangerousness of an opponent. So I told him, "That's very different than most people think, Herr Grosz. The big, bad-looking fighters with the cauliflower ears are never very dangerous. It's the ones who are unmarked, who have had dozens or hundreds of fights without the slightest mark, those are the ones I respect—even if they don't appear to be physically imposing."

Then I came to my favorite point, that in the ring as elsewhere, it's intelligence that is the decisive factor. With tactics and strategy, even a less physically gifted boxer can outmaneuver a giant. "You see," laughed Grosz, "we've discovered yet another similarity between us. With painters too it's not a matter of who has the biggest box of paints."

Two or three days later my portrait was ready. Flechtheim was extremely satisfied, and so was I—as well as a little flattered to have been "immortalized" by the controversial George Grosz.

Grosz and I remained friends up to his emigration to New York, even before Hitler's takeover. And then we got together there a few times in the thirties. But as the times got increasingly dangerous and violent, Grosz began to mellow. The biting satire and combativeness of his pictures from the twenties began to disappear. As everything moved towards the great catastrophe, he began to search for beauty.

The portrait was lost in the war. But then it surfaced again after the war at an auction. An acquaintance of mine bought it and presented it as a gift to my old friend, the publisher Axel Springer.*

The society of which I was becoming a part had its meeting spots in the western part of Berlin, each with its own atmosphere and identity. It was mostly writers, actors, and artists who met at the apartment of Viktor Schwannecke, then director of the Bavarian State Theatre. His daughter Ellen appeared a few years later in the film *Mädchen in Uniform* [*Girls in Uniform*].

It was at Schwannecke's place on Rankestrasse that I met the sculptor Rudolf Belling* for the first time. He had become the talk of the town by way of his bold sculpture, in particular his mannequins. These were bodies reduced to mere aluminum stick-figures, which were then draped with flowing silks. I still remember being somewhat embarassed and tongue-tied when Schwannecke introduced me to him. But Belling greeted me with a worldly cordiality and immediately involved me in a boxing conversation. To my amazement he knew everything about my latest fights and spoke knowledgeably about technical and tactical details. He must have noticed my astonishment, because he soon said, laughing, "You're speechless, right? But I've been boxing myself for a few years and even train regularly." Then he added with irony, "But you don't have to worry about your title, I won't challenge you." When Belling had left, Ellen came to my table and explained that he was totally sports-crazy. He played tennis, he was a regular fan at the Sports Palace and soccer matches, and he didn't only box, he was also a gifted wrestler. He had repeatedly won his sports club's championship in Greco-Roman wrestling, lightweight division. And in the sports-related discipline of tournament dancing, he was an outstanding dancer, who had even established some of the judging criteria that are still used today. Now, many years later, it has become clear to me that this man embodied the spirit of the times even more than most; he was a man of society, who managed to combine and master the passions of that society: artist and sophisticate, boxer and fashion designer, dancer and wrestler.

A few months later Belling invited me to his studio. "Do you want to model for me?" he asked. I told him that George Grosz had already painted me. "Yes, of course," replied Belling, "without realizing it, you have become much more than just a successful athlete." Then I heard for the first time that for many, the boxer had become a sort of ideal for the times. As a sculptor Belling had, along with Brancusi* and Archipenko,* started to make abstract sculpture popular. His *Triad* had attracted international attention. But to everyone's surprise he made of me a completely realistic figure, the well-known *Male Torso.*

Aenne Maenz's bar on Joachimstalerstrasse was where movie actors met. Ernst Lubitsch* had discovered the bar and brought with him an entire entourage. Originally a bar for carriage drivers, it was now considered chic for the very reason that it completely lacked any pretensions to being chic. Alfred Döblin,* the famous writer and physician to the poor, hung out there, as did

Erich Carow,* whose Laugh Cellar had been played by Charlie Chaplin during his triumphal visit to Berlin.

I got to know the legendary Cafe Grössenwahn [Cafe Megalomania] on Kurfürstendamm only after its heyday with Herwarth Walden,* Else Lasker-Schüler,* Gottfried Benn* and Georg Kolbe.* One day the owner became sick of the whole nest of bohemians and threw them all out. So everyone picked up stakes and went across the street to the Romanisches Cafe next to the Gedächtniskirche. This cafe was an uncomfortable, ugly waiting room without any atmosphere, which, up until this time, had been avoided by the public but which was now on any given day turned into a caravan of Berlin's intellectuals and artists. The uncrowned king of the Romanisches Cafe, next to Max Slevogt,* was the bon vivant Emil Orlik,* who, despite his advanced age, would pursue the youngest women. In order to appeal to journalists, the owner had stocked the Cafe with reference works; I often saw famous reporters writing their stories at the little marble tables.

But the Romanisches Cafe really wasn't my world. What attracted the painters was more the older generation, which held court there and which knew as little of me as I did of them. The literary circle was really too esoteric for me and too far into its own little skirmishes and intrigues. The hierarchical structuring of the Romanisches Cafe—its "small pond" for the literary big shots, and "big pond" for the career-climbers, "wannabes," and flashes-in-the-pan—really didn't appeal to me; nor did the cold and sober room itself. It may have also been that you were nothing there if you hadn't made a name in art or literature.

Michael Bohnen,* the celebrated singer and my closest friend at that time, dragged me to Eric Charell's Stalactite Cave, where he was singing the title role in the wildly popular *Casanova,* for which he had taken a hiatus from the State Opera Company. No one gave it any thought that a great opera singer would sing in a nightclub—much less a nightclub where a young dancer with little talent aside from her flawless body would hold a crowd breathless as she was carried almost naked onto the stage on a silver tray by twelve men. Her name was "La Jana." A short time later she became the companion of my friend Michael.

Michael Bohnen was also fascinated by boxing, which quickly brought us together. The powerful man, who hadn't trained and who wore glasses on top of that, started taking boxing lessons and proved himself to be not without talent. The general "boxing fever" of those years had captivated him so completely that he came up with the absurd idea of giving up his singing career to become a boxer. "But Michael," I repeated time and again, "let it go! I don't want to become a singer!" Bohnen laughed, "That would be even more beautiful. You, with your voice you could ruin every opera house

in the world!" Only with effort was I able to talk him out of his fixation on a
boxing career.

But Bohnen's foolishness was significant. One day at Sabri Mahir's
gym I met the actress Carola Neher—a celebrated beauty of the time—who
was wearing boxing gloves and trying to learn some of the basic moves. As I
came into the room, which had a ring in the middle, she was being instructed
in some defensive moves by Franz Diener. I casually strolled up to the ring and
called out a few joking remarks to Carola Neher, but Diener told me to back
off. He took the whole thing as seriously as did his student.

Soon thereafter I was also asked to give boxing lessons. One day after
a performance I went to visit Fritz Kortner in his dressing room and he said
right away, "Max, I have to learn how to box. Want to teach me?" I looked at
him with surprise. Then he told me that he would soon have a part in *The
Rivals,* an American play that had been translated by Zuckmayer,* in which he
would have to do a fight scene, and he wanted to learn a few boxing funda-
mentals. "I'm small," he added, "and maybe I'll have to go up against some
Germanic behemoth. You must teach me how to fight someone like that."

The boxing lessons with Kortner became a very amusing change of
pace. In his apartment we cleared the furniture of one room off to the side
and, between the bookcases, faced each other in boxing trunks. Kortner
showed that he had not wasted his time running from one boxing match to
another; he really had studied the boxers and their techniques. He added to
everything he had seen a kind of squirming quickness; he danced around me
excitedly, seriously, like a whirling dervish, popped me in the nose every now
and then, until I finally had to give him a shot back—otherwise he would have
gotten too cocky.

After those sessions, when the furniture was back in place, we would
often sit out on his balcony or in his living room. I remember once asking him
what it was about boxing that so fascinated him. "It's the times," he said. "What
happens in the ring is a reflection of life. Merciless, raging—the way you go after each other—it's the way we all fight for our existence." He sat across from
me with his chin resting on his fists and spoke to me in his unmistakable high,
strangely urgent voice: "You see, Max, we on the stage portray that fight. But
with us it's only play-acting. If I kill dozens of people playing Richard III, the
curtain falls, we all stand up and take our bows before an applauding audience.
With you, it's really a matter of life and death. Whichever of you is lying on the
canvas—it can really be over for him. Your blood isn't makeup. We only fight
against the critics and once in a while each other."

Kortner stood up and went into the kitchen to get another pot of tea.
And as he clattered around on the stove, he yelled in to me, "That's the most
exciting thing about boxing—nowhere else is the lust for fame and success so

tangibly, so dead seriously there, right before your eyes!" Then he came back in and poured more tea. "I think you see it a bit too dramatically," I said. "You're letting your theatrical temperament run away with you. Because it's really not as deadly serious as it seems to you. We sit around afterwards too; I'm pretty good friends with a number of opponents—Franz Diener, Paul Samson-Körner, and Hans Breitensträter."

But Kortner wouldn't hear it. "No, no, I have a better understanding of it. I sat three meters from Bonaglia when he was down on one knee. I saw it in his eyes—that was drama, Max! It was naked fear!" After some reflection he continued, saying that it wasn't just coincidence that "boxing fever" had come to Germany only after the war. "Why did you all rush to it? Why do we all sit there gawking when you guys go after each other. Because we're all Bonaglias and know this fear. Go out on the street and look at people's faces! You'll see it in all their eyes! No, no, Max," he said by way of conclusion, "when you all sit together afterwards, it doesn't mean anything. Don't kid yourself! Boxing isn't a sport! It's all of life's struggle compressed into a dozen rounds."

Kortner had become increasingly excited as he spoke. His face, always interestingly ugly, was now completely distorted. His last words had been spoken more to himself than to me. It was clear—he had wanted to explain to himself, not to me, why he was so captivated by boxing. In conclusion, he made fun of himself: "The dervish declares that life is a boxing match! You should read Lessing,* Max!" Then, going to the window, Kortner began the great monolog from *Nathan the Wise.* He turned his back to me. He spoke the words simply and to himself—a sweaty little man in a bathrobe. But I've never heard it spoken more impressively.

Ernesto de Fiori took me to his favorite bar, the Jockey Bar, because he loved to make quick informal sketches of his subjects before he sculpted them. The drawings themselves didn't mean anything to him, and the dozen or so sketches he made were mostly thrown away as soon as he memorized a line or feature that he had been looking for.

De Fiori was the bon vivant among Berlin's artists. His striking appearance, his elegance, and his early fame made him the stereotypical romantic artist and the center of attention. In the Jockey patrons spoke of his countless affairs with amusement, indulgence, and envy. He had liasons with the ladies from the salons and love affairs with the daughters of many an upstanding *Bürger,* and even the wives of his friends weren't safe.

After Flechtheim had started to represent him, Ernesto de Fiori quickly became rich. He held court in his apartment on Budapester Strasse, where girls with starched caps and white aprons greeted you at the door. The arbiters of Berlin's cultural life, Max Liebermann* and Georg Kolbe,* officially sanctioned the doings.

～～～

But people forgave de Fiori a lot; often his strikingly attractive Russian wife, Barbara Dju, had her hands full trying to smooth the ruffled feathers of those whom the sculptor had offended. It was only with the art historian Carl Einstein that her charm was in vain. Einstein, an admirer of the sculptor, hadn't even mentioned him in the art history volume that he had just done for the Propyläen Press. When the two met the next time at Flechtheim's gallery, de Fiori, in front of everyone, hit Einstein on the head with the book.

In the Jockey there was great camaraderie. Everyone greeted not only the owner, Freddy Kaufmann, as a friend but also the piano player, Ernst Engel, who sometimes added Bach fugues to his set.

But my true stomping grounds were my friend Heinz Ditgens' Roxy Sportsbar. Here you could sit for hours over a soft drink, and no one expected that you drink a lot, even champagne. It was the meeting spot mostly for athletes and their circle of friends. Famous jockeys hung out there; Gottfried von Cramm* and Sonja Henie were among the regulars, also Gustav Jaenecke and Hans Albers,* as well as the sports-loving nobility. Often famous racing drivers came here—Manfred von Brauchitsch, Rene Dreyfuss, world-record holder Sir Malcolm Campbell, Rudolf Caracciola and Prince Georg Christian Lobkowitz.

Lobkowitz, whose estates were in Bohemia and Mähren, was only one of the many aristocrats in the twenties who could be found at the starting line of Europe's Grand Prix circuit. Auto racing, along with riding and tennis, were the aristocratic sports, and many of the nobility took part in one or the other of them. The Hungarian Count Tivadar Zichy was an international tennis ace, who also competed in all the great auto races. From England came Earl Howe, whose blue race car was known around the world, from Poland there was Count Stanislaus Czaykowski; the Baron Rothschild from the French line of that family kept a stable of race horses, and from the German nobility, aside from Max von Brauchitsch, there was Ernst von Delius, Prince Hermann zu Leiningen, Hans-Joachim von Morgen and Fritz von Opel, son of the auto magnate. But the race drivers weren't all aristocrats. The Dresden cigarette manufacturer Hans Levy, the 1931 champion of the Avus,* would drive to the starting line wearing his monocle and wear it for the entire race. It wasn't until the early thirties that the landed gentry began to hire professional drivers to race for them. Back then, one had to be wealthy oneself to compete in auto racing. Usually the drivers owned the race cars or they were financed by wealthy patrons. It was not so much a battle of the auto companies as it was between the racing personalities.

It was in the Roxy that one of the eeriest scenes of those times took place. A few days before the 1933 Avus race, practically all of the Roxy regulars sat together one evening, among them Eric Jan Hanussen, who had been appearing at the Scala for weeks as a clairvoyant and whose presence guaranteed a full house. As before any great sporting event, people were speculating on the outcome of the race. Hanussen, who usually made somewhat forboding, ambivalent predictions, reacted this time very differently. He asked Ditgens for a piece of paper and an envenlope, after which he sat way back so that no one could see and wrote something down. Then he calmly folded the paper, stuck it in the envelope and wrote: "Don't open until Sunday evening after the race." Ditgens gave it to the bartender and laughed, "Eric's making a big secret out of this one. Lock it up!"

The race was one of the most dramatic that the Avus had ever seen. Never before in the Weimar years had the box seats facing the north curve seen a more prestigious turnout. Next to the ministers and state secretaries sat practically the entire diplomatic corps, among them the English ambassador Sir Horace Rumbold, as well as his French colleague Andre Francois-Poncet. Of course the crown prince was there with his retinue, as well as Emir Faisal, Viceroy of Mecca, with his colorful following.

The elite of auto racing was at the starting line—Rudolf Caracciola and Hans Stuck, Luigi Fagioli and Earl Howe, Rene Dreyfus and Manfred Brauchitsch. One of the crowd favorites was the twenty-five-year-old Prince Lobkowitz, ever since he had had an accident in his Austro-Daimler 100 meters from the finish, crawled out of the wreck and finished the race in some old bucket-of-bolts parked near the track.

Lobkowitz was one of the favorites to win, and he had played that role to the hilt in the days before the race—after a recent string of bad luck, he would put it all on the line and win the big one. Three weeks earlier he had bought the newest, most powerful Bugatti, which was said to be the equal of the sixteen-cylinder Maseratti, the legendary Mercedes SSKL, and even the Type 8C Alfa Romeo.

But this time the young prince's irrepressible fighting spirit was fateful from the start. As the pack came off the straightaway for the first time into the north curve, Lobkowitz wasn't there. His Bugatti had left the track on the south curve, had gone over the infield at 200 kilometers an hour, flipped over and over until it lay in pieces at the *S-Bahn* embankment almost 100 meters away. On that same afternoon Lobkowitz succumbed to his injuries in the hospital.

That evening everyone came to the Roxy Bar. A gloomy mood reigned, as conversation kept coming back to the tragic accident of that afternoon. Everyone debated whether it had been recklessness or unfamiliarity with the new car that had caused the fatal accident.

Suddenly Ditgens was called to the phone; it was the race winner Manfred von Brauchitsh. And as Ditgens returned, he had the envelope in hand that Hanussen had given him a few days before. In the excitement of those last days, we had all forgotten about it. "That was Brauchitsch," said Ditgens as we all watched him expectantly, "he wanted to know what Hanussen had actually predicted." With a weary gesture he threw the paper down on the table. Someone picked it up and read, "Winner: Manfred von Brauchitsch; fatality: Prince Lobkowitz."

As I look back from a distance of half a century to Berlin of that time, I see a city of enormous energy, a hectic lust for life as if the whole world knew that it stood before an approaching catastrophe. Berlin was an open city, a city of cafes and bars, revues and dance palaces. Everything happened in public and no four walls could contain it. Whoever went into a bar could in a single evening see the entire register of the artistic and social scene.

The guestbook of my friend Heinz Ditgens read like a catalogue of the culturally prominent in Berlin of the twenties. Written there were the names of Fritzi Massary* and her husband Max Pallenberg;* Erwin Piscator* had signed next to his nemesis Alfred Kerr,* Oskar Homolka* was on one page with Otto Zarek, and Werner Krauss* was next to Conrad Veidt.* Shortly before his death, the fragile and tubercular poet, Klabund,* had signed, along with his wife Carola Neher. Upon the death of the actor Albert Steinrück at the start of 1929, they all gathered for a performance of Wedekind's* *Marquis von Keith;* at least half of that Berlin society stood on the stage, while the other half was sitting in the audience.

The incomparable hurly-burly of the twenties also brought lesser talents to the top. Dancers like Anita Berber would hardly turn a cosmopolitan city upside down today. But what a scandal it created back then when the attractive dancer answered public protest over her too-explicit erotic dancing with even more obscene dance movements; or the time she came into the crowded dining room of the Hotel Adlon accompanied by two young dandies, sat down at a highly visible table, ordered three bottles of Veuve Clicquot, and then, after the waiter had poured, unclasped the diamond broach on her expensive fur, let the coat fall casually from her shoulders, and drank to her escorts stark naked.

Maybe I was letting myself get too far into this new world. I was starting to catch myself breaking my training routine of going to bed by ten, and it was beginning to show. A few days after a particularly late night I had a bout at the Frankfurt Festhalle against the Englishman, Gypsy Daniels, whom I had beaten three months earlier. Without my usual concentration, I was caught coming off the ropes in the first round by a haymaker that dropped me for my first knockout loss.

That caused a sensation. At the same time there was a six-day bicycle race in the Berlin Sports Palace, where it was announced over the loud-speaker that I had been KO'd at two minutes forty-seven seconds of the first round. The crowd broke into laughter—they thought it was a joke. Fourteen days later I got some revenge by beating Daniels's countryman Ted Moore over ten rounds.

The laughter at the Sports Palace over the presumed joke gave me a sense of my growing popularity at the time. When I went up against Franz Diener three weeks later in April 1928, the anticipation was so great that a Berlin theater manager feared for his premiere, and then postponed it. In fact the bout, happening at the time of my moving up into the heavyweight division, was the sporting event of the year, and it was sanctioned by the Berlin Sporting Press Association and designated as the Championship of All Classes. The rules were also changed for the first time. Instead of the usual twelve-round distance for a German Championship match, the bout was extended to the European and World Championship distance of fifteen rounds. The Berlin Sports Palace was chosen as the venue.

The Sports Palace on Potsdamer Strasse had been there forever and overshadowed all other arenas. The enormous building, whose sober facade was framed by two awkward columns, stood sixty meters back from the bustle of the street. The entrance doors faced the street at that time with an open court directly behind them. This gave the effect of an open-air foyer during the intermissions.

Above all boxing, but also ice hockey and the Berlin six-day bicycle races had made the Sports Palace a sports shrine. It had its own anthem, the so called "Sports Palace Waltz," which had been written by the Viennese composer Translateur but was then co-opted by the Berliners; it was always immediately followed by a barrage of whistles, usually started by the handicapped newspaper vendor, "Crutch," who was more popular than the mayor. With his catcalls he could get Richard Tauber* or Gitta Alpar to sing for free during intermissions, or he could extort free beers from prominent visitors by getting the crowd to chant in unison.

During the six-day bicycle races there were continuous announcements of cash bonuses for the riders—bets made by businessmen, artists, and athletes on who would win a particular lap. One evening in particular occurs to me, when the announcer said that 500 marks would go to the winner of the next three laps. He added, "From a six-day fan in Oels." Everyone in the Sports Palace knew that Oels was the estate of the German crown prince who had just returned from exile in Holland.

When the arena, which had been rebuilt after 1945 from the bombed-out ruins, finally closed down after brief success, it felt as if a little piece of Berlin's history went with it, and also a part of my life.

⤬⤬⤬

I took the Diener fight very seriously. Four weeks before the bout I moved out to Lanke with my trainers, and Max Machon and I went through every available film of Diener's fights round for round. Machon was especially concerned with my left hand, which was critical to the strategy of keeping up a barrage of jabs against the stronger Diener until that split second when I could bring my right into play. Diener, being trained in the western part of the city by the Turk Sabri Mahir, had ten pounds on me, was stronger and, most of all, had a number of tough American fights under his belt—he was my most dangerous opponent up to that time.

On the evening of April 4 there were cloudbursts over Berlin. But more than an hour before the start of the fight, every seat was taken. As I made my way through the crowd to the back entrance, tickets were being sold out front on Potsdamer Strasse for five and six times their original price.

The official program, which I have kept to this day, brought together contributions from authors who would normally only write something for a big theatrical production. Leopold Jessner,* Carl Zuckmayer,* Dr. Kurt Pinthus,* Herbert Ihering,* Egon Erwin Kisch,* and Leo Lania had written pieces. And my friends Werner Krauss* and Curt Bois,* Friedrich Hollaender,* and Willi Schaeffers* were represented as well. Even Berlin's popular assistant police commissioner, Dr. Bernhard Weiss had written something.

Spotlights illuminated the entrance gates, in front of which cars were backed up along the street. Celebrities made their way through the crowds and puddles. As I climbed into the ring and the crowd began to cheer, I realized that boxing in Germany had finally become a social occasion: at ringside were only tails, tuxedos and starched shirts, bare shoulders and elegant eveningwear. "The Sports Palace," wrote the press next day, "had it's biggest evening to date."

The prelims had already finished, hands were wrapped and gloves pulled on as Paul Samson-Körner, chosen as the impartial referee by the German Boxing Authority, called us to the middle of the ring and gave us our instructions. Tension crackled in the arena.

The fight went the distance. Diener attacked without letup for the full fifteen rounds. He punched wildly and with little accuracy, but his physical reserves were unbelievable. Again and again he attacked my defense. In the first round I managed to fracture my left thumb, but I was no longer a fighter who depended solely on a knockout to win. During training in Lanke I had improved my style, so that I could now win a fight with a variety of punches, I could go the distance and win by boxing if necessary.

The pain in my left hand was a hindrance, but the excitement of the fight, along with Diener's aggressive style, made me forget the pain. After fifteen

rounds I stood in my corner totally exhausted as the decision was announced. I was the winner on points. The next day the newspapers wrote that the result was unequivocal and one-sided.

With the victory over Franz Diener, for which I earned 30,000 marks, I now held three titles—German and European light-heavyweight champion as well as the German champion of all classes. Boxers from all over were suddenly drawn by the purses and title chances that a Schmeling fight could bring. Right after the Diener fight I received a challenge from the top contender, Ludwig Haymann of Munich, but the doctors said that my injured left hand needed more time to heal.

The medical delay started to cause some anger. Although impartial doctors prohibited my return to the ring, more and more I heard complaints that I wasn't putting my title on the line. I began to get the feeling that public opinion was turning. Suddenly I started to hear criticism that I was arrogant and a social-climber, that my new circle of friends had turned my head. It reminded me of how Gene Tunney had been criticized because he read the classics, corresponded with George Bernard Shaw, and modelled for the Swiss sculptor Hermann Haller. The same accusations were now being directed at me, especially in the tabloid press.

It was during this time of starting to see some of the downside of success, as I sat in Berlin depressed and with an injured hand, that I received a telegram from the American promoter, Tex Rickard: "Offering Schmeling a fight on the undercard of the July 27 Tunney versus Heeney championship bout / $6,000 / travel costs paid / reply." It was a tempting offer, however I felt obligated first to defend my title against Ludwig Haymann. But when I resumed training in Lanke a month after the Diener fight, the pain in my left hand only got worse. My doctors shrugged their shoulders and ordered more rest.

So I had to postpone indefinitely a Haymann bout. But I saw the opportunity to go to America and at least see the Tunney-Heeney fight as a spectator. My titles and recent victories had fired up Arthur Bülow's entrepreneurial spirit. He said: "Son, let's go to America and seek our fortune! That's the only place to make the big money!" It was a bold move.

On May 18 Arthur Bülow and I boarded the liner *New York* in Cuxhaven. My hand was heavily bandaged. On the day before, the Boxing Authority had vacated all of my titles for failure to defend them.

---

[1] The remaing ruin of the Kaiser-Wilhelm-Gedächtniskirche [Kaiser Wilhelm Memorial Church] at the upper end of Kurfürstendamm is one of Berlin's most recognizable landmarks; the damage of World-War-Two bombing is intended as a constant reminder of what war has done for Germany.

෴

5
The New World

Like everyone else, I had already heard a lot—countless stories and descriptions—about New York. But as our ship neared land, and the Statue of Liberty loomed before us, I felt like most first-time travellers to America—the actual sight exceeded all expectations. Manhattan's skyline, although the old-fashioned skyscrapers would be overshadowed by the gigantic glass boxes of today, made a stronger impression on me then than in any later visits. Standing at the railing, I watched the swarm of people and smaller boats that came from all directions. It was all so overwhelming compared to the Hamburg harbor back home.

Even as we slowed into the docks, reporters were storming aboard and checking the purser's passenger list. "No one important on board," they yelled to each other. The whole churning scene—the horns of passing ships, the aggressiveness of the press—all made a lasting impression on me. From the first moment, I had the feeling that I was in the capital of the world. Franz Diener had recently been to the USA with his manager, Mabri Sahir, and had had some fights there. Of course he lost all but one, but his all-out style had made him popular with the fans. On the return voyage, Mabri Sahir had consoled him with, "You weren't crowned king, Franz, but at least you saw the castle!"

Bülow and I took a room at the Hotel Ransby on 84th street, not far from Central Park. It was a favorite hotel of many boxers. "Mr. Smeling [sic]," said the owner, "I have a beautiful room for you. Two world champions have stayed there, Dempsey and Tunney." The room was modest and medium in size; at that time only the luxury hotels had suites with a bath. Here we only had a washbasin behind a screen. But every morning when I got up I could look out over Central Park and the sea of New York's buildings.

〜〜〜

Bülow and I had been sure that we would be greeted by offers and invitations. After all, I was European champion and had received an offer from New York's biggest promoter, Tex Rickard, just a few weeks earlier. But the days went by and nothing happened. Only later did I learn that New York at that time generally did not pay much attention to European fighters. Year after year they came from England, France, and Germany, as well as Italy and Spain, to try their luck in American rings. At first they were greeted expectantly, but, since so few succeeded against tough American competition, the interest gradually died.

My deteriorating mood wasn't improved any by the fact that my left hand still hurt and had to be put back in a sling, while attacks in the German newspapers said that I had broken contractual agreements for a rematch with Franz Diener—that my trip to America was an escape. And for the first time I started to have problems with Arthur Bülow. Every time I asked him to start contacting fight promoters, he begged off. He always replied that we weren't going to be "kept in the waiting room," which would only weaken our bargaining position; you had to have nerve and be able to wait it out. They would come to us soon enough. I, on the other hand, became increasingly impatient.

Living in New York was turning out to be surprisingly expensive—a dollar was worth over four marks, and our stay was beginning to eat up our funds. When still nothing had materialized after several weeks, we gave up our hotel room and rented a cheap bungalow near the water. As the days went by, we became more nervous and on edge. We walked aimlessly among the tall buildings, our initial excitement having long since disappeared. I took the Lexington Avenue subway to 161st Street to see the renowned Yankee Stadium, where I gloomily stared at the 60,000-seat colliseum. My dream of someday fighting there seemed more remote than ever.

Four weeks after our arrival, Max Machon came with some of the boxers from Lanke; they too were hoping to strike it rich and were just as in the dark as we were. When I asked them what was going on back in Germany, they gave only vague or evasive answers, leading me to believe that the intrigues and attacks against me were continuing. After a short time and a few unsuccessful fights, they returned to Germany. Only Max Machon stayed on. At that time he became my trainer, which he remained until the end of my career.

Machon introduced me to Madame Bey—the exalted wife of the retired Turkish ambassador—who had a training camp in Summit, New Jersey, about sixty kilometers from New York. So there's where Arthur Bülow and I took up residence. In this country setting there were cabins, two rings, running tracks and a huge assortment of training equipment. We each had a single room with a bath. The boxers followed a strict daily regimen, and our health and conditioning were closely monitored. There were a bunch of us, American and

European fighters, among whom were the French future featherweight world champion Andre Routis and the Spaniard Paolino (whose real name was Uzcudun), nicknamed "The Basque Bull." Madame Bey has long since died, but the camp is still there, still serving the young boxers of later generations.

Right after arriving in camp, hungry for some activity after so long a layoff, I started working out. But the first time I hit the heavy bag I screamed out in pain—the hand injury had actually gotten worse. Madame Bey recommended a specialist, the New York sports surgeon Dr. Fralick.

He operated on me for three hours and removed a small bone splinter that had been causing a painful inflammation. When I went back a few days later for a follow-up visit, I met a good-looking young man. The doctor introduced us: "Mr. Schmeling" and then turning to me, "Mr. Sharkey." We shook hands. It was Jack Sharkey, one of American boxing's most promising stars. Two years later I would stand in the ring with him for one of the most important fights of my career.

Dr. Fralick's operation was successful. After just a few days the inflammation went down and I could finally start training. On July 26, about two months after my arrival in America, the Tunney-Heeney fight took place—the bout for which I was supposed to fight on the undercard. Together with Machon and Bülow, I went into the city.

The fight was a one-sided affair. The great technician Tunney gave an incomparable demonstration that a battle in the ring doesn't have to be a brutal slug-fest, that it can even be an elegant sport. With his stinging left he wore down the New Zealander for ten rounds, then showed his power by knocking Heeney out in the eleventh round.

On that same evening, directly after the fight, Tunney relinquished his title. And despite many attractive offers in the years that followed, he never laced up the gloves again. He had gotten $600,000 for his last fight, a fortune for those times. Since he had made over $2 million for his previous two fights with Jack Dempsey, he retired from the ring a wealthy man.

In the course of time it became increasingly clear to me that you couldn't get far in America without a manager who knew the local scene and who had a license from the official boxing authority. Bülow just didn't want to hear that. One day at Madame Bey's camp I turned to Andre Routis and asked him how he had managed to get ahead in the tough American fight game. Routis answered, "You'll never get a fight here with Bülow. I'm telling you. You need an American! Get my manager, get Joe Jacobs! He knows his way around and he has the best connections in boxing."

Joe Jacobs, as I later found out, came from New York's East Side. His parents were Hungarian Jews who had emigrated to America before his birth.

But the small, agile man spoke a mishmash of English and Hungarian as if he had just stepped off the boat. He knew nothing about boxing, but he knew how to negotiate and get his man the best deal possible. And he was as nice as he was clever.

Of course, my interest in Jacobs had to lead to conflict with my manager up to that time. Bülow really had two sides. On the one hand he was trying to promote my career for both our sakes, but sometimes his intensity even took on a comical aspect.

Once, during the time that we shared a room at the Ransby Hotel he awakened at three in the morning and began to hold forth excitedly: "I've got it! Your left has to be thrown as if you were trying to snatch a fly out of midair. Do you understand?" The whole time he was motioning wildly, throwing determined hooks just inches above my nose.

On the other hand he was here in a strange country, helpless, and doing nothing to change the situation. He would go on for hours about how with Tunney's retirement there were too few headliners in American boxing, and matchmakers would soon be beating down our door. But I was tired of waiting. One day in camp I saw Joe Jacobs and asked him directly, "Mr. Jacobs, can you get me a fight?" Without even taking the ever-present cigar out of his mouth he said, "Nothing easier. You can have one tomorrow if you want."

When Bülow—whom I'd been trying in vain to motivate for months —heard that, he suddenly became active. He came to an agreement with Tex Rickard's representative Tom MacArdle that I would fight the American Joe Monte on the undercard of a fight taking place on November 23 in Madison Square Garden. I was elated. After almost eight months of waiting and personal crises, I was looking at a fight in the world's greatest sports arena.

Bülow, who had just sat back and done nothing for months, was apparently now awake. He seemed finally to realize that something had to happen soon if we didn't want to go back to Europe with our tails between our legs. But he signed the contract too impulsively, without any American advisor, and took the fight for a total purse of only $1,000. That wasn't only a pittance compared to my German purses, it was also a big disappointment after Tex Rickard's initial offer of $6,000.

Angry, I told him that I thought he had blown the deal. I decided to take matters into my own hands and went to the New York Boxing Commission. An assistant commissioner named Farley showed understanding for my anger, but he shrugged his shoulders, "Bülow had the right to sign," he told me, and, further, it was a legally binding contract. "Fight a good fight and move on," he added, and advised me to finish out on good terms with Bülow. He told me that Bülow's take of 40 percent of my earnings was extremely high by American standards, and I actually did get Bülow to come down to 33.3 percent. But the relationship between us cooled considerably from that point on.

A few days before the bout everything was up in the air again. I woke with a high fever, chills, and muscle pains, and the doctor said it was the flu. But I was well aware that this was my last chance to make it in America. The doctor emphatically forbade me to fight in this condition. But I was determined to go through with it. With chattering teeth and a cold sweat I climbed into the ring of a half-filled Garden. My memory of the fight is somewhat clouded, but Max Machon alone stood in my corner—Bülow had claimed to be sick and Joe Jacobs wasn't yet licensed to handle me. "You've got to pull yourself together, Max," whispered Machon, "Tex Rickard is sitting down there."

Nothing much happened in the first or the second round. I was so out of it from the fever and medications that even Tex Rickard didn't matter to me. By the end of the seventh round I had had it, more from my condition than from my opponent. "Machon, I can't continue," I gasped, "I really can't! Let me quit!"

Machon wasn't buying it. Before pushing me out for the next round, he let me have it: "If you quit on this one, you can throw in the towel for good. You'll be finished in America and you'll be finished in Germany." Just before the bell he added roughly, "Either you pull yourself together, or we pack our bags tomorrow and head home."

In this round Joe Monte let down his guard. For a second I saw his unprotected chin in front of me. With my last strength I let go with a short right. Joe Monte suddenly collapsed as if his legs had been ripped out from under him. I found myself in a neutral corner hearing the referee count from what seemed to be a great distance. Behind me at ringside Tex Rickard jumped up and yelled, "What a right hand!"

Next day the same words were repeated by boxing experts in all the papers: "What a right hand!" This sentence started my career in the United States. After the fight Bülow came into the locker room and congratulated me, "We did it! You were fabulous!" But at this point I really didn't want to hear that from him. Sure, I owed him a lot. But my anger over his inactivity and stubbornness, which had cost me months, had really destroyed the old friendship. And my disappointment over his absence from my fight didn't help either. My decision stood firm—I wanted to sever our ties and move on to Joe Jacobs. Before the year was out I had signed a contract with Jacobs.

Right away Bülow complained to the Boxing Commission, accusing me of breach of contract. Farley brought us in for separate interviews. The members of the commission sat behind a long table while I stood before them like a defendant. The hearing gave me the impression that Bülow had used his white hair and polite, dignified manner to turn them against me. In any case, the questioning got pretty aggressive and I finally lost it, slamming my fist on the table and bolting out of the room. But Farley followed and calmed me down. "Be reasonable, young man." he said, "nobody here is out to get you. We only want to get at the truth." Then he took me by the arm and led me back into the room.

The commissioner was suddenly transformed. In an almost fatherly tone he said to me, "Don't get us wrong, Max. But we're dealing here with large sums of money and people's livelihood—not just yours but your manager's too." Finally it was agreed that I could leave Bülow, but that I would pay him his percentage until our contract ran out. Afterwards Jacobs came up to me in the hall and said that he wouldn't take any cut until my contract with Bülow was up. That impressed me a great deal.

Only later did I realize that Farley probably saved me from making the biggest mistake of my life when he brought me back into the room. A lot of boxers were suspended for months and even years for less serious behavior. Almost a quarter of a century later Farley would again play a part in my life.

Joe Jacobs took over from then on. He began with a big campaign. "You don't have a name yet," he said, "you need publicity. Not a single day can go by without your name being in the papers." To make me popular he gave me the name "The Black Ulan of the Rhine."[1] He put the reporters on me and arranged receptions and invitations; he dragged me through schools, monasteries, and churches, had me photographed atop skyscrapers, had me meet politicians, and skillfully played up my resemblance to Jack Dempsey. Amid all this he scheduled four fights right away in 1929.

In Hamburg, Walter Rothenburg (who considered himself something of an astrologist) published horoscopes at the beginning of the new year. His public prognosis for 1929 read next to my name: "A string of luck begins for Max Schmeling—he's going to achieve a great deal." We had always made fun of Walter Rothenburg's hobby, but when the stars are in your favor, you're less likely to scoff at fate. So we began the new year with high hopes.

Three days later, on January 4, 1929, I beat the technician Joe Sykra. He had just moved up from the light-heavyweight division, so he was very fast. He pushed me hard for the entire ten rounds, and, really for the first time, I had to use my left again. I had become accustomed to only using it tentatively, and I was surprised that I now felt no pain. When I hit Sykra with a hard left and he went down, I automatically ran over and helped him to his feet. That was a gesture that was unusual in American rings. It probably cost me a knockout victory, but it did win over the crowd. The Garden went wild.

Just eighteen days later I faced the Italian-American Pietro Corri. The bout lasted fifty-nine seconds; then my right found its mark. In barely eight weeks I had three wins in three fights. In the boxing world of 49th Street between Broadway and 8th Avenue my name was starting to mean something. Madison Square Garden now showed interest. Joe Jacobs arranged a bout for February 1 with the tremendously strong Johnny Risco; I was to get $25,000 for this fight. The former baker's apprentice from Cleveland had never been knocked out, and with his boxing ability, his strength and toughness, he'd managed to frustrate a number of world-class boxers.

On the night of the fight people flocked to the Garden, which had been sold out for days. And for the first time in the States, tickets for one of my fights were being sold at black-market prices. The fight was, in the opinion of the press, one of the most dramatic heavyweight contests in the history of boxing. Risco, whose explosive power had brought him victories over boxers like Jack Sharkey, Phil Scott, Max Baer, and Paolino, attacked from the first round on with dangerous combinations. He threw left hooks and straight rights from everywhere, and I started to lose my bearings. The many German-Americans in attendance suddenly became silent. It appeared that I wasn't up to the merciless assault.

Risco went all out. This night would decide his career too. Only with a victory could he position himself for a shot at the vacant world title—he was the toughest competition I had faced to that point. And even though I was being outfought at the moment, the victories over Joe Monte and Joe Sykra had given me back my self-confidence. In the middle of Risco's swarming attack I staggered him with a hard right, immediately followed by another. He went down.

The spectators jumped from their seats. But Risco showed why he was at the top of the American rankings. In the second round he had already pulled himself together and began again with devastating combinations. But I boxed him methodically and undermined his attack with hard counterpunches. I floored him again in the seventh and eighth rounds. In the ninth round something happened that momentarily stunned the crowd. The ironman Johnny Risco, who had never been knocked out, suddenly turned away, wearily shook his head and lifted his hands in a sign of defeat. As if on cue, the crowd exploded.

From this moment on I had a name. Jacobs no longer had to drag me through schools and skyscrapers. I now received offers from broadcasters, newspapers and magazines, from large companies. The German ambassador, Baron von Prittwitz, gave a reception for me. And I started to get a sense of how hard it is to be a "public figure." In Berlin my victories had made me a figure in society, in the USA they had made me a hero on the street. In Berlin they had passed me around, in New York they lined up to meet me.

A few days after the fight Tex Rickard died at only fifty-eight—Tex Rickard, who had really been the soul of American boxing. Tex Richard, whose "what a right hand!" had launched my American career, had had a typically American background. He had been a cowboy, blackjack dealer, gold miner, real estate salesman, porter, and dogtrack owner before he promoted his first fight card at the age of thirty. From that time on he devoted himself to boxing.

In the remaining quarter of a century he was really the mover and shaker of New York boxing. And with his passion, dignity, and perfection he had organized boxing of his era and kept it clean. Upon learning of Rickard's death, Jack Dempsey is said to have broken into tears, while thousands passed by the coffin, which had been placed in Madison Square Garden. With his passing ended a piece not only of New York boxing history, but also of an entire era of the sport.

On the day after Rickard's wake I signed a two-year contract with "his" Madison Square Garden. Then I shipped out for Europe. Joe Jacobs, Max Machon, and I booked cabins on the *Deutschland.* On the voyage back to Germany I had already decided to make my career in America. The feeling of relief and freedom stayed with us for the entire trip. It was a relaxing voyage.

We had barely passed the three-mile limit (Prohibition was in effect) when Joe Jacobs ordered the champagne. When he saw on the wine list that a bottle of champagne—which sold for fifty dollars on the New York black market—could be had for only three dollars, he decided to buy the ship's entire stock. Machon gave the steward a sign and followed him into the pantry. The steward returned with more champagne and presented Joe Jacobs with the bill; it was for 20,000 bottles of champagne at three dollars each. At the bottom of the bill read: "Immediate payment is requested."

We were all in our twenties, relaxed, and perhaps foolish, and the pressure of the past few months had been lifted from us. As the coast disappeared in the distance, I said to myself, "You've at least seen the castle from the inside."

[1] Joe Jacobs's colorful nickname for Max Schmeling derives from *"die Ulanen,"* a unit of cavalry lancers in the Prussian army from 1807 to the end of World War One; the resulting *nom du guerre* combines two elements that have very little to do with each other (except for their "Germanness"), but that somehow sounded good to Jacobs.

~~~

6

In Front of the Camera

Controversy and abuse had accompanied my departure from Germany, and the mail I received in America had continued the onslaught—it was like reading my own obituary. But now everything had changed. At the pier and on the train platforms I was now greeted by large, cheering crowds. The Boxing Commission rushed to give me back my title and even staged a reception in my honor at the Hotel Adlon. The mayor of Berlin invited me to the city hall and thanked me for my services on behalf of Germany's international image. Of course I enjoyed all of that, but now with the knowledge of how precarious fame and popularity—and, therefore, one's career—could be.

Another personality had also achieved overnight fame during my absence. I had often seen the young man with Paul Samson-Körner; he stood mostly in the shadow of the massive heavyweight—shiny leather jacket, quiet, strands of hair combed over his forehead, shifty, angry eyes looking through his wire-rimmed glasses. It was Bertolt Brecht.*

In the Schiffbauerdamm Theater, Brecht and the composer Kurt Weill* had had a smash hit with the musical satire *The Three Penny Opera*. Up until then Brecht had made something of a name for himself in the literary world, but he had not been considered in a class with dramatists such as Ferdinand Bruckner,* Georg Kaiser,* and Fritz von Unruh.* At the time of my departure for America, most of my friends in the theater had spoken of him as simply an eccentric young outsider. By the time I returned, he had achieved that which no one had believed possible—the greatest theatrical success of the twenties.

Soon after my return I was approached by the well-known film director Reinhold Schünzel* on behalf of the Terra Film Company; he suggested that I take on the leading role in a boxing film. It was a somewhat sentimental story of a naive young boxer who, after winning the title, comes under the spell of a man-eating femme fatale. I would play the part of the inexperienced young man who becomes caught in a web spun by the evil beauty, yet who is set free by the love of his childhood sweetheart, returning to his true self in the ring.

Although I was being offered a considerable amount of money to play the lead, I hesitated at first. But Schünzel said, "What can happen, Max? You don't have to speak, it's a silent film. You only have to act, and every now and then you say 'the weather is nice' or 'autos go fast' or whatever. We only need your mouth to move, nothing more." I laughed and agreed to do it.

At first I really enjoyed the work in the Terra Studio. I especially liked working with the comedian Kurt Gerron, who made the most out of the fact that here in the studio he was the pro and I was the amateur. Like many of my friends, he was later murdered in Auschwitz.

One morning, Reinhold Schünzel showed up with news that was a pleasant surprise for most, but which scared me to death. Terra Studio had decided that silent films were no longer competeitive and, therefore, the remainder of *Love in the Ring* would be shot as a sound film. "So from now on," continued Schünzel, "you have to speak lines. The screenplays are already on the way. You, Max, are even getting a song."

I couldn't believe my ears. It had to be me, whose only failing grade in school had been in singing. I refused. But Schünzel could be very persuasive. He promised to get me singing lessons and finally gave permission to leave the scene out if I really didn't like the result. After all, he didn't want to ruin his own film.

Unfortunately, I let myself be talked into it. The pitiful text went as follows:

> The heart of the boxer
> knows only one love:
> the battle for victory alone.
> The heart of a boxer
> knows only one care:
> In the ring to be number one.
> And if for a woman his heart beats,
> makes him want to sing and shout,
> the heart of a boxer must forget all this,
> or the boxer will be knocked out.

The poetry of this verse was horrible, and even today I shudder if I happen to hear my miserable baritone singing it on the radio or an old recording. But thanks to the cast, the film did well, both with the critics and the public.

~~~

In the meantime, America was looking for a successor to Gene Tunney. According to an unwritten law, it had to be an American, because no European had ever carried the championship away from the United States. Jack Sharkey—twenty-seven years old, born Joseph Paul Chusauskas of Lithuanian parents—appeared to have the best chances of a title shot. Yes, Jack Dempsey had knocked him out in the seventh round two years ago, but since then he had fought his way back to the top with victories over Johnny Risco, Jack Delaney, Leo Gates, and Arthur Kuh, and just recently K.O.'d Kristner and Young Stribling. The Garden Corporation, now headed by Tex Rickards' successor William F. Carey, was looking for a "house star" to show-case, and Sharkey looked like a strong candidate.

This was the situation in the American boxing business early in 1929. Only the occasional reports from Joe Jacobs, who was trying to get me into the title picture, gave me a sense of what was going on behind the scenes. After the excitement of my time in America, I decided to relax for a while, visit some old friends in Düsseldorf and Cologne, and travel to Prague for a few days to visit the Czech actress Jarmila Vacek; I had met her on the voyage from New York to Germany as she was returning to Europe after filming in Hollywood.

Jarmila showed me the city, we walked hand-in-hand over the Nepomuk Bridge and through Prague's old quarter. We had afternoon tea in a cafe at the Waldstein Palace and later found a little pub on the heights over-looking the palace.

She told me of her life, how she had studied at the Drama Academy in Prague and then travelled to America to try her luck in film. "It was a mis-take," she said, "it's practically impossible for a newcomer to make it over there. You have to have already become a star here to get anywhere over there. My best friend had the right idea. She went to Berlin. Maybe you've heard of her—she's supposed to have become quite well known in Germany. Her name is Anny Ondra."

Nobody knew about my trip to Prague. It was only when Jarmila and I went to a soccer match that we were discovered by a reporter who made it into a big affair and even had us engaged. I later learned that Anny Ondra's mother wrote to her daughter: "Dearest Anny! Just imagine what Jarmila's been up to! She's engaged to a boxer! A boxer! Why just recently they caught and locked up a boxer who was trying to break into a local bank."

The days in Prague were fun and carefree. But in Berlin I returned to a very different climate. The conflicts in the *Reichstag* [Parliament] were more and more spilling over into the street; confrontations in the working-class neigh-borhoods of Wedding and around Alexanderplatz were the first signs of the street battles for which the political parties would soon be calling up virtual armies. Communist agitation was increasingly less about specific grievances,

and more about the "exploitive system" in general; while their opponents on
the right disparaged the "system" or the "System of Versailles" in the form of
the Weimar Republic.[1]

The "Nazis," as Adolf Hitler's party was commonly called, had ap-
pointed themselves the moral guardians of the nation, and their commandos
marched against everything that displeased them. At the premiere of the anti-
war film of Erich Maria Remarque's novel *All Quiet on the Western Front,*
white mice were released in the theater by the Berlin *Gauleiter* [district com-
mander] Joseph Goebbels and the radical nationalist and former reserve officer Ernst von Salomon, who had already been involved in the Rathenau*
assassination. Shortly before that, Hitler appeared for the first time in the
Sports Palace and brought a crowd to its feet, many of whom had only come
to satisfy their curiosity and desire to see a good show.

At this time I heard from Joe Jacobs that he had been successful. He
had arrranged with the boxing commission that I would face the Spaniard
Paolino as part of an elimination tournament to determine the new world
heavyweight champion.

The commission's decision came as a big surprise to me and everyone
else. Among the other contenders, after all, were boxers who had dozens of
tougher fights behind them, and some of them had even done well against
Tunney and Dempsey. With Bülow it never would have happened—without a
doubt it was Joe Jacobs's skill and savvy that had made the critical difference.

In order to promote his plans, Jacobs had also gotten the support of
the Hearst Corporation. He had made an ally of publishing Czar William
Randolph Hearst's charity-conscious wife by offering to donate a portion of the
fight profits to a milk fund for needy children. In America, the first signs of the
impending financial crisis were becoming visible. Further, the Garden was en-
ticed by Jacobs's proposed arrangement with the Hearst Corporation to have
their 300 newspapers coast-to-coast extensively cover the fight preparations.

Only forty-eight hours after hearing from Joe Jacobs, Max Machon and
I were on the ocean liner *Reliance* bound for New York. As I entered the dining room on the first evening, whom did I meet but Michael Bohnen,* who was
also headed to New York to sing the role of Hagen in Wagner's
Götterdämmerung at the Met. We became inseparable for the entire voyage,
and the stories from that week, which still come to mind, give me a sense of
how free and high-spirited we both must have felt as we approached the
greatest challenges that we had yet faced.

From time to time, on the sun deck or at shuffleboard, I had spoken
with a German-Chilean family that I had met. They owned saltpeter mines in
northern Chile, and it was Señor Ricardo Neumeier's mission to convince the

෴

entire world that, in light of Europe's situation at the moment, the future belonged to South America. He was as talkative as he was gullible, and we couldn't resist playing tricks on him and his plump señora.

One evening as Bohnen and I were standing at the railing, we discovered that Señor Neumeier, his wife and three daughters were taking a leisurely stroll on the deck. Quickly we came up with a plan. Bohnen disappeared behind a tarpaulin while I—staring out to sea like some romantic creature of the night—began to sob the aria from *Don Carlos,* "She Never Loved Me." Of course it was none other than Bohnen who was singing from his hideaway.

Señor Neumeier froze on the spot, energetically motioning his family to be quiet. As the aria, which I accompanied with dramatic breast-beating gestures, came to a close and I gazed a moment longer at the horizon, a frenzy of excitement erupted from the Neumeier family. Señor Neumeier rushed over to me: "I am so moved," he said effusively, "you have a magnificent voice. You are not only a great boxer but also a great singer. Señor, I thank you. You simply can't keep your great talent to yourself! It can't remain that we alone, who by sheer coincidence witnessed your art, are the only ones permitted to enjoy your singing! I insist, Herr Schmeling, that you give a concert tomorrow evening!" Urgently he added, "You must, señor! I will arrange everything with the captain." Then he took his family and they all disappeared through the door leading to the upper deck.

My embarassment was considerable. As Michael Bohnen crept out of his hiding place, he took particular pleasure in my dilemma. With a show of mock concern he offered to give me singing lessons in his cabin next day.

At a loss for how I could reasonably get out of this mess without hurting poor Señor Neumeier, I went to Max Machon. After thinking about it, he came up with the solution. "Just say you're indisposed," he recommended. "The evening outing on deck made you hoarse. Tomorrow morning you let yourself be seen wearing a heavy wool scarf, and everyone will believe you. And so as not to disappoint anyone, Bohnen will jump in for you." And that's what we did. Michael Bohnen's performance in the dining room of the *Reliance* was a rousing success.

I had to disembark in Halifax. William Carey of the Garden Corporation would play out the weeks leading up to the fight according to time-honored rules of show business. He had rented a special train from Northern Railways, with which he brought close to two hundred reporters to Montreal to witness the contract signing firsthand and then attend a gala banquet.

The Garden and the Hearst Corporation took turns calling the shots. From now on every step I took was planned according to the publicity agenda. Even the border crossing into the U.S. was played up as a major event, covered by dozens of reporters and the *Fox Weekly Report.*

Joe Jacobs had secured an ideal training camp in Lakewood, New Jersey. It was owned by William Dwyer, co-owner of New York's hockey team and a well-known figure on the sporting scene.

America's boxing fans received daily—and as the fight approached almost hourly—reports from both training camps. Reports included not only my training sessions, but also my diet, sleeping, and even the brand of my boxing shoes.

The training camp was adjacent to one of eight private golf courses owned by the legendary millionaire John D. Rockefeller. One afternoon a golfball came flying into camp, and before we knew it, the easily ninety-year-old lemon-faced magnate came running by—with incredible agility—to fetch his ball. I had heard about Rockefeller's thriftiness bordering on stinginess, which was almost as famous as his wealth. This little episode demonstrated to me how true that was.

Dwyer introduced me to Rockefeller, and the eccentric old man proved to be very interested and knowledgeable. "You've beaten Risco, young man," he grumbled, "then you'll beat Paolino too. Sharkey has already qualified, so you'll soon be going up against him. I don't need to wish you luck for the Paolino fight, but for Sharkey you'll need it. Give it your best shot!" Without saying another word he turned and scampered, with dignity, back to his game.

Around 40,000 spectators surrounded the ring in Yankee Stadium on the evening of June 27, 1929. It wasn't a record attendance like a Dempsey or a Tunney fight, but considering that two foreigners were facing each other, it was an astonishing turnout. The gate was almost $400,000.

I was to get around 17 percent of the gate; regardless of the outcome I would earn about 300,000 marks. Only a few years earlier I had walked (to save train fare) the almost thirty kilometers from Cologne to Bonn to cash a check for three marks, only to find the bank closed and walk back to Cologne empty-handed. I was so naive and inexperienced at the time that I believed that I could only cash the check at the Bonn bank from which it was drawn.

The Paolino fight went the full fifteen rounds. The bullnecked Spaniard put up a tremendous fight. He won a total of two rounds, two rounds were even, and the other eleven went to me. For Paolino it was the toughest fight of his career. He took countless hard rights without going down, convincing many boxing experts that he had the best chin of all time.

Mrs. Hearst was among the first to congratulate me. Just after the fight, at the celebration party, the first numbers were already in: 35,000 spectators had paid $364,000, of which $130,000 went to the milk fund. So the match had paid off for Mrs. Hearst's charity as well.

❦

Joe Jacobs also told me that the fight had benefitted the Hearst Corporation in other ways—the week of reports from the training camps, as well as the interviews given exclusively to the Hearst papers, had boosted circulation considerably. So the kindness of his wife had also been a business advantage for the tycoon.

The Paolino fight also represented the debut of a new media advance in Germany: it was the first time that a sporting event in America had been simultaneously broadcast on German radio. From the flood of telegrams that I received that night and into the next day, I could see the possibilities that this innovation brought with it.

Joe Jacobs took advantage of my newly won fame and arranged a series of exhibition matches to take place in thirty American cities over several weeks. I remembered how I had admired Dempsey in 1924 when he had travelled through Germany with his entourage—now I was doing the same thing in America! From the observation car of the Southern Railway and Pacific Express, from cars and planes, I was finally seeing the America that lies behind the New York skyline. I met Buffalo Bill's son, I saw the Ford Motor Works, took part in crowning Chicago's "Blossom Queen," and saw the Grand Canyon and the Golden Gate Bridge.

But the details are lost. The American experience of that trip is today a jumbled memory that all runs together, a flood of images, which were always new yet often repetitive: train stations, reception committees, Main Streets, country clubs, arenas, and hotel rooms; and always a pack of reporters—hat pushed back with cigar in mouth, pushy and rude, yet cordial at the same time.

In Hollywood I was taken from one party to the next—continuous and exhausting festivity. The high point was the reception that Ernst Lubitsch* gave for me. Douglas Fairbanks and Clara Bow came, Ludwig Berger,* Emil Jannings,* Gloria Swanson, Walt Disney, and Mary Pickford.

After everyone else had left, we Berliners stayed and sat together for another hour. Lubitsch asked longingly after Aenne Maenz and whether the pig's knuckles and sauerkraut at her place were still as good. And Jannings took on a dreamy expression as we spoke of her *Königsberger Klopsen* [a kind of meatball in cream sauce]. They were all successful in the new world and longed for the old. They had achieved fame and the big money, but they were homesick.

[1]At the conclusion of World War I, Germany's "quick-fix" attempt at a progressive, western-style democracy in the form of the Weimar Republic (1919-1932) was really doomed from the start, being constantly undermined by those from the right (the National Socialists and other nationalist parties) and from the left (the Communists). By the late twenties and early thirties the polarization became increasingly extreme, and the scene was set for the emergence of Hitler's Third Reich.

7
World Champion

By the time of my return to Germany, the country we had all longed for from Hollywood found itself on the eve of a crisis. The first shadows were already falling. On the surface hardly anything had changed. The unemployment figures weren't yet alarming, the political parties seemed relatively stable, order had finally been established. But no matter whom you spoke with, everyone was afraid of some non-specific, intangible something. Even at the sendoff reception with Baron Prittwitz in Washington, every conversation had been marked by this sense of crisis. Now, as I arrived in Bremerhaven, more people seemed to be just hanging around the docks; their clothes seemed shabbier to me, their faces wearier and more sullen.

With his innate sense of publicity, Joe Jacobs recognized an opportunity. In northern Berlin, in the back-courtyard world of the working-class, he rented a hall. There we played host to several hundred needy kids whom I would ask their wish; and to the extent that it was possible, we filled those wishes. What moved me most was the modesty of their requests: usually a few crayons, a top, a pencil case, or a bathing suit. The biggest wish of one little boy was a toy Zeppelin balloon. I was especially touched by a five-year-old girl whose thin, strawlike braids were done up in bows and whose wish—that her father stop drinking—we couldn't fill. But the idea was a great success, and Joe Jacobs came up to me afterwards and asked, "How did we do that?" For once, he took the giant cigar out of his mouth.

But Joe's flair for public relations didn't always work out. A year and a half later we were together again in Berlin, where he arranged some exhibition bouts to keep me in the public eye. Jacobs came up with the idea that we would all be wearing black-red-gold tee shirts, which he thought would be popular in "red Berlin."[1] But he had overlooked the developments of recent months, in which the National Socialists had seen landslide gains in the popular elections; they had gone from a struggling splinter party to the second strongest party in the Reichstag.

So of course the crowd in the Sports Palace also had a large number of Hitler's followers. At the sight of the hated black-red-gold colors of the Republic the crowd broke into piercing whistles [the German equivalent of booing], and when I climbed into the ring wearing a red-black-gold helmet the hooting only increased. And since this only provoked the spectators on the other side of the political spectrum, it looked as though the program might have to be cancelled. It took over twenty minutes before enough order could be restored to at least go on with the exhibition matches. Hitler's takeover was still two years away.

In the meantime, I had gotten myself into a difficult situation. On the one hand, I was contractually bound to the Madison Square Garden Corporation and could only box elsewhere with their permission. On the other hand, I was finding myself at odds with the American boxing authorities. Instead of the original agreement that I would get a title shot at Sharkey if I beat Paolino, I was now being told that I would first have to fight the Englishman Phil Scott. Even before leaving America I had refused this condition and told the commission, "If you can't offer me a final fight for the championship, then I'm returning immediately to Germany. Whoever here thinks that I need America is mistaken. I'll do just fine in Europe. But you need me in this tournament. That's the way it is."

The members of the Boxing Commission were furious. As a way of getting leverage, they immediately suspended my license. Max Machon later described the last hours before our departure for Germany: "Schmeling's hotel room was jam-packed with thirty or forty people—reporters, officials from the German Embassy, boxing officials—all talking to Schmeling at once. 'Max, go along with it! Fight the Englishman! He's no competition for you! You're going to ruin your career!' But Schmeling, the barely twenty-four-year-old, stood fast: 'If I stay and give in, I'll become your puppet,' he shot back. 'You're not going to make a fool of me. If your people don't know what it is to keep your word, then I'm going home to cool my heels until America calls; and you can bet that that call will be made.'"

I really wasn't that sure of where I stood, but Joe Jacobs had promised me just before I sailed for Germany that he would take care of everything, that I shouldn't worry. But nothing happened in the next few months. I passed the time as usual, going to premieres, hanging with the old friends at the Roxy Bar, going on outings to the surrounding area. And of course I didn't neglect my training.

∼∽∾

My parents, brother, and sister. My father was a navigator for HAPAG (Hamburg America Line, a Hamburg-based shipping firm); he died before my boxing career began.

The house where I was born in Uckermark, west of Stettin, about three hours from Berlin.

My first passions in sports were track and wrestling, and I also played goalie for the St. George youth soccer team. I'm wearing the dark tunic.

A film of the
Dempsey-Carpentier
fight had awakened
my enthusiasm for
boxing. The sport
soon became my life.

Only in the capital city of Berlin was a real career possible. On the morning of my arrival, I strolled through the city, awe struck by the glamour and the chaos.

I was "discovered" by Arthur Bulow, editor of *Boxsport*. With his help I began training at the camp in Lanke.

After my early victories I was challenged by Hein Domgorgen, the German middleweight champion, in 1927. Since his manager, Willi Fuchs, insisted on "all or nothing," I won the 20,000-mark purse by a seventh-round KO.

I won my first German title from Max Dieckman.
The bout lasted thirty seconds.

The Dieckman fight took place in Berlin's Luna Park
at the upper end of the Kurfürstendamm. It was an
amusement park in the turn-of-the-century style.
Shooting galleries, restaurants, carousels, and acrobatic
tents were arranged in a colorful maze of narrow
streets. A houseboat was moored on the bank of
the adjoining Hallensee; it was on this boat that
we celebrated my victory.

A favorite of the
Sports Palace crowds
was figure skater
Sonja Henie.

The uncrowned king of the six-day bicycle races was Reinhold Franz Habisch, nicknamed "Crutch." He led the crowd in boos, whistles, and chants, and was more popular than the mayor.

The Berlin Sports Palace was the city's premier sports arena. For boxing, ice-hockey, and six-day bicycle races the Sports Palace was a mecca for Berlin's sports fans in the twenties and thirties.

One of the biggest events at the Sports Palace was my bout with Franz Diener, which I won on points to become German heavyweight champion. I only met Diener once in the ring, but we became good friends in the years that followed.

The official program (right), which I kept, had pieces written by authors who normally only wrote for theater programs.

Deutsche Meisterschaft

Diener=
Schmeling

Programm-
Magazin

Mittwoch, den 4. April 1928

und vor allem: ich bitt mir aus, dass anständig geboxt wird!"

Preis Mk. 0,50

Berlin society of the twenties did not consist of the most important or powerful people, but rather of those who were talked about — a varied mix from every sphere — artists and bankers, showgirls and actors, journalists, writers, race car drivers, and scholars.

Ernst Lubitsch and Pola Negri belonged to the "society" of which I became a part.

Berlin was a city of cafes, bars, revues, and dance palaces. E.A. Dupont shot his film, *Varieté*, in the Wintergarden.

The Romanisches Cafe
— "an uncomfortable
waiting room" without
atmosphere — was the
oasis for the cultural
and artistic elite.

Mama Schwanebeck's "Kleine Scala" [Little Scala] was the meeting spot for countless artists, such as Greta Garbo (left) and Lya di Putti (far left).

The twenties rediscovered the naked body — in film, on stage, in revues. The UFA film, *Paths to Strength and Beauty*, offered a history of the naked body. The suggestive movements of dancer Anita Berber (right) caused quite an uproar. The dancer "La Jana" (left) became the companion of my friend Michael Bohnen. Alfred Flechtheim's *Querschnitt* showed boxers in poses reminiscent of Classical and Renaissance sculptures. I am pictured below.

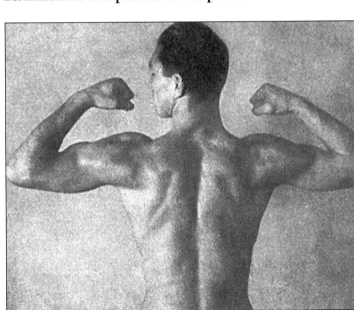

The premiere of
the film, *All Quiet
on the Western Front*,
was sabotaged by
Goebbels and
other right-wing
extremists, who
released white
mice in the theater.

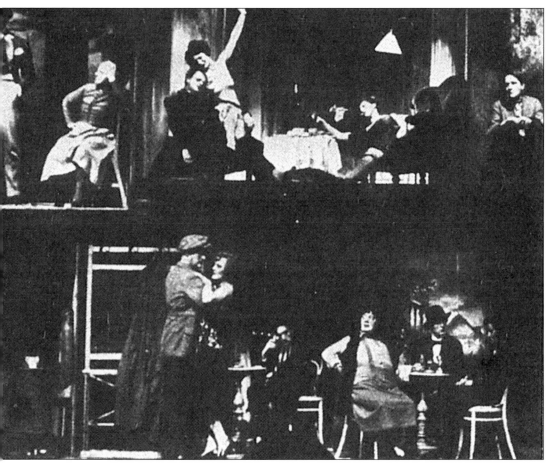

When I returned from New York, Bertolt Brecht had
scored a smash hit with his *Three Penny Opera*.

At a performance of Wedekind's *Marquis of Keith* in memory of Albert Steinrück, almost ninety of Berlin's most noted actors took the stage.

| Max Pallenberg | | Hermann Valentin | Max Hansen | Jacob Tiedtke | Heinrich George | |
| Fritzy Massary | | Tilla Durieux | Werner Krauss | | | Fritz Kortner |

tto Wallburg   Leopold Jessner   Lothar Müthel   Viktor Schwanecke   Albert Florath Alfred Fischer

enore von Mendelssohn   Maria Bard   Carola Neher   Heinrich Mann

Elisabeth Bergner   Mady Christians   Trude Hesterberg   Tilly Wedekind

At our meeting spot, the Roxy Bar, I often sat with Ernst Deutsch (above).

The singer Michael Bohnen was my friend for a long time, until the night that he reported our circle of friends to the Gestapo.

Fritz Kortner turned out to be a passionate devotee of boxing. During rehearsals for *Rivals*, in which he had a fight scene with Hans Albers, I gave him boxing lessons in his living room. He also followed me throughout Germany to my important fights.

Clara Bow, whom I met with Ernst Lubitsch in Hollywood, was an avid boxing fan.

A magician and psychic was needed for the wild twenties — Eric Jan Hanussen.

I rarely missed the auto races at Avus. It was a great day in the capital whenever the race cars screeched around the famous course. The whole city of Berlin followed these races.

"Tempo" was the catchword of that period; the pace was now much faster. Where fashions had once lasted for decades, now they changed continuously.

Film stars set the standards for fashion and beauty.

Sports, dance, theater, film, literature, culture, the high-life — that was one side of the "Golden Twenties." The other side: the aftermath of war, inflation, unemployment. The mark lost its value ever faster. In Berlin, publishing firms' printing presses were used to make bank notes.

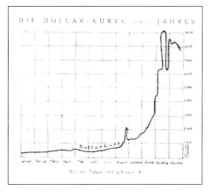

A billion-mark note.

A trillion-mark note.

The purchasing power of the mark sank
daily. In front of lending institutions
and pawn shops stood long lines of
those who still had anything to pawn.

Wages were paid in cash. By 1922, the large
firms picked up the money from the banks
and delivered it in wash baskets.

I had already heard a great deal about New York, but my first look at the skyline still left me speechless. Especially fascinating was the view from the Zeppelin.

On trips between America and Germany I met many actors, singers, and athletes who also "commuted" between the Old and the New World. Here I am with tennis player Roman Najuch, figure skater Gillis Grafstrom and singer Gota Ljungberg, among others (below).

At receptions in New York, I often met the German ambassador, Baron von Prittwitz.

During an exhibition tour throughout America, we took a break in Florida, where I met "Tarzan," Johnny Weissmuller.

After the victory over Stribling, I travelled back to Germany on the *M.S. Europa*. The tennis aces Hans Nusslein and Roman Najuch were on the same voyage.

My friends picked me up in Hamburg in a 10/50 Stoewer-Wagen.

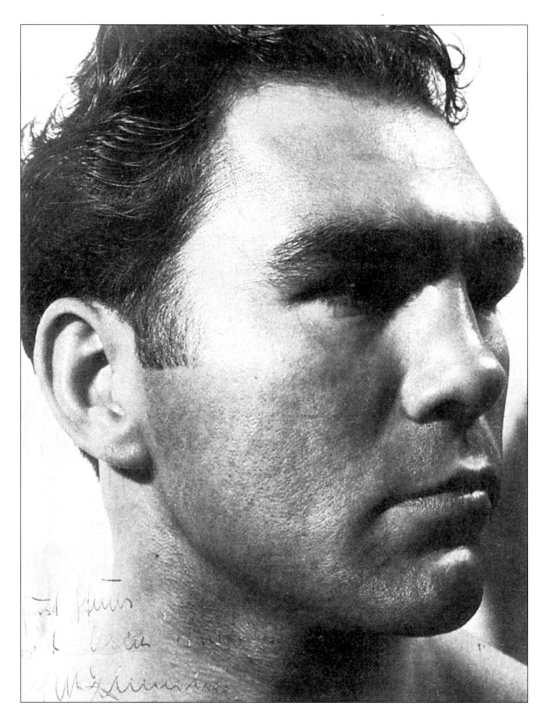

I dedicated this picture to August Steuer, owner and publisher of the 100-year-old *New Yorker Staatszeitung*, an important publication for German immigrants in the U.S.

Around this time I went to a reception for Heinrich Zille* at the Sports Palace, at which a friend of mine brought me to Zille's table to meet the feisty old man who was Germany's leading satirical artist. I felt more at home here in the unpretentious atmosphere of a beggars' banquet than I did in the social world of Flechtheim's soirees. Heinrich Zille also came from a humble background, which wasn't hard to imagine as the famous but somewhat shabby old man sat hunched over his beer.

On another evening I participated in a charity function at the Scala for underprivileged children. We sat on stage in a group of eight or ten. I believe that Lil Dagover,* Josef von Sternberg,* Conrad Veidt,* and Fritz Lang* were there. At the conclusion we were each called on to say a few words. Only a pretty blond with Sternberg was not called up. She was still too unknown then, although within a few weeks she would be world famous as Marlene Dietrich.*

As I look back, it seems that I spent most of that time running from one benefit to another. At one such function at Max Reinhardt's* Deutsches Theater I was called to the stage to take a bow. I was coming on stage—half climbing and half being pulled—when I suddenly felt a sharp pain. The next day the doctor found that I had torn a ligament in my leg, and he prescribed strict bed rest. But I refused to listen and hobbled on a cane to the German Amateur Boxing Championships at the Sports Palace, where a lanky young boxer named Walter Neusel took the heavyweight title; I climbed into the ring to congratulate him.

After this appearance, which produced a lot of questions, I had to more or less stay home in bed. At Machon's insistence I went under the sunlamp for a few minutes each day to maintain at least the appearance of good health. He didn't want rumors circulating that would hurt my chances in America or lower my market value. If I did get out, it was only with a broad-brimmed hat and dark glasses. As a professional boxer I had become a slave to the image of health and strength.

To be out of the public eye, we escaped for a few weeks to Taormina, a beautiful spot in the southeast corner of Sicily, which had remained undiscovered by tourists. Mussolini was already in power, but his reign had yet to be felt in this part of Italy. We swam in the ocean and lay in the sun, and as soon as I could throw away the cane, we returned to Berlin.

In Berlin the news was waiting that the American boxing officials had given in. Joe Jacobs's campaign, called "Bring Max Over," had finally done the trick. A short time later, Jacobs himself came to Berlin and told me the new fight date. I would fight Jack Sharkey for the world heavyweight title on June 12, 1930 in Yankee Stadium.

First off, in order to get back in shape and make weight, I undertook an exhibition tour throughout Germany. After three weeks of intensive work

I felt myself getting back into form. Jacobs had already left for the States on April 1 on the *Bremen.* On board was the young Marlene Dietrich, who had just been signed by Hollywood on the very eve of the triumphal premiere of Josef von Sternberg's *Blue Angel;* she had been put on the night train to Bremen and from there was whisked off to America.

Shortly before my own departure, I drove out to my old training camp at Lanke to receive the well-wishes of my friends there. Carefree and happy as I was, I put down the top of my Maybach in order to enjoy the ride out to the country on this mild spring day. Maybe I was overtrained, because the next day I came down with the flu—a bad sore throat, aching joints, and a high fever.

Once again I had to lay low. The doctor came secretly to my Steglitz apartment and prescribed strict bed rest. On April 18 Jacobs telegraphed that I had to leave for America no later than April 25. A postponement was impossible because the contract-signing could not be put off any longer.

Despite a rising fever I was determined to go. Only a few people knew of my condition. On board the train departing from Berlin, I acted relaxed and posed for the many photographers and camerapeople there. On the morning of April 25 I sailed from Cuxhaven on the ocean liner *New York.*

This time everything was planned right up to the day of the fight. We avoided the publicity circus by leaving right after the contract signing; our destination was Endicott, a small town outside of Boston. It was there that the American "Shoe King," George Walter Johnson, allowed us to set up our training camp on his estate—complete with tennis courts, a golf course, swimming pools, bridle paths, and every other luxury imaginable. But my contract with the Garden ruled my private life, and activities such as tennis or riding were prohibitted on account of possible injury. Similar clauses were in most important fight contracts—boxing ruled us, not the other way around. Too much money was at stake for promoters to take chances. George W. Johnson, whose shoe empire stretched from coast to coast, picked me up at the train station. He then drove to a hill overlooking the idyllic little town and said with a sweeping gesture, "The city is yours!"

He meant what he said. His generous hospitality fell to me because Sharkey had refused an earlier invitation extended after one of his recent victories. Before our fight, Sharkey's manager had suggested to the industrialist that he forget the affront and let Sharkey train at his estate. But Johnson wasn't that forgiving. Sharkey had to find another camp, while I basked in the lap of luxury. Again it was Joe Jacobs who explained to me the advantage that Johnson's patronage would bring to the mogul. During the weeks that followed practically every newspaper in America made daily mention of Endicott

❧❧❧

and Johnson's shoe empire; the publicity was worth millions and more than compensated for the expense of the camp.

Like the old billionaire Rockefeller, Johnson was also obsessed with not wasting a penny of his fortune. When I sent him a postcard from Florida a short time later with a three-cent stamp instead of a two-cent stamp, he immediately sent me a telegram full of reproach: "Dear Max, you'll never amount to anything in the business world. Whoever overpays the post office by exactly 50 percent is on the wrong track." Right away I cabled him back: "Dear Mr. Johnson, whoever wastes $4.30 on a telegram concerning one cent is also on the wrong track and will soon have squandered his fortune."

In camp there was always a gang of reporters around me. Since my leg was still giving me problems, we started getting up at an ungodly hour, usually around five, to do a run in the woods. Every few hundred meters I had to stop and let Machon massage my ankle. Regular roadwork was still out of the question.

It was only three weeks until the fight. This time as well, Joe Jacobs had arranged with Mrs. Hearst to donate a portion of the gate to the milk fund. Of course that got the Hearst Corporation on board again, and pretty soon all of America was buzzing about the fight. Every day our chances were reevaluated, the experts were interviewed, and Sharkey and I were hounded by reporters. It was the first time I had really experienced the "big ballyhoo": "First I'll cut his face to ribbons and then, around the seventh round, I'll knock him out," explained Sharkey; or, "What does he have going for him other than his resemblance to Jack Dempsey?"

As for myself, I tried to get into the spirit of this war of words, and we had a lot of fun trying to come up with the most swaggering threats. What I really couldn't get into was the mandatory tearing down of one's opponent —even though it was mostly a put-on—as part of the American pre-fight hype. Once when a reporter was trying to provoke me into a more hostile tone, I finally laughed, "What do you want me to say? Will you finally be satisfied if I say that I eat Sharkey every morning for breakfast with or without kraut?" His eyes lit up as he asked, "What's kraut?" Machon explained that we were speaking of the world-renowned sauerkraut. Now the reporter was excited: "If I were you, I would say just that. Sauerkraut sales would skyrocket. You could get a great endorsement contract with a sauerkraut maker."

Jack Sharkey was totally convinced that he would win. And, in fact, he was one of the best boxers in the world, and he had come up at a time when there were a number of first-rate heavyweights. He had brought his boxing skills against most of them, and had even toyed with the great Jack Dempsey for six rounds until he got careless and was KO'd in the seventh.

He considered me to have just been lucky: "In the entire history of boxing," he explained to a reporter, "there has never been anyone with the luck of Schmeling. He pokes his nose into our country and gets a title shot just like that. If our leading boxers had demanded that when we were coming up, we would have been slapped right down, and with good reason. And this German comes over here and expects that after two ridiculous elimination bouts he's earned the right to face me, Jack Sharkey."

As a boxer, Sharkey had what they call "fighter's instinct." What he needed in the ring wasn't so much an opponent as a personal enemy. He was at his best in fights where his emotions came into play. Not that he was a killer possessed. Highly intelligent, he focused his emotional energy. He tried to play up statements that I could have made in order to get himself into a rage. Then add to that the statements attributed to his opponent, which were constantly fed to him by his people—all designed to get him fighting mad and keep him that way.

On the day of the fight we drove to the weighin at the Boxing Commisssion offices accompanied by a police motorcycle escort with sirens screaming. I met Sharkey there, and he looked in tremendous shape; at 178 pounds he outweighed me by eight pounds. After an extremely thorough examination, the doctors declared us both fit. Then the gloves were given to the responsible persons.

Sharkey confidently assured reporters present, "I'm going to come into the ring wearing the American flag around my shoulders and then leave the ring as world champion, still wearing the stars and stripes."

I was more reserved: "I've never made a prediction, and I'm not going to make one now, before the toughest fight of my career. But I will do everything in my power to bring honor to my fatherland."

The stadium had 80,000 seats; 22,000 cheaper tickets had been held back that were only released for sale at the box office at noon on the day of the fight. This was due to the practice of some scalpers buying up blocks of cheap tickets, selling them at inflated prices, and then splitting the profit with the fight promoter. In this case the promoters wanted to show that they had nothing to do with that type of manipulation. But within a very short time, these tickets were gone too, and thousands who had stood in line all night had to go home empty-handed.

On this day New York stood in the shadow of the fight. Public transportation to Yankee Stadium carried double the usual number of passengers. Airlines flying from Los Angeles to New York announced a whole squadron of special flights for film stars and other prominent Hollywood personalities.

❧❧❧

As for myself, after lunch Max Machon and I drove a short ways out of the city to take a walk and relax a bit. Two detectives followed us step for step, and driving at a snail's pace behind them was Mr. Caswell, the head of a small security agency and a brother of Joe Jacobs. He was one of the leading private detectives in the country and provided our security before every big fight. Even around-the-clock security of this type was called for by the fight contract.

But we were on guard, too. Even the mineral water for between rounds was picked up by Max Machon from German ships anchored in New York harbor. He then wrapped the neck of the bottle with tape so that even a boxing glove could hold it.

Late that afternoon I returned to my hotel room for a short but very deep sleep. My three bodyguards were sitting in front of the door. During that time Machon packed the suitcase with the necessities: a mouthguard made by one of Berlin's top dentists, collodium to stop bleeding, smelling salts, vaseline, handwraps, salve, scissors, and towels.

Yankee Stadium was filled to the last seat by the time I arrived, and the preliminaries were already under way. In the sterile, shabby basement area where the dressing rooms were located the rumble of the crowd sounded far away, sometimes broken by cheering or a mass groan. Then came one of the seconds from Sharkey's corner to observe my hands being wrapped, just as we had sent one of my men, Doc Casey, to watch the same procedure in Sharkey's dressing room. In the meantime it had become quiet in the arena above us. As I sat waiting on my dressing table, the door suddenly opened. "Come on, Max!" yelled one of the promoters, and we followed him.

As we walked into the arena, the crowd came to life. Cheering broke out, mixed with loud booing; hats, little flags, and handkerchiefs were waved in the air. Then the ring announcer introduced us and announced the prominent figures in attendance. In the general commotion I could barely hear the names of New York mayor Jimmy Walker, the auto magnate Chrysler, Florenz Ziegfeld, Jack Dempsey, Gene Tunney, Paolino, and Risco. In addition, Ernst Lubitsch, Josef von Sternberg, and Marlene Dietrich were announced and cheered.

Finally the referee, Jim Crowley, called us to the middle of the ring. He gave us the usual instructions—fight a clean fight and remember the rules. And as the last of the stadium lights went down, so that just Sharkey and I were facing each other in a harsh light, the referee said, "And now go back to your corners and come out fighting. . . ." Then came the bell.

Jack Sharkey was known as a fast starter, while I generally took several rounds to get on track. Machon had been afraid that Sharkey would overwhelm me with a barrage of punches, so we had worked on a number of defensive strategies in training. As he gave me a little shove into the ring, Machon whispered a final time, "Be careful, don't get caught cold!"

And in fact Sharkey did go all out from the first bell. He clearly wanted to get it over early, because as wary as I was of his fast start, he had to know that I would come on strong in the later rounds. He was wound up and kept coming straight at me, while I concentrated on slipping his punches and countering. In the last minute of round one I caught him flush on the chin with a hard left, and he went into a rage, swarming over me with a hailstorm of punches. The round plainly went to him.

The second round went pretty much the same. Sharkey continued his enraged attack without letup and fully lived up to his reputation as a madman in the ring. But at first he didn't succeed in catching me with one of his left hooks, either in the infighting or at mid-range; then about halfway through the round, while we were still in a clinch, he unleashed a powerful left hook to my stomach. He hadn't seemed to notice that I went with the punch, neutralizing much of its effect, and while he registered a moment surprise, I caught him flush with a hard right.

But now I was the one who was surprised, because Sharkey took the punch with no apparent reaction. I followed up with two left hooks that did seem to bother him and forced the tempo to pick up. I took two left hooks to the face and an uppercut to the body and had to go into a clinch.

After the referee separated us, Sharkey came at me with a flurry of punches, which, however, lacked any real power. And even though I had to take a couple of left hooks to the face, I could now hear Sharkey breathing heavily in the infighting. He had really picked up the pace and therefore won this round decisively as well. But I had the feeling that his attacks had taken more out of him than me and that he could maintain this pace for only one or two more rounds.

When I came back to my corner Max Machon was still concerned, but his expression had begun to lighten up a bit. "You're doing OK out there," he said, "but now we're going into Sharkey's favorite round. Just keep it up for the next two rounds; then we've held to our fight plan and we have him." The simmering stadium appeared to be dotted with thousands of fireflies as far as the eye could see—the lighters and matches of the eighty thousand, now melting together in the stadium's haze, reacting as a single body.

The third round really was Sharkey's strength, and I remembered that in 1927 he had even had Jack Dempsey on the verge of a knockout in this round. While Machon and Casey were working on me in the corner, I went over my fight plan again in my mind. Sharkey was a wild man, but he lacked nerve. If he couldn't pull it off in the third round, I could count on him losing momentum and starting to go downhill.

࿇

And at the bell Sharkey really did come at me with everything, catching me with several shots, including a hard right to the body. In the hail of blows he missed a few, too, but I couldn't seem to get any good counterpunches past his guard. But for all his rage, none of his punches really rocked me or put me down.

Sharkey was breathing heavily as he went back to his corner. I had had to take a few good shots, but I still felt pretty fresh. Max Machon, however, was fuming: "You've got to be more careful! For God's sake, wake up in there!" Out of sheer nervousness, he held the smelling salts under my nose, which I batted away angrily. "OK, he hit me—it happens. Don't make such a big deal out of it!"

In the fourth round I tried to turn the tide and take the initiative. I managed to block or sidestep Sharkey's first wild rushes and had him missing badly. I also started countering effectively, backing him up. I rocked him twice with hard rights to the body, but he kept his chin covered. I kept attacking, and he let himself fall back into the ropes in order to bounce back with a counter. Then came his left.

In this moment a stabbing pain shot through my entire body. I felt my legs buckle and went down to my right knee before collapsing completely. Instinctively I tried to get up, but it was as if I were paralyzed. I heard the referee counting from what seemed to be a great distance. They told me later that he got to six before the bell ended the round.

I only know what happened after that from what my handlers told me. The referee went over to the judge at ringside who had been sitting right behind me when the blow came. Without hesitating, the judge told him, "Yes, Crowley, it was a blatant foul!"

Throughout Yankee Stadium the crowd had become quiet, seeming not to know exactly what had happened. While Crowley appeared to hesitate and conferred with the judges, you could hear Arthur Brisbane, America's leading boxing writer, vehemently shouting, "If Sharkey isn't disqualified, then I'll see that boxing's done for."

For a moment Crowley just stood there weighing the options. During all this, Joe Jacobs and Sharkey's handler, Buckley, were arguing in the middle of the ring. Suddenly Crowley went over to Sharkey and said, "You've been disqualified for a low blow; the fight's over." Then the ring announcer Joe Humphrey climbed into the ring and, without a microphone, yelled into the the stadium's breathless silence, "Jack Sharkey: disqualification. The winner and new champion: Max Schmeling!"

The last word wasn't even out when all hell broke loose. It was the first time in the history of boxing that a champion owed his title to a disqualification, although the disappointment and anger seemed to be directed mostly at Sharkey. Still only half conscious, I was carried from the ring.

In the dressing room I was examined by the ring physician, who confirmed the damage of the low blow. This was announced over the loudspeaker, which unleashed a new round of boos and whistles. Even Gene Tunney, whose title we were fighting for, agreed that the disqualification was fully justified, as did former Heavyweight Champion Tommy Burns and almost all of the reporters from America's leading newspapers. Even Sharkey himself didn't protest.

After I had more or less come around, I realized that I had reached the goal that I had always wanted, but in a way that could only make me new enemies. Depressed, I sat hunched over in the dressing room. I said to Machon, "I can't accept the title! To win it this way doesn't mean anything to me." But Machon, Joe Jacobs, Doc Casey, and everyone else shouted me down: "You're crazy, Max! The whole world would be laughing. You're the champion and you'll stay the champion." I shook my head, "I don't want the title." Jacobs got more and more wound up: "Defend the title in your next fights! Then you can show them whether you deserve it or not!" Everyone was worked up, everyone was talking to me at once, all trying to persuade me to come around.

Tired and disappointed, I finally gave in and then was driven back to the hotel. But it wasn't long before I regretted my decision. For while forty-seven American states recognized me as the new champion, the New York Commission withheld recognition. They also refused to engrave my name on the Muldoon Trophy in Madison Square Garden with those of previous world champions.

Similarly, my purse of 747,000 marks was initially withheld. But Jim Farley and General Phelan of the New York Boxing Commission finally prevailed and the purses for me and Sharkey were released.

After all this, I wanted to get back home. But in the press releases from Germany I heard some of the old spiteful tones, which only intensified my somber mood. I stayed down for the entire return voyage, and every congratulation only made me more depressed. Now, in the words of Sabri Mahir, I had not only been in the castle, I had also been made king. But my crown was without glory.

---

[1] The black, red, and gold colors chosen by Joe Jacobs represented the Weimar Republic (as opposed to the old Imperial Reich), which by the early thirties pleased practically no one. Certainly those on the far left (hence "red Berlin") and the far right (the Nazis and other nationalist parties) had despised the Republic from the start. Germans were increasingly gravitating to one end of the political spectrum or the other.

～〜～

8

Love at First Sight—Twice

When I returned to Germany I tried to avoid public attention to the extent that that was possible. But when the president of the German Boxing Association suggested to me that I consider giving the title back, I cut him off: "You can save yourself the worry—I've already thought about that one long and hard. The future will rehabilitate my reputation." I didn't even want to attend the receptions and parties that people tried to give for me. I was just so tired of all the talk and only wanted to be with my closest friends.

I rented a new apartment on Sachsenplatz in Berlin's West End, which was larger and nicer than my place in Steglitz. This was an area they called "the New West," a kind of fashionable suburb in the extreme western part of the city. About thirty years earlier, prominent people started moving away from the old heart of the city near Unter den Linden,* following the Kurfürstendamm* westwards. Now artists, writers, and actors were moving even further west.[1]

Since I had appeared in *Love in the Ring* with Olga Tschechova, she and I had become good friends. We spent many evenings together, and one or the other of us would often swing by and pick up the other on the way to visit mutual friends. One afternoon as we sat over a cup of coffee at Schilling's on Kurfürstendamm, Olga suggested that we take in a movie. "In the Gloria Palace they're showing *The Girl from Rummelplatz*," she said. "They say that your neighbor Anny Ondra is supposed to be dynamite in it."

In fact Anny Ondra did live next door; her blue, chauffer-driven Cadillac was often parked out front. But my first impression had been somewhat negative due to a baby carriage—in which an apparently unattended baby cried continuously—which was always parked on what appeared to be her balcony.

∽∾∽

The film featured the spunky, pretty blond in a role tailor-made for her, and she showed herself to have a rare talent—especially for the stars of those times—for comedy. I was captivated at first glance. Even as we left the theater and strolled down Kurfürstendamm, I had to confess somewhat tactlessly to Olga Tschekova, "I'd like to meet Anny Ondra—could you help me out?" She replied, a little hurt, but mostly amused, "You're going to have to do that yourself! I'm not a very good matchmaker." We walked on a little further, and I really don't remember what we talked about—probably about Olga's new film roles and my tribulations and plans. But one thing is certain: my thoughts were only on how I could meet Anny Ondra.

The very next day I got together with Paul Damski, a well-known boxing promoter who was hardly a shrinking violet. He was the only one of my friends whom I trusted to be uninhibited enough to simply ring Ms. Ondra's doorbell and put in a word for me. "No problem, Max," said Damski, a White Russian who had fled the Revolution to Germany.

A few days later he made his way to Anny Ondra's door and unceremoniously rang the bell. She must have stared, unimpressed, at the somewhat stocky man with the garish bouquet of flowers as he explained his mission in broken German: "I have this friend, Frau Ondra, you know, Max Schmeling, the world champion. He's asking gracious lady if gracious lady wouldn't go with him for a cup of coffee or something."

The conversation apparently ended there. Anyway, Damski came back—upset and still holding the bouquet—and told me, "I can tell you right now, it's hopeless. Your ladylove isn't interested."

But fourteen days later I sent him back: "This time say 'Herr Schmeling may be the world champion, but he's too scared to approach you himself. It's his birthday tomorrow and his only wish is to meet you—even if it's only for two minutes." This time Damski had more luck. Anny told me later that she had made some calls to check me out: "There's this crazy man, the boxer Max Schmeling. He keeps sending some character around to see if I'll meet him."

Whatever her sources told her apparently wasn't too bad, because she agreed to meet Damski and me at Cafe Corso on Reichskanzlerplatz at four. I waited there along with Max Machon, whom I had brought for fear of having nothing to say. By way of greeting, I said the only Czech sentence that I had learned from Jarmila: "Jak se vam dari? How are you?" She was clearly relieved and immediately began bubbling over to me in Czech.

When I explained that this sentence constituted my entire Czech vocabulary, she laughed; and when I told her that I had learned it from Jarmila Vacek, she seemed reassured and began to loosen up a bit. The fact that I didn't dare meet her alone seemed to convince her that I was harmless.

∽∽∽

And now we had a few things that we could talk about. She told me of her parents, that her father had been an officer in the Austro-Hungarian Imperial Army. She and Jarmila had both come up together at the Drama Academy and Prague's Svanda Theater, and she had had her first theatrical success in the role of Candidia in Wedekind's* *Pandora's Box*. A director named Carl Lamac had seen her skating one day and signed her to a film contract. Then we chatted about Prague, its bars and cafes that I knew through Jarmila. Incidently, I also learned that the bawling baby on the balcony wasn't her's but her neighbor's.

It wasn't long before I felt comfortable enough to invite her to drive out to Lanke bei Bernau with me. At first she said no, but I persisted, and she finally agreed to telephone and see if she could break a previous engagement. A half hour later we were in my car driving along the Reichsstrasse out of the city. Only much later did she tell me that she had made up the previous engagement and hadn't telephoned at all.

When we said good-bye, she promised to call me in the next few days. But when she still hadn't called eight days later, I finally took the initiative and dialled her number. She apologized and then, as if to repair the damage, invited my friends and me to tea on Sunday.

I made Max Machon and Paul Damski promise that after a short time they would remember a previous engagement and excuse themselves. After a half hour I saw Machon give Damski—who was visibly starting to relax and enjoy himself—a good kick. Damski winced and looked under the table: "Ah, I'm glad you reminded me," which made little sense since no one had said anything, "we have an important engagement." They both stood up abruptly, barely giving me time to add, "But I have nothing to do with this engagement."

As Machon and Damski said their awkward good-byes in the hall, Anny Ondra invited me to stay. Then she disappeared for a few moments and returned, asking "Shall we listen to some music?" When I nodded yes, she called her maid and asked her to put on a record.

We listened to soundtracks from the latest hit movies, but it was somewhat annoying that exactly as each record ended—about every three minutes—the maid would promptly reappear to put on a new record and crank the record player. Pretty soon I was cursing this infernal appliance that was ruining my visit. But of course that is what Anny had intended. She watched my nervousness with amusement and finally asked with feigned innocence if I didn't care for music. As I squirmed nervously she finally laughed out loud, at which point I relaxed and joined her. From this moment on we were friends. During the weeks that followed I left a bouquet every morning on the blue Cadillac parked in front of her door.

The wisdom of my decision to stay as much as possible out of the public eye became clear to me at a boxing night in the Sports Palace, where I was to be officially presented as the new world heavyweight champion. But when I was called into the ring, a barrage of derisive whistles started in! Attacks in the press—especially from Rolf Nürnberg's *Twelve O'Clock Gazette*—against the "Low Blow Champion" had convinced the public that I didn't deserve the title.

It was the first time that Anny Ondra had accompanied me to this type of an occasion. But instead of the expected ovation for her boyfriend, she experienced his humiliation. But that wasn't the only reason that the whistles and putdowns got to me. I was also hurt by the fact that every evening in the city's cabarets I was an object of ridicule. Max Pallenberg* had written a sketch about me, the *Kabarettist* Paul Nikolaus* did a satire, and Will Schaeffers* performed an ironic lesson on how you could become a winner by losing.

Throughout all of this, however, I tried to keep reminding myself that there is a certain price to be paid when one leaves the private sphere. Whoever enters the spotlight expecting only cheers should stay out of it in the first place—that's a simple rule. The true professional has to play by the rules: sign autographs when and wherever, be able to take the abuse that comes with celebrity, don't show fatigue or a bad mood in public. The people are your public, and there is only one way to win them over—through achievement. Others may feel differently, but this was always my outlook.

Nevertheless, a new tone could now be heard in the rallies and demonstrations of recent weeks—a disturbing aggressiveness that I had never noticed before. Looking back, it almost seems as if the public mood had unconsciously changed with the calendar, the boisterous good times of the twenties were over, and they wouldn't return. The faces of the people in the Sports Palace were like those you saw on the street: serious, tired, bitter. The public's passion and devotion had up until now been for actors, athletes, and adventurers—the mountain-climber Hans Stuck, Charles Lindbergh, or Gustav Jaenecke. Now people were turning more and more to political demagogues and "saviors."

Of course, this was the effect of the sudden economic downturn. In October and November of 1929 the crash of the New York stock market unleashed an immediate crisis in Germany. Business failures and mass layoffs led to a landslide of ever increasing unemployment. Month after month the army of relief recipients grew by the hundreds of thousands. The crisis affected all professions without distinction, in the cities and country alike. The earlier skirmishes among the various political parties, the rapid succession of chancellors, and even the occupations mandated by the Treaty of Versailles really hadn't brought the masses to the streets; that didn't happen until the lines in

༉ཊ

front of the unemployment offices and at the soup kitchens—the unemployed languishing in the city parks—awakened the fear of the "little man" of sliding down the economic ladder. Suddenly the streets were filled with gangs of thugs, the private armies of the warring political parties. And in the arenas where yesterday's matadors of sport had been cheered, now were crowds of desperate people singing the "International" or the "Swastika Song."

The same fears were apparently affecting me too, because at this time of uncertainty I decided that I should invest my money in a place of my own. I ended up choosing Saarow-Pieskow, an idyllic little spot on the Scharmützelsee, about an hour's drive southeast of Berlin. I had been there a couple of times and seen the growth of a quaint artist colony, separated from the former fishing village by a small patch of woods. Among the residents were the actor Harry Liedtke* and painter Bruno Krauskopf, Walter Kollo,* and Victor de Kowa.*

The gabled house with the thatch roof was another case of love at first sight, although it wasn't finished when I bought it. Next door lived Josef Thorak,* a talented sculptor whose star was very much on the rise. Anny and I quickly became friends with him and his wife and spent many a pleasant evening at their home.

Thorak was a Tyrolean with a broad, somewhat frightening face and a lion's mane of silver-gray hair. Although he was always broke and often had to fall back on pottery and wood carvings to make ends meet, he still managed to be a gracious host. And there were also a number of art patrons who were always ready to buy his works or give him an advance on forthcoming works.

Like Thorak himself, his parties had a simple, peasant quality, and he preferred to serve his guests hearty dishes with beer from the keg. Wearing an apron, he stood behind a wooden table and carved huge, juicy slices of smoked ham or pork.

I still remember one of those parties at which a butcher from a neighboring town had been summoned to provide his famous sausage soup. The whole colony was there, as well as people who had made a special trip from Berlin. But pretty soon everyone had pushed their bowl aside—the watery grey brew was horrible.

Frau Thorak was beside herself and telephoned the butcher, who came immediately. "What in Heaven's name have you served your guests?" In the kitchen he pointed to the unopened pot of *Wurstsuppe*. Thorak had mixed up the pots and served his guests dish water instead of soup.

Anny was just as excited by Saarow-Pieskow. Before long we were planning the building completion and finishing the interior. Our new friends and neighbors helped as well, and we soon put in a swimming pool, which was a big deal in those times. We called our house "Auf dem Dudel."

❧❧❧

Right in the middle of this time of relaxing and pulling back from the spotlight (early 1931) came the news that the New York Boxing Commission had designated the opponent for my first title defense. It was neither Jack Dempsey, as many had expected, nor was it Jack Sharkey, but rather an incredibly strong fighter with 270 fights behind him and an astonishing record of 127 knockouts. His name was William Young Stribling.

[1] Whether intentional or not, Schmeling's observation on the westward movement of Berlin's cultural elite is ironic indeed. Much of the cultural life of the Weimar Republic had been characterized by movement in a westward, modernizing direction, drawing heavily on American popular culture; many of these same people would soon be forced to flee westward as well.

∽∾∾

9

Belated Atonement

At the beginning of February I was back in New York. The talk of the town this time was the world's tallest building, which was just being completed on the corner of Fifth Avenue and 34th Street. William Frederic Lamp had built a 102-story building that could house thousands workers. It was 381 meters high not counting a 67-meter-high radio tower on top. The Empire State Building loomed over the former world's tallest building, the Eifel Tower, by over 100 meters and wasn't surpassed for nearly half a century.

In order to build up the gate for the upcoming fight, Joe Jacobs had arranged a series of exhibition matches, which had me once again crisscrossing the country. We finally took a break for a few days in Florida and put up at Miami's luxurious Beach Hotel.

But even during this break I still kept up a daily training routine. One day as I was working out I was called to the phone and was greeted on the other end by none other than Count Luckner,* the legendary writer and sailor whose exploits in World War I had brought him world fame. He invited me for that evening aboard his three-masted yacht, the *Mopelia,* which was modelled after his famous *Sea Devil.*

Luckner was popular in the United States for the cat-and-mouse games he had played with allied ships during the war. And the fact that he had done it in an old–fashioned sailing ship was particularly appealing to the American sporting mentality. His knightly demeanor had earned him a great many fans as well—he had been made an honorary citizen of a number of American cities.

Sitting that evening in his cabin, we asked him if he would perform some of the tricks with which he had amazed his "audiences" around the world. Count Luckner could rip telephone books in half, bend silver dollars between his thumb and forefinger, and, the one that I couldn't believe, break through a pencil with a sharply creased dollar bill.

Luckner, whose chiseled features gave him the appearance of a pirate out of Robert Louis Stevenson, was an optimist who believed that his popularity in America foretold a reconcilliation among the peoples of the world, that old hatreds belonged to the past. He believed that technology, adventure, and sports brought people together better than diplomacy and politics ever could. Ten years later Germany was at war not only with America, but with practically the entire world.

While we were in Miami we received another invitation that caused us a little more concern. Al Capone, king of the Chicago underworld, had heard that I was in Miami and invited us to a party at his place outside the city.

Like many gangsters of the time, Al Capone's surface life was that of a businessman whose guests included pillars of society—whether they came out of fascination or fear of offending him. And I was also curious and concerned at the same time. I asked Joe Jacobs to find out how the public and the police would react if we accepted the invitation.

People told us not to worry. Three days later a limousine pulled up in front of the Beach Hotel and a short, stocky man in a blue pin–striped suit came and got us. The chauffer was a giant with curly red hair and a gap-toothed smile. The wrought-iron gate in the double wall around the property was opened by guards who were also wearing pinstripes and felt hats, saluting us as we passed through. We had been told that all autos were searched before entering the property, but this didn't seem to be the case. Yet as we drove up the long gravel driveway to the villa, we were sure that we had seen the barrel of a machine-gun poking from one of the arbors off to the side. Everywhere on the parklike estate—behind hedges and bushes—stood bodyguards.

A uniformed servant took our coats in the entrance hall. Mrs. Capone greeted us with arms outstretched and led us to the reception rooms buzzing with the conversation of several dozen guests. We were told later that these were friends from Miami, as well as guests from New York, Washington, and Chicago—lawyers, doctors, bureaucrats, and businesspeople. Champagne, wine, and whiskey were in abundance, despite Prohibition. The tables were practically groaning under the weight of the choicest of foods—pyramids of lobsters on heavy silver trays, flanked by pheasant, partridge, turkey, as well as bowls of salad, ice-cream confections, cakes, decoratively arranged mountains of pineapples, strawberries and other fruit—it was all overdone, all too lush, as is often the case with those who have come to wealth quickly and easily.

We waited in vain to be introduced to the head of the house. "That must be him," said Max Machon, pointing to a squat, pockmarked man with a receding hairline. His restless eyes almost disappeared beneath bushy eyebrows that had grown together over the bridge of his nose. He stood there holding court in a circle of similar-looking individuals. We tried as inconspicuously as possible to drift closer and hear what was being discussed.

Suddenly he turned to us with a big smile and said, "Hello, boy! You're Max Schmeling, the Black Ulan of the Rhine." And as I smiled back somewhat uncertainly, he grabbed my hand and continued, "And I'm Joe; they call me 'Joe the Boss.' Nice to meet you." Then he introduced me around, and one of his people whom they called "Augi" asked me cordially, "Are you absolutely sure, mister, that you're going to win the fight?"

My answer must have sounded pretty convincing. Anyway, Augi finished with, "That's good to know, Champ! We'll see you later." I wasn't quite sure what that meant, as he turned and walked back to his circle of friends.

When Al Capone still wasn't to be seen after quite a while, I asked Mrs. Capone if she could introduce me to her husband. "I'm awfully sorry," she said "I'm expecting him any minute. He was called out very suddenly. But I'm sure he'll be right back."

But Al Capone didn't come home on that evening or any other for quite some time. He had been arrested—not for the crimes that all America was talking about, but rather for a comparatively harmless case of income-tax evasion. His armies of lawyers couldn't get him off this time, and he spent the next eleven years in Alcatraz, returning home a broken man.

It turned out that "Joe the Boss" had his own set of problems around this time. Two days later the papers reported that he had killed two men in broad daylight and then fled to Florida to avoid arrest. But his flight hadn't done him much good, as he was himself gunned down by a rival gang a short time later.

The Stribling fight had gone to Cleveland. An escort of blaring sirens brought us into the city. Ten carloads of reporters followed my car and then a further police escort led us to the hotel. All along the way were crowds of waving, cheering people. My training camp was outside the city in Conneaut Lake Park, an ideal spot to recover from the exhibition tour and get in my final training for the fight.

My daily regimen consisted of distance runs, films of Stribling's fights, workouts on the training apparatus, massages, and afternoon sparring sessions. The camp was closed off to spectators, not only for the sake of the quiet and concentration I needed before the coming fight but also to keep out any posssible spies.

But at exactly the same time every afternoon a light plane would fly over the open-air training ring, circling at nearly tree-top level, turning around and coming back before leaving with some loops and other fancy stuff. The pilot was none other than Young Stribling, a passionate sport pilot whose acrobatics drove his handlers insane and certainly violated his contract.

But Stribling was in every respect an amazing man and, more than that, one of the most likeable athletes that I ever faced in the ring. Yet the same carefree, youthful quality which had him playing this kind of trick right before a fight that could bring him a world title would only a short time later cost him his life. The amateur racing driver was the victim of a passion for speed mixed with too much recklessness. As his wife was about to give birth, he raced to the hospital on his Harley-Davidson, proud and happy at the same time. On the way, however, he lost control of the motorcycle and crashed. At the hospital they tried to save him by amputating his shattered leg, but he succumbed to his injuries and died on the operating table.

Two hundred fifty arc lights bathed the new Cleveland Stadium—the fight was its first event—in a sea of light. Thirty-two overhead lights were directed at the ring, only intensifying the brutal summer heat. With a deafening roar, special machines sucked the myriad of insects from the air. The betting odds were at 7:5 for Stribling.

Stribling, whose trainer/father was in his corner, had the reputation of being a savvy boxer who knew all the tricks. In the first round he took the initiative from the opening bell, taking advantage of my usual slow start to try to put me away early. I had expected that, but I hadn't expected to be repeatedly thumbed in the eyes.

"I can't see anymore," I said as I came back to my corner after the second round. "Stribling keeps sticking his thumb in my eye." Machon blew up, "Why don't you do the same? This isn't a kindergarten!" Then he shoved me out into the next round. The next time Stribling thumbed me, I gave it right back to him. He looked at me with surprise and didn't try it again.

I started to go on the offensive in round six. Now I was catching him with hard rights, which, despite all his conditioning, began to take their toll. After a seventh round in which he seemed tired and ready to go, he came out of his corner for the eighth like a new man. Although his face was pretty badly marked up, his combinations of left hooks and straight rights were lethal.

But then I decided to turn the fight around for good. I came at him with combinations that drove him all over the ring. And while his legs buckled a number of times, Stribling refused to go down.

Then came the bell for the fifteenth round. Determined to end the fight, I hit Stribling with a devastating left hook to the chin. As if paralyzed, his arms dropped and he fell slowly to the canvas. He managed to rise by nine, but then staggered and fell back on the ropes. There were twenty seconds left in the fight when Stribling's father threw in the towel to end the fight.

⚬〜⚬

Without hesitating, referee Blake came over to me and raised my hand. "Winner by TKO and the old and new heavyweight champion of the world: Max Schmeling!" The crowd gave us both a standing ovation. It had been a great fight.

Only with this victory did I become the true world champion and silence the critics. The New York Boxing Commission finally recognized my title and had my name engraved in the Muldoon Trophy. The sudden change of mood—the unanimous acclaim that came to me from Germany—finally set me free.

It was belated atonement. Only now did I realize how dissatisfied with myself I had been for all those months. The criticism of others only hurt so much because it confirmed my own self-doubt. I hadn't ever been sure that I was the best. Now I was awarded the championship belt by Nat Fleischer's *Ring Magazine*—now I deserved to wear it.

Shortly after the fight I travelled to New York where I would board the liner *Europa* for the trip back to Germany. As I was busy packing in the Commodore Hotel, there came a knock at my door. Before I could even say, "Come in," Augi Scalfaro was standing there in my room. Dapper and awkward at the same time, he pressed a small package into my hand. Then he congratulated me again, tipped his hat and disappeared.

Since I was in a hurry, I tossed the package in my bag; only after a couple of days on the Atlantic did I remember it again. I opened it to find a watch elaborately inlaid with jewels; on the back was the inscription "To Max Schmeling from Augi."

Augi, one of the best-known gamblers in the United States, had bet heavily on my "tip," and my victory had won him a small fortune. The watch was a token of his gratitude. Incidently, I had it appraised in Germany, and it was valued at 4,000 marks.

That summer Anny and I spent as much time as possible together. We had grown very close, sharing our joys and cares, and in the eyes of our friends we were inseparable. In public we kept a lower profile, bending to the unwritten law that a "star's" market value was determined by image—no past, no private life, no family. Consciously or unconsciously, we played the same game.

In the meantime I was looking at a year of forced inactivity. In New York they couldn't seem to decide on an opponent for my next title defense. Along with Jack Sharkey, Mickey Walker had also become a contender. And the manager of the Italian giant Primo Carnera was ready to move heaven and earth to get his man into the title picture.

Anny, on the other hand, was being swamped with offers. In London she had just finished a young Alfred Hitchcock's first sound film, *Blackmail,* and now she was working on a German-French collaboration. A short time before, she and a few Prague friends had started their own production company, with her old friend and discoverer Carl Lamac as manager. The Ondra-Lamac Company produced about eight films a year, most of which featured Anny in the lead role.

At this time there were three screenplays waiting for Anny, and she usually came home late and exhausted, while I spent my days on the shores of Scharmützelsee, walking in the nearby woods, or visiting Josef Thorak in his studio, where in recent weeks he had been sculpting a half-relief of me. It was an idyllic time, maybe the most carefree of my entire life.

Only later did it occur to me that as the Weimar Republic neared its end, the hit songs and films became increasingly light and upbeat. When we drove into Berlin from Saarow-Pieskow, we would come through the grey, impoverished neighborhoods of the unemployed in the eastern part of the city, while along the Kurfürstendamm people flocked to see Lilian Harvey* and Willy Fritsch* in *The Gas Station Three* and everyone was singing the hit song "Darling, My Heart Beats for You." At the movie theater next door they were showing *The Private Secretary* and Renate Müller sang "Today I Am So Happy." The culture of the Weimar Republic is remembered for its serious, revolutionary art—Brecht's *Three Penny Opera* or Ernst Krenek's* *Johnny Spielt Auf*—but for every such work there were a dozen lighter, popular pieces. The city was filled with catchy melodies while the Brown Shirts and Red Front staged brawls in the street.[1]

---

[1]In the early thirties street brawls between Hitler's "Brown Shirts" (*Sturmabteilung* or SA) and the Communist *Rotfront* were increasingly common in Berlin.

10

A Lost Title

At the start of 1932 I was back in New York to do another exhibition tour and discuss my next title defense with Joe Jacobs. Since his defeat, Sharkey had worked very hard to earn a rematch. He had mobilized some powerful supporters among the press and the boxing officials. During my last exhibition series I had been well received, but someone would always yell from the crowd, "What about Sharkey, huh? Give him a chance, Max!"

During my layoff Sharkey had had several fights, all of which he had won, thereby earning himself a title shot. Joe Jacobs, however, was of the opinion that we shouldn't automatically give Sharkey a rematch right away —it wouldn't hurt him to have to wait a bit.

When the exhibition tour came to Boston, Sharkey's home town, the press was waiting with baited breath. Sharkey had let the newspapers know that he would sit ringside and drive me crazy, make a fool of me, offer to take me on then and there.

But it turned out somewhat differently than Sharkey had predicted. No sooner was he called into the ring to take a bow, which he did dancing around with his arms in the air, than I went up to him and greeted him like an old friend. A hush fell over the arena. And before Sharkey could get a word out, I gave him a big hug, clapped him on the shoulder, and gave him a friendly pat on the rear. Then I held the ropes for him and, with a hearty smile, shoved him out of the ring.

Sharkey was somewhat dazed by this, and when the crowd saw that I had mastered the situation, they broke into loud applause. On that same evening I made the official announcement that I would defend my title not against the most frequently mentioned contenders, Primo Carnera or Mickey

Walker, but rather against Jack Sharkey. A few days later the contracts were signed in New York. We agreed on June 21, 1932 as the fight date.

After a short trip to Germany, I came back to the States to start training seriously for the fight. Six weeks before the fight I set up camp at Greenskill Lodge in Kingston, New York, a small, attractive vacation spot about an hour and a half outside New York City.

A few days later I received a phone call from Albany. Governor Franklin Delano Roosevelt's secretary was calling to let us know that he would be paying us a visit. Joe Jacobs and the promoter were ecstatic. As the Democratic candidate for president, and probable winner, Roosevelt was at the center of national attention. His visit meant publicity that money couldn't buy.

Roosevelt came on a Sunday right before training started. The reporters and photographers had already been alerted by his headquarters; after all, a visit to the world heavyweight champion's training camp wasn't bad publicity for him either. Everyone knew that Governor Roosevelt was crippled since contracting polio a few years earlier, so we had put together a platform to help him get out of his car when he arrived. But Roosevelt's response to the platform was a good-natured "Take that thing away!" as he climbed out of his car unassisted and with a broad smile, showing the press that he could get around with his crutches, that he was no cripple and more than up to the office that he was seeking. Then I approached him to recite the official greeting that we had decided on: "Your Honor, Sir, Mr. Governor . . ."

I got about that far before Roosevelt cut me off with, "Oh, never mind, Max! *Wir wollen Deutsch miteinander reden* [let's speak German]!" And as we sauntered over to the open-air practice ring, he said in German, "I know your homeland quite well. I may have even seen more of your country than some Germans."

In fact, Roosevelt had visited Germany as a boy and returned later as part of his study. He knew Heidelberg and Göttingen, he loved Munich and raved about the dark evergreen stretches of the Black Forest. "I love Germany," he said, as he returned to English. From everything that I had heard, Roosevelt's love of Germany was genuine. But some years later Hitler would force Roosevelt to abandon his friendship and become Germany's most determined enemy.

I took Roosevelt over to the seats that had been reserved for him in the shade and climbed into the ring. Then I started my workout. While my visitor watched with great interest for over an hour, his wife Eleanor covered her eyes during the sparring session. She told me later that she couldn't watch two grown men hitting each other like that.

"Of course I'm an American, Max," said Roosevelt when it was time to go, "but I still wish you good luck with the fight!" As we shook hands, I replied, "And you, Your Honor, good luck with the election!"

⤫⤬

After Roosevelt had become president he sent me a picture with a personal dedication, and in an accompanying letter he reminded me of our meeting at Greenskill Lodge. I returned the favor by sending the avid stamp collector special-issue German stamps.

For the upcoming fight, the promoters wanted to avoid the enormous rental cost of Yankee Stadium, so they built a new sports arena with a seating capacity of 70,000. The gates were opened almost before the last nail had been driven. Due to the worsening of the economy, we were pretty skeptical about ticket sales.

But the fight was a sellout, with ticket sales of almost $500,000. The odds were 13:10 in my favor, and I felt in peak condition. Our only worry was that Gunboat Smith, one of Sharkey's closest friends, had been chosen as referee. I tried to reassure a ranting Joe Jacobs, who wanted to register an official protest with the Boxing Commission, that a fight couldn't be bought and sold, that it would be decided by our fists.

Shortly after ten the bell sounded for the first round. I was the champion and Sharkey wanted my title, so he had to attack and come after it. But to everyone's surprise, Sharkey remained cautious in the early rounds, feeling me out and seeming to wait for an opening.

During the break after the fourth round, Max Machon told me to go on the attack myself and force the pace of the fight. Only after Sharkey had been tagged hard by my left did he show the rage that made him so dangerous. By going all out, he managed to score some needed points, but the desperate attack also took a lot out of him. Only in the tenth round did he manage another rally, but I handled his rushes without any problems. Exhausted and with his left eye closed, Sharkey returned to his corner on leaden legs.

The last five rounds belonged to me. Sharkey was tough and clever, but he didn't have much left. He clinched a lot and had to eat the hardest punches of those rounds. But he didn't go down. After the thirteenth round, the early press release was "Winner: Schmeling."

In the fifteenth round I put it all on the line to finish Sharkey. I had to be far ahead on points, but after our last fight, I wanted to win this one all the way. Despite hard shots to the body and head, however, Sharkey managed to survive the round. After the final bell, a badly marked-up Sharkey groped his way back to his corner. The anticipation in the arena wasn't nearly as great as for some of my earlier fights. The match seemed to have been clearly decided and the decision a foregone conclusion.

Gunboat Smith conferred with the judges at ringside. Then he gestured Sharkey and me to the center of the ring and raised Sharkey's arm, yelling out, "Winner on points and new world champion—Jack Sharkey!"

I couldn't believe my ears; dazed, I looked over to Max Machon in my corner, then to Doc Casey and Joe Jacobs. Shaking my head, I forced myself to move; with tears in my eyes and an exhausted smile, I went over to Sharkey and congratulated him.

Joe Jacobs, however, stormed into the ring. "We wuz robbed,"[1] he yelled angrily when the reporters gave him the microphone. "They stole the title from us!" I was also asked to comment, and I simply said, "I don't believe that I lost the fight." Then I didn't want to hear or see any more. Depressed, I left the ring and went to my dressing room.

It wasn't long before New York's Mayor Jimmy Walker came down to see me. "Max, that was a bum decision," he said as he put his hand on my shoulder. "There was only one winner as far as I'm concerned, and that was Max Schmeling." Suddenly Gene Tunney was there, too. "That decision is a scandal," he said; "Sharkey was on the defensive for the entire fifteen rounds—nobody ever won the title that way." And to the reporters on hand he said even more vehemently, "This decision is a disaster for the sport. On my card Schmeling won going away." And the next day Tunney's words were in all the papers.

As everyone was trying to drown out everyone else, another reporter stormed into my dressing room and shouted that he had just taken an unofficial poll of boxing experts at ringside. "Of the twenty-five I asked, twenty-three voted for you. Even Muldoon," he added, "said that he was shocked by the decision." He went on to report that Sharkey was sitting in his dressing room with a badly battered face and was refusing to let any photographers in.

The American press was unanimous in condemning the decision as one of the worst in boxing history, which still didn't help me any. I had lost the title, and it was clear to me that I wouldn't be getting a return shot anytime in the near future. America wasn't about to let the title go back to Europe.

The fight had another consequence as well. The Boxing Commission rescinded Joe Jacobs's license for an indeterminate time for "unbecoming behavior." Resigned to the situation, Max Machon and I booked passage back to Germany on the *Columbus*. On July 3, 1932 I was back in Berlin. Sooner than I expected, however, I was again in New York. Despite his license suspension, Joe Jacobs had succeeded in getting me a fight with Mickey Walker, who, along with Primo Carnera, was one of the top contenders for a title shot. So in three months I was standing in the ring at the center of Long Island's new stadium facing the "Nebraskan Wildcat." Counter to my usual strategy, I went on the offensive from the opening bell, overwhelming Walker with a hail storm of punches. In the first minute of the fight he went down from a hard right, and in the seven rounds that followed he never had a chance despite his courage. He went down a number of times, but always managed to stagger back to his feet. Having again been knocked to the canvas, he barely made it to the end of the seventh round. Since I didn't want to keep beating on an opponent who was beyond defending himself, I made the unusual request of referee Denning to stop the fight; of course that wasn't allowed, and he ignored the request.

But as the bell rang for the ninth round, Walker's corner had seen enough. His manager, Jack Kearns,[2] signalled that his man was through. The referee then declared me the winner by TKO. Mickey Walker later told me that from the first round on he had been seeing "three Schmelings" in front of him. That was his last important fight, but he went on to become a well-known painter whose works were widely exhibited in galleries and museums.

With the Walker fight I felt that I had secured the right to another title shot. After all, Sharkey had only boxed Walker to a draw. The champion then declared himself ready to face me a third time. But in this situation Joe Jacobs, whose negotiating talent had done so much for me, made a bad mistake. When Sharkey's management offered us 12 percent of the gate, which was customary for the challenger in a championship fight, the normally so astute Jacobs turned it down.

Without knowing it, Joe Jacobs had played right into the hands of the promoters and the Boxing Commission, because the commission really didn't want to see another Schmeling versus Sharkey fight. They were much more interested in giving a chance to an exciting young newcomer. He was the new crowd favorite, a California native who had all the qualities of a world-class boxer; and he had already destroyed journeymen like Ernie Schaaf and Tuffy Griffith—his name was Max Baer.

Back in Berlin I decided to take a few days off to go hunting with some friends. After a day in the forest we came back to the hunting lodge, and almost immediately the phone rang. It was Anny Ondra, and she was in tears. She stammered that everything was out, that our relationship was through. "Everything's out! Out!" she repeated.

In vain I tried to get from her what she was talking about. "What in God's name is wrong? What's out?" She sobbed, *"The Herald!"* "What *Herald?*" I asked. "What are you talking about?" Finally I got her to tell me that a Berlin tabloid, *The Herald,* had come out with the headlines "Love Affair: Max Schmeling—Anny Ondra!" Anny thought that I would be angry and want to break off our relationship.

But to me it seemed to be damage that could be easily repaired. On that very same evening I left the hunting lodge and drove back to Berlin. I didn't say much, I just took Anny in my arms and asked her to marry me. Her answer was a happy smile, and we sat together and wrote a letter to her mother in which I formally asked for her daughter's hand in marriage. A few days later we published the banns and set the wedding for the coming summer.

[1] Joe Jacobs's justified outrage gave birth to one of the most enduring sports clichés.

[2] Jack "Doc" Kearns achieved even greater notariety as Jack Dempsey's manager. He created a great deal of controversy years later when he claimed to have wrapped Jack Dempsey's hands in plaster of paris for Dempsey's title fight with Jess Willard in 1919.

11
The End of an Interlude

As caught up as I was in my own triumphs and setbacks, I really didn't notice the change that turned out to be Hitler's takeover. On January 30, 1933 Reich President von Hindenburg named the "Bohemian Corporal," as he called Hitler in private, to the office of Reich Chancellor. Days later my friends from downtown Berlin told me of the torchlight parade through the Brandenburg Gate, of the mass celebrations and hysteria. Outside my apartment in the West End, however, there was none of that. After the fact, people spoke of an awareness of history in the making, but mostly it wasn't like that at all. Surviving newsreels give the impression of a city and a people wild with excitement and change. But in reality the celebrations were limited to the inner city and a few neighborhoods controlled by the National Socialists.

Still, you could soon sense that something new had begun, a bustling energy had come over the country, new confidence, new hope. The most visible sign of this was to be seen in a both emotional and silly new form of expression that had suddenly swept through the entire country: there were marches practically everywhere.

A week or so later I was at my Jewish tailor's shop on Unter den Linden; his name was Molldauer, and he was married to an actress. City traffic hummed on the street below while we looked at material and checked measurements; but then a stomping rhythm gradually began to mix with the normal street sounds—fife and drums and brass instruments becoming louder and louder. Everyone ran to the windows—the tailors, customers, and finally Molldauer and I.

Following the musicians down Unter den Linden* marched a division of SA Brown Shirts. With their banners and uniforms, they looked threatening;

it was one of those "propaganda marches" whose purpose was to instill the public with a mixture of fear and excitement.

And those were the reactions that ran through Molldauer's shop; even Molldauer turned around and said, "Isn't it tremendous!" He was a nice, older gentleman, and I wasn't sure whether he was really excited or had lost his mind. Mostly I think he was trying to keep up a good front while preparing to leave. In any case, it was the last time I saw him; a few weeks later he was gone.

Other seemingly contradictory behavior was that of the clairvoyant Hanussen, himself threatened, yet, through his friendship with Count Helldorf,* somehow close to a clique of the Nazi inner sanctum. In the Romanisches Cafe, the bastion of the liberal literati, the clairvoyant and charaltan forced his rival Max Möcke to stand on one of the small marble tables and with outstretched arm swear his allegiance to Hitler. Was he playing up to those whom he feared? Was it a perverse desire to humiliate a rival? Certainly he didn't really share the sentiments that he had forced Möcke to express. Whatever sham, arrogance, or desperation was at work, the result was the same—both Hanussen and Möcke would be swallowed alive by the storm that followed.

But it wasn't as if the country had been divided into two opposing camps—followers and opponents of the regime. We were so used to frequent changes in the government—the previous year and a half had seen three Reich Chancellors—that no one viewed Hitler's appointment as a "final chapter."

It's very difficult to recall even one's own feelings after so much time. In my own circle of friends I think there were some who were hopeful, some concerned, and some deeply depressed, especially Fritz Kortner, Ernst Deutsch, and Renée Sintenis; but most seemed to have the feeling that it wouldn't last, that the whole thing would be over in six months.

One day towards the end of April, I was having dinner with some friends in the Hahnen Restaurant on Nollendorfplatz where the German Motorclub had its regular table. Among the prominent racing drivers there were Rudolf Caracciola, Hans Stuck, and Bernd Rosemeyer. As we were having dessert, an SA officer came into the restaurant, saluted the room with outstretched arm, and then came over to our table. "Herr Schmeling, the Führer requests that you join him for dinner at the Reich Chancellory." I replied that I had just eaten, but that I would gladly come. We drove to the Reich Chancellory in a big government limousine, and as we turned into Wilhelmstrasse, people stopped and stared into the limo to see who was in it.

It was the same Reichstag building in which Bismarck had carried out his official duties. Some adjutants who were waiting at the door led me into an anteroom and asked me to wait a moment. I had barely walked over to the window when the door opened and Hitler appeared, surrounded by Göring,

❧❧❧

Goebbels, and most of the other cabinet members. Without hesitating, Hitler came directly over to me and said, "Good day, Herr Schmeling, how good of you to come. I wanted to invite you to join me for dinner." He was shorter than I had imagined, but, more than anything else, there was none of the rigid, overdone intensity of his public appearances. When we had driven into the city from Saarow-Pieskow in the last few years, we would see his election posters in the villages and towns that we drove through, and Anny would always laugh at his resemblance to Charlie Chaplin. But in this moment there was nothing comical or absurd in his bearing; he moved about in a relaxed way, he was charming and seemed quietly confident in these surroundings. I answered, "Herr Reichskanzler, thank you very much, but I have just eaten." Hitler accepted that in a friendly manner and said only, "Well, let's at least just chat a bit."

Then one by one his cabinet ministers came into the room. Göring clapped me heartily on the shoulder, Goebbels made a joke about the Sports Palace, and Papen* asked me some trivial question about America. His response to my answer was a bleating laugh. I've forgotten who else was there. We stood there talking for about twenty minutes, and it was a very relaxed atmosphere. As I left, Hitler wished me luck in my upcoming fight. "I've heard that you're going to America," he said. And then casually added, "If anyone over there asks how it's going in Germany, you can reassure the doomsayers that everything is moving along quite peacefully." Standing at the door as I left, he asked me to let him know if I ever needed anything.

As I was being driven home it occurred to me that Hitler had probably summoned me for exactly that reason—that I carry his message to America. He was the master of public relations and must have realized that I would give dozens of interviews in America, which would appear in hundreds of American newspapers.

Since becoming chancellor, Hitler had often invited athletes and actors to tea in the Reich Chancellory. He courted the worlds of stage, art, and sports with congratulations for success, with flowers and invitations. Anny had also received this attention after more than one premiere. He probably enjoyed this milieu and surely wanted to win them over. I had the impression that with him everything was multi-layered and that at that time there were still some positive layers to be found.

On the ride home I couldn't help but feel a little flattered; let's face it, one can also be bribed by small favors. At that point I had been German and European champion for years and the first European to win the world heavyweight championship. But never once in Germany—it was different in the States—had a politician paid me the slightest attention, not a minister and certainly not a Reich Chancellor. I can't remember even a telegram.

∾∾∾

For years it had been my wish, just once to meet the Reich President, and through some friends I had let Hindenburg's office know this. But with Hindenburg you had to be from the nobility. The only athletes received by him were the equestrian Freiherr von Langen and the "Tennis Baron" Gottfried von Cramm.* As for me, I never got beyond Berlin's mayor, Dr. Böss.

Maybe this small bribery did have its effect on me at first; anyway, I did, here and there, see some positive things in the new regime. Hitler really had begun to achieve some of his election promises within a few short months. Unemployment had been significantly reduced. The street disturbances, violence and shootings had stopped. But the crimes and acts of violence perpetrated by the new masters were covered over by a shrill carnival atmosphere.

Certainly there were those in middle-class circles who found the National Socialists offensive, who took them to be nothing more than loudmouths and rather ordinary braggarts. I and many of my friends didn't take such offense at first. After all, it was a revolution, and wasn't Hitler correct when he said that compared to the Russian Revolution, this was "the least bloody revolution in world history?" But mostly my friends and I weren't offended by the vulgar carnival atmosphere that the new regime brought with it because all of us had more or less come from that very same circus milieu: it seemed to be just another aspect of our show-business world.

How ignorant we all were of what lay ahead! Sometimes we would joke that if Hitler didn't make it in Germany he could have a spectacular career as an entertainer in the "New World." And in fact he did draw huge crowds to his public appearances—like a circus star in the arena, accompanied by banners and fanfare, drums and flourishes.

But the awakening came soon enough. From early in 1933 on, we started to miss at least one person a week from our usual crowd at the Roxy, at Aenne Maenz's place, at the Romanisches Cafe. Molldauer had been the first, and soon we looked in vain for Fritz Kortner, Ernst Deutsch was simply gone one day, as was Ernst Josef Aufricht. Then Ludwig Bergner* was gone, then Richard Tauber,* and finally Albert Bassermann.* We heard that Bertolt Brecht* and Kurt Weill* had also emigrated. We gradually became aware that there was a price to be paid.

In New York I met again with the German Consul General, whom I had come to know well since my first New York fights. When I told him of Hitler's "assignment" for me in America, he said, "It's all going to end in disaster. Believe me, Herr Schmeling, there's going to be a bloodbath in Germany. It's all going to end in war." To which I replied, "But there can't be a war—who's going to attack whom? Hitler with his 100,000 men?"[1] But the Consul General stood fast: "There's going to be a war, I'm telling you, there will be a war."

My New York friends were almost all Jews, Joe Jacobs foremost among them. When I told them about the reception at the Reich Chancellory, they kidded me and asked what Hitler had said when I told him that I would be boxing a Jewish Max Baer. Wouldn't that be forbidden in the new Reich as a form of athletic "race crime." We just laughed.

A few weeks before the Baer fight I received a visit at my training camp from Jack Dempsey, who was one of the backers of the fight and wanted to feed the ballyhoo with a personal appearance. Since he had announced that he would spar with me, several thousand spectators showed up.

Dempsey greeted me cordially as in the old days; politics hadn't yet entered our world. Then he asked me if I would go easy on him in sparring and try not to hit him in the face. Dempsey had also entered the movie world and had recently gotten a nose-job for an upcoming role. I jokingly promised that I would be careful. But Max Machon had barely left the ring when Dempsey stormed over to me—as he would have in his prime—and decked me with a barrage of punches. For a moment I had the wind literally knocked out of me, but I felt compelled to be a good sport about it. However when Dempsey continued to attack and landed a hard right on my headgear, I forgot our deal. I countered with a hard right to his nose, whereupon he staggered backwards and, laughing, put up his hands in surrender as the crowd applauded. To the reporters Dempsey said, "Max is in excellent shape and still has an outstanding right hand."

Despite the weeks of training, I decisively lost the fight against Max Baer. I can't say why. Maybe it was the brutal heat that day in New York. Even before the fight sweat was pouring down my body. During the whole fight I felt paralyzed.

"Move, for God's sake, move!" yelled Max Machon between rounds. "Move away from him, get him missing." But my legs were like lead and only rarely did I manage to avoid or neutralize Baer's punches. Standing still, I offered the Californian an easy target. By the time Baer's corner told him to finish it in the eighth round I could barely hold up my arms. After several knockdowns, referee Authur Donovan finally stopped it in the tenth round. In the dressing room Max Machon said, "That wasn't a defeat, that was a disaster."

Then the reporters swarmed in and asked how such a defeat was possible. I didn't have an answer. I just shrugged my shoulders and took refuge in the adage that one could only win if one were prepared to lose as well. In the newspapers of the following day it was reported that I had been way off my form, barely recognizable as the Schmeling of earlier fights. It was the worst defeat of my career.

෴

What really bothered me wasn't so much the defeat itself, but rather the way it happened. Max Baer had simply outclassed me as no one had before. I was completely awake and saw practically all of Baer's punches coming. But my body no longer obeyed me—I gave it commands, but it didn't react. Long before Max Baer's punches rocked me, I was demoralized by the fact that I was no longer the master of my reflexes.

And that was the reason for the personal crisis that plagued me now. I swore to myself that I wouldn't hang up my gloves; I wasn't going to retire after so humiliating a fight. But in the months that followed I continued to torture myself. The following winter I fought the young American Steve Hamas in Philadelphia; as a college football hero he was extremely popular, but certainly not in the first rank of heavyweight boxers. Yet he decisively outpointed me, and I fell into a deep depression.

In endless conversations with myself I went around and around, tormenting myself with the same thoughts: you can't quit now, not after losses like those. After all, you were the heavyweight champion of the world. This can't be the end of your career, defeated by a kid just starting out! I also told myself that I hadn't been defeated by better boxers. In my normal form I would have beaten Baer and Hamas without that much trouble. And finally, I was only twenty-seven. In the history of boxing there had been plenty of fighters who had made it to the top in their early thirties.

But did I really need to be dragging myself from ring to ring suffering defeat after humiliating defeat? After all, I had earned millions of marks and didn't have to worry about the future. No one was forcing me to travel the boondocks fighting second-rate talent, only to destroy what reputation I had left.

The little accidents to which I had suddenly become prone were symptoms of the crisis: getting out of a car I fell flat on my face; I fell down some stairs in a hotel; I dropped a cup at breakfast.

It was never so clear to me as in this time how precarious a boxer's career is. I had told myself that during the good times, but I had never experienced it. It was only now that I was beginning to realize what a boxer's existence can become.

It was during this time that our wedding was scheduled. Anny and I had set the date, and everything was ready. We had said "yes" to each other when both our careers were at a high point. Anny wasn't only one of the most sought after stars of her time, she was also an extremely successful businesswoman. I had lost my title, although not by a convincing defeat. But as we stood before the altar of the little church in Saarow-Pieskow on July 6, 1933, things had changed quite a bit. My string of bad luck hadn't changed, and Anny was deeply hurt by nasty letters she had received about my slump.

There were even articles here and there that implied that I was having an affair with another actress.

Still, our wedding turned out to be a happy occasion. On the invitations we had reminded guests to bring bathing suits, and on that hot July afternoon we all jumped into the pool. The celebration lasted into the night, but I think I felt somewhere in the back of my mind that for all our happiness there was a touch of regret. Had we really forgotten the friends who were no longer with us, or was our partying a sign of wanting to forget. What were our true feelings as we looked at the Japanese maple that Hitler had given us as a wedding present?

A few months earlier, Fritz Kortner and Ernst Deutsch would have been among the guests; now they had both been forced to leave the country. George Grosz was also missing, gone to New York. Most of Anny's partners in Ondra-Lamac Productions had returned to Prague. It seemed more and more that we were all now living in two worlds.

We spent our honeymoon at the Baltic Sea resort of Heiligendamm. While the newspapers speculated on the Riviera or Venice, we were building sand castles, swimming in the waves, and learning how to skeet shoot. We had each other and didn't need to make headlines.

When we returned there was some bad news waiting for Anny. She had never given any thought to the fact that four of the six partners of her production company were Jews and the other two Czechs. Now even the mighty Gugenberg, a minister in Hitler's cabinet, could not protect his UFA;* there too, Jewish directors, cameramen, and actors had to get out. The prospects for Anny's little company on Friedrichstrasse were not good. Suddenly they were getting no more work, and there were no longer half dozen scripts waiting to be considered.

Berlin had become so international that no one asked your nationality or where you were from. Robert Sidomak had been an American, Billy Wilder* came from Austria, and Anny Ondra from Czechoslovakia. Now suddenly one's passport took on an unexpected significance—not only for those in danger who had to flee the country, but also for those who ran a business. For a time Anny considered moving the firm to America; she had had a number of offers from Hollywood. But then, after much consulting with lawyers, it was decided to liquidate Ondra-Lamac Productions.

Not until three decades later did I read the memoirs of Carl Zuckmayer,* whose premieres the old Berlin crowd used to attend. There he wrote what all had felt who were driven from Berlin. "From no other place in Germany was it so difficult to separate oneself," he wrote. "Half of our life remained back there."

In the meantime on the other side of the Atlantic there was a changing of the guard in the heavyweight division. Primo Carnera, approximately six feet five inches tall and weighing around 260 pounds, had always been considered by the experts to be only a mediocre boxer. They said he couldn't really punch, that he just sort of clubbed his opponents. In fact, his reach was much greater than that of any opponent, and the leverage that that gave him enabled his punches to penetrate almost any defense. In contrast to the experts, I had always considered Carnera to be a technically sound boxer, so I wasn't surprised to hear that he had knocked Sharkey out in the sixth round to become the second European to win the world heavyweight title. Within the same year he successfully defended his title against Paolino; he did this in Italy in front of Mussolini.

Most American experts, however, felt that Max Baer was the world's best heavyweight, and everyone was eagerly awaiting a Carnera-Baer matchup. And this fight did take place a few months later, with the young Californian knocking out the Italian in the eleventh round.

So these were the boxers who ruled the scene. I had to fight one of them successfully in order to get back into the heavyweight picture, to start doing business in America again.

Paolino must have had similar thoughts after losing to Carnera. He too needed a decisive victory over a big name—preferably a former champion—to regain his drawing power in American rings. Logic told us that we needed each other. At the start of 1934 I received Paolino's challenge to even the ledger after his 1929 loss to me in New York. Our managers quickly came to an agreement and the fight was set for April 1934. The bout would take place in Spain, where Paolino's popularity would guarantee a full house.

Five weeks before the fight I left for training camp, accompanied for the first time by Anny. But the string of mishaps wasn't over yet. In sparring, an eyebrow cut I had received in the Hamas fight reopened, and for a few days I could only work out on the apparatus. My old friend Douglas Fairbanks, Jr. had come to Barcelona with his wife Lady Ashley (who later married Clark Gable), and we played some golf together during this time.

I found out just how popular Fairbanks was in Spain as we sat at dusk in an open-air cafe along the Ramblas. Douglas Fairbanks, Jr., young, dashing, with the hint of a mustache, seemed even in private life to be the hero of a Three Musketeers movie. We kidded him with the nickname Count Douglas. This was Hollywood fame—we were surrounded by people, and Fairbanks couldn't even take a sip from his cup without unleashing an admiring chorus of "oohs" and "aahs."

In the very last round of sparring I slipped and fell, landing badly. Machon tore off my gloves. The thumb was broken; the doctors determined that it was actually split. The fight had to be postponed. I went back to Germany and tried to stay in shape with running and calisthenics. The fight date was pushed back to May 13.

The staging of the fight was very Spanish, something like a grandiose fiesta. Three rings were set up in the middle of an arena, and for the entire day seventy boxers fought thirty-five bouts leading up to our main event in the evening.

As the gong for the first round sounded, I felt as if I were fighting not just Paolino, but, also his 30,000 countrymen cheering him on with latin enthusiasm. But I didn't have any problems with him. The thumb injury didn't hurt anymore, and, as in our first fight, I didn't give him an opportunity to get on track.

Paolino, normally an attacking boxer, never got a chance to come off the defensive. With the first exchange of punches I felt like my old self and knew that Paolino couldn't hurt me. Again and again he ran into my left; but he took these punches along with my hardest rights. He didn't go down once. Breathing heavily and with a swollen face, he wearily returned to his corner after the final gong.

To the amazement of even Paolino's most dedicated fans, the decision was a draw. There was even a storm of protest. A local paper had, in order to scoop the competition, been calling in results after each round. As the fans exited the stadium, that paper's headline read: "Schmeling beats Paolino."

The decision was a farce. All the Spanish papers said that it was a bad decision, even ludicrous, and the Catalonian paper *Diagraphico* wrote that from the first round on, Paolino had been nothing more than a punching bag. *La Vanguardia* wrote: "There can be no more decisions like this one, which hurts the prestige of Paolino, Spain, and the sport of boxing."

I was disappointed by the decision, but not depressed. There wasn't a single moment of the fight in which I didn't feel in control. The old ability, my punching power and most of all my reflexes—which had been missing in the Baer and Hamas fights—were back. In this condition I could confidently go against a world-class American boxer.

I returned to Germany feeling good and with my old self-confidence. Since Anny was shooting a film in Munich, I joined her there instead of Berlin. We had planned to take a few days to just relax.

Then the phone rang. It was Heinrich Hoffmann, Hitler's personal photographer, whom I knew as a member of the *Motorclub von Deutschland*. "The Führer would like to invite you to an outing. We're going to have coffee at Franz Xaver Schwarz's on the Tegernsee."

Hoffmann was chatty, business-minded, and vain, but not unpleasant. As we were getting decked out for the drive to meet Hitler, a long procession of cars pulled up in front of the Regina Palast Hotel, and Hitler himself got out. He greeted Anny and me with courtly Austrian politeness: "I am extremely pleased to make your acquaintance, gracious lady," and "it has been my wish for a long time. . . . We're fortunate in the weather, at Schwarz's we will be able to sit outside in the garden. I hope you brought a shawl. I have left the top down in the car."

Then he galantly motioned Anny—his manner seemed to come from the world of the operetta—toward the car. But we ended up sitting in another car, and I don't remember who rode with Hitler.

At Tegernsee we sat down at one of the large coffee tables in Schwarz's garden. Franz Xaver Schwarz, the Reich Treasurer of the Nazi Party, was one of the longest–standing of Hitler's followers. Frau Schwarz had decorated the table with elaborate place-settings, and there was pound cake and strudel with lots of whipped cream.

I don't remember that anything in particular was discussed, only that everyone seemed to be fairly relaxed. Only once did Hitler bring the conversation around to the Paolino fight, and he didn't say a word about my loss to Baer.

I noticed a young woman who appeared to be in her mid-twenties, pretty in a simple way, with a charming laugh that often seemed to have no reason. She remained in the background and, despite all modesty, seemed to speak to Hitler in an open and extremely intimate way. When I asked Hoffmann at the coffee table who she was, he brusquely waved me off. Only later, away from the group, did he tell me, "That's Eva Braun; she works for me." He said this with a certain pride. Somewhat surprised, I asked him what the big secret was all about, at which point he flashed a smile that said volumes and turned away.

After Hitler's particularly hearty good-bye at the Schwarz's, we took an unpaved country road along the lake shore to Sankt Querin, where another of Hitler's long-time followers, the pudgy, hard-of-hearing Adolf Müller, had prepared an evening meal for the group. Müller was a printer whose press published the Nazi Party newspaper, *Völkischer Beobachter.* This time Hitler beckoned us to his car. As always, he sat in the front passenger seat, but turned around often to point out the beauty of the landscape, the mountains, or the quaint Bavarian villages.

It was a strange contradiction. The black cavalcade of six or eight large Mercedes followed by the dust cloud they pulled through the idyllic countryside; this man in the front seat who couldn't seem to get enough of the peaceful landscape through which our convoy roared.

When I returned to Berlin a short time later there was an official notice waiting for me which stated that I had been sentenced to six months in prison and a 10,000-mark fine for a currency violation. It further stated that because of my "celebrity," the penalty would be waived in favor of probation.

The whole thing was pretty trivial. After the Hamas fight an American acquaintance came to my hotel and asked me if I would buy some stock shares and gold bars from him, as he desperately needed the cash. More to help him out than to make a killing, I agreed and gave him the amount he asked for. After my return, I went to my bank in good faith and had the stocks and gold put in a safe-deposit box. Without knowing it, I had circumvented some currency regulations and was notified by the currency office.

I alerted my lawyer and asked him to take care of it. When I asked him before the Paolino fight how things stood, he assured me that everything had been taken care of. But now there was a serious case against me, and during my absence the press office of the Justice Authority had even published the finding.

At this point I remembered Hitler's offer to let him know if I ever needed his help. I called Wilhelmstrasse and spoke with Hitler's chief adjutant, Wilhelm Brückner. After I had explained the problem to him, he promised to get me an appointment with Hitler. The next day I received a call notifying me of a five o'clock appointment in the Reich Chancellory.

Hitler listened attentively and voiced his dissatisfaction with "the bureaucrats in the Finance Ministry." Clearly annoyed, he finally put a call through to the state secretary of the Justice Ministry, Roland Freisler.* When Freisler, who later became notorious as the president of the *Volksgerichtshof* [Peoples Court of Justice], tried to give an explanation, Hitler cut him off abruptly: "There will be no discussion! Take care of the matter immediately!" Then he hung up.

Two weeks later I received official written notification that the verdict had been overturned and the case dismissed. Six months later I was notified by my bank that the stocks had risen twenty-one points in the interim, so I even came out of the whole affair a little on the plus side.

---

[1] One of the provisions of the Treaty of Versailles was that the German army be limited to 100,000 men. Even before Hitler openly defied this condition, however, there were any number of paramilitary organizations in the form of veterans groups and police forces, as well as troops being secretly trained in the Ukraine.

❧❧❧

12

Hitler's Shadow

In the boxing world the heavyweight championship had changed hands. Primo Carnera had defended his title against Max Baer and lost it by an eleventh-round knockout. Among the boxers who were rising quickly and starting to be noticed by American promoters was the young German heavyweight Walter Neusel.

Four years earlier at the 1930 German Amateur Championships in the Sports Palace I had presented the heavyweight-championship belt to Walter Neusel. At that time he was still a tall, lanky boy, still with lots to learn, but he had a great fighting spirit. He could stay with any pace and wear his opponent down systematically.

None other than Paul Damski had taken Walter Neusel when he went pro and turned him into a good-looking headliner. For three years he remained undefeated in dozens of fights. He won against excellent boxers such as Rudi Wagener, the much-feared Larry Gains, my nemesis Gypsy Daniels, the Englishman Bobby Shields, and the behemoth Guardsman Gatern.

Among those who left Germany shortly after Hitler came to power was my friend Paul Damski. But just as he had done well in German business after fleeing the Russian Revolution, so he had quickly established influence and connections abroad after leaving Germany. Through astute management he had succeeded in bringing his protégé into the American boxing scene.

In America Walter Neusel had great success right away. His first opponent, Les Kennedy, only lasted six rounds, and he scored impressive wins over Stanley Pareda and the American Carnera, the six-foot-seven Ray Impelletiere. He fought the world-class boxer Natie Brown to a draw, despite a dislocated thumb. And as I had been labelled "The Black Ulan of the Rhine," so he was called "The German Tiger" because of his aggressive style. When Neusel, in his first fight in the Garden, outboxed the great King Levinsky, he was suddenly a title contender. His American manager was the shrewd Jimmy Bronson, who had at one time looked after Gene Tunney's interests. Everything pointed to Neusel picking up where I had apparently left off in America.

But there was a difference. Walter Neusel met all the requirements of a great boxer: a fighting heart, toughness, endurance, ring intelligence, punching power, sportsmanship. Still, with all his victories and ballyhoo, he never quite achieved the status of a boxing "star." That was most evident in his purses. When he fought Impelletiere, for example, he had to guarantee his opponent $5,000. After everyone had gotten their cut, the remainder amounted to only $5,003.19. So Neusel had fought his heart out for a check amounting to $3.19. His largest purse never exceeded $4,000, which just wasn't enough to finance two managers, a training camp, and sparring partners. For all his success in the ring, Neusel never made any money.

The inevitable question after my losses to Max Baer and Steve Hamas was: who's better, Schmeling or Neusel? Walter Rothenburg who, despite a Jewish grandmother, was still active as a promoter, had put together a fight card for June 26, 1934, in Hamburg that would answer that question. The cite was to be a dirt track next to the Hagenbeck Zoo. Within a few weeks Rothenburg had managed to revamp the facility into a model arena which could hold 95,000 spectators.

I set up training camp in Travemünde, while Neusel got ready in Orry-la-Ville near Paris, where Paul Damski was living. Just twenty-four hours before the fight, Neusel returned to Germany like a gladiator with a large following: he was the man of the hour, not I.

It was a brutally hot Sunday afternoon, with over 90,000 spectators gathered in the covered outdoor ring. As far as a live attendance is concerned, no fight in Germany or Europe has ever surpassed this.

Walter Neusel and I were essentially two different types of boxers. He was impulsive, always on the attack, ready to go for broke anytime. I, on the other hand, was cool, cautious, always studying my opponent, only going on the offensive after a few rounds when I had my strategy set. Ideal for me was an aggressive opponent against whom my countering style would be most effective.

It was the first fight on German soil that drew international attention. Almost all the major newspapers sent correspondents, and my friend Sparrow Robertson, the boxing writer for the *New York Herald,* told me the predictions of some former opponents and world champions. Dempsey and Baer predicted a clear win for me inside the distance, while Tunney felt that Neusel's aggressiveness and youth would be the deciding factors.

࿇

When the prelims were over, referee Pippow called us to the center of the ring. In my corner was, as always, Max Machon, while Neusel had Jack Diffson, the important American promoter and owner of the Paris Sport Palace; because of the Gestapo, Paul Damski had remained in Paris.

Politics or, more precisely and honestly put, the increasingly visible signs of Hitler's rule of violence and power had begun to cast a shadow over boxing as well. I had looked forward to seeing my old friend again, and upon hearing that he had decided to stay in Paris, I thought of Joe Jacobs. He had wanted to visit me at the end of the year, but now I had to ask myself whether he would still want to come to this Germany.

On the evening before the fight I had dinner at the Hotel Atlantic with Max Machon and a few friends. There was a moment in which it suddenly became clear to all of us what was happening. The circle of friends—artists and actors—had long since scattered to the four winds; now reality was taking hold of sports as well, shattering bonds that had never cared about borders, skin color, or race.

I hadn't been wrong. At the opening bell Neusel came after me with furious but not very accurate combinations. A few times I slowed him with hard left uppercuts, and pretty soon Neusel wasn't finding any opportunities to use his superior reach or weight advantage. As he kept coming forward, I would try to force the infighting, and before the first round was over I caught him with a powerful right hand to the the mouth.

The following rounds went much the same. Neusel nervously forced the fight while I waited, slipped his punches, and caught him with accurate counterpunches. Another advantage for me was the infighting.

From the sixth round on, Neusel started to slow down, and I noticed that his punches were becoming less and less effective. Now all of his efforts to open or punch through my defense failed. In the seventh round I succeeded for the first time in catching Neusel with an explosive short right hand that visibly shook him up. Tired and on heavy legs, he dragged himself back to his corner between rounds.

But to my and everyone else's surprise, he came out for the eighth round fresh and back on the attack. Yet that was his fatal mistake. Because as he was going all out and trying to force a toe-to-toe exchange, I kept finding openings for sharp, accurate counterpunches that continued to take their toll. A hard left knocked him back into the ropes, and for that instant he let his guard fall such that one punch could have finished him there. But something made me hesitate and not finish off the beaten opponent. Walter made it to the end of the round on his feet.

As the bell for the ninth round sounded and I headed to the center of the ring, the referee came between us and stopped the fight. The gutsy Neusel didn't want the fight stopped, but the referee decided that he had had enough.

As the 90,000 plus cheered, I went over to Neusel. The usually up-beat Neusel had come into this fight dead serious; now, with cuts over his eyes and a swollen face, he smiled for the first time. After the fight, one boxing article said that it had been lucky for Neusel that I didn't have a real killer instinct: "As Tunney used to do, Schmeling was satisfied to punish his opponent, where he could have destroyed him. . . . That could have been the end of Neusel's career."

While Walter Neusel was set back considerably by this loss, I was now back in the American fight picture. Max Baer, who enjoyed the good life (at one point he had something like five women taking him to court at the same time), had put his title on the line against a lightly regarded Jimmy Braddock and had been beaten badly by the supposedly washed-up fighter.

But New York wasn't talking about the new champion at this time. Suddenly a young black boxer who had scored a string of early-round-KO victories was in the spotlight and the talk of the town—a boxing genius that comes along only once in several generations: Joe Louis. After seventeen victories, fourteen of which he had won by KO, he had become a sort of myth. From the start of his career on, Joe Louis had a tremendous following that just kept growing, most of all in Harlem and the black ghettos of other large American cities. They called him the "Brown Bomber," and when the almost delicate-looking Joe Louis knocked out the white giant Primo Carnera, it was a symbolic victory for all of black America. The experts whispered among themselves that no living boxer could stand up to Joe Louis.

While I was counting on Joe Jacobs's diplomatic talent to promote my career in America, it was Walter Rothenburg in Hamburg that brought me back into the American boxing scene. At the start of 1935 he made it clear to me that I had to atone for the "downright dishonorable" loss to Steve Hamas that still marred my record. "I will," said Rothenburg with cool confidence, "bring the man to Hamburg."

We were all somewhat skeptical, because what Walter Rothenburg was planning was really an American matchup on German soil, and no American promoter would go for that. And when we pointed out to him that the weather was still too cool for an outdoor fight, he simply replied, "Then we'll put up an arena."

This is how Hamburg's famous Hanseatic Hall came to be. In a record time of forty-two days, Walter Rothenburg built the largest indoor boxing arena in Europe, with a capacity of 25,000. But his biggest coup was, with the help of his American friend Charlie Harvey, outmaneuvering the Garden Corporation, which had an option on Steve Hamas. The head of the Garden Corporation, Jimmy Johnston, tried at the last minute to get the fight for New York. But Rothenburg handled the situation and got all the signatures.

Steve Hamas, who set up his training camp in Hamburg, knew what was at stake, and for me it was all or nothing. Only a convincing win would give me the chance for a comeback.

I had asked Joe Jacobs to come to Berlin a few days before the fight. We would spend a couple days together and then travel to Hamburg. On a morning late in 1935 I got a call from the desk at the Hotel Bristol on Unter den Linden, asking me to please come quickly to the hotel. As I came into the lobby, the head desk clerk came up to me with a look of embarassment.

"Herr Schmeling, a few days ago you reserved a suite for a Mr. Jacobs from New York," he said. "I'm afraid we won't be able to accomodate him." Concerned and not understanding, I asked how it was possible that they could have overlooked my reservation. The head clerk shook his head. "That isn't it, Herr Schmeling. Mr. Jacobs is . . . you know, don't you? We simply can't give Mr. Jacobs a room." Only then did I get what this was all about. "You mean you can't give him a room because he's a Jew?"

The head clerk raised his shoulders in embarassment. "Then I'm going to tell you something! If Herr Jacobs isn't given a room here, then something's going to happen. You don't know who Herr Jacobs is! When this shows up in the New York papers, then you've seen your last American guest. And you can be sure that my guests will never stay here again."

The head clerk again raised his shoulders helplessly and mumbled something like, "You have to understand . . . the new situation. . . . Where we have so many guests from Wilhelmstrasse . . . I regret . . ." et cetera.

But I wasn't going to accept any explanation. "I've said all that I'm going to say," I said sharply. "Is the room that I reserved available or not?" Apparently the clerk wasn't enjoying this either. After a short pause, he turned and beckoned us to follow him to the reception desk. Wordlessly he pushed the registration form across the desk to Joe Jacobs.

Like Walter Neusel, Steve Hamas also tried to force a steady exchange from the opening bell. He seemed very sure of himself. He knew that my strength was as a counterpuncher, but his previous victory over me, overconfidence, and his youthful enthusiasm made him forget caution. Even in the opening round I could feel that I had my old reflexes, movement, and punching power back—there wouldn't be a repeat of the fiasco in Philadelphia.

As early as the break after the fourth round I said to Max Machon, "The kid has really had it! I don't want to hurt him!" Hamas hadn't gone down, but appeared to be finished and no longer able to defend himself.

∽∾∽

In the sixth round Hamas got nailed with a hard right. He hit the canvas for an eight count, got up, but only for a moment, and went down again. After the break for the seventh round, his corner wanted the fight stopped, but Hamas protested loudly and they let him continue. The finale came in the ninth round. The Belgian referee Faloney finally ended the one-sided bout over the objections of a dazed Steve Hamas. After this, March 10, 1935, Steve Hamas never returned to the ring.

A jubilant victory celebration followed the stoppage. As had happened in 1928 after the Bonaglia fight in the Sports Palace, the 25,000 fans spontaneously stood and broke into the *Deutschlandlied* with arms raised in the Hitler salute, which was required when singing the national anthem.

Joe Jacobs, who had come into the ring to congratulate me, seemed not to know what was happening for a moment. Then he mechanically raised his right arm—the inevitable long Havana cigar still in his hand—in the Hitler salute. After a few seconds he turned to me and winked.

The incident had its repercussions. The victory scenario had been caught on film by dozens of camerapersons and photographers: the picture of the small, somewhat ironically smiling man holding a cigar in his outstretched hand made it into newspapers around the world. A few days later I got an extremely terse—and given my recent victory, almost insulting—letter from the newly installed head of the Reich Ministry of Sports, Hans von Tschammer und Osten, a former equestrian, who owed his appointment (according to a then-circulating rumor) to a mixup with his more famous brother. Even before Hitler's takeover he had been high up in the SA.

Tschammer received me in his office with his press secretary in attendance. Spread out before him on his desk were numerous clippings showing the ominous photo of Joe Jacobs. "You should really box more often in Germany, Herr Schmeling," Tschammer opened with a forced friendliness in his voice. "That would really be a more appropriate surrounding for you."

I made a gesture of regret: "Fights and fight locations are decided by who makes the best offer, *Herr Reichssportführer*," I answered. For a moment Tschammer stared straight ahead, as if he were trying to think of how to begin the conversation again. Then he suddenly said, "Our youth need role models to emulate, to inspire them." I persisted, "Role models can be everywhere. What I accomplish in America can inspire German youth, too."

Tschammer was beginning to show anger: "It's athletes like yourself that are needed in our new Germany," he shot back at me, his tone increasingly irritable. But I held my ground: "When I box in America, I represent Germany!"

Now Tschammer raised his voice: "You shouldn't be so short-sighted, Herr Schmeling—think of your age! You're going to want to be a trainer here some day. Over there no one's going to care about you when you're washed up. Force yourself to listen! It's dumb to burn all your bridges behind you!"

The angrier Tschammer got, the calmer was my response. I even smiled as I said, "I hope, *Herr Reichssportführer,* to be able to live off my savings and investments when I'm old." Astonished, Tschammer wanted to know my income and how much I got for a fight. "That depends," I replied, and then picked my largest purse up to that time: "When I fought Sharkey I got around a million marks." I didn't mention the immense expenses and taxes. "How much?" asked a disconcerted Tschammer. "A million," I answered casually.

Tschammer paused and studied the ruler he was holding from every angle. No one spoke. The press man sitting wordlessly in the corner cleared his throat. Then Tschammer suddenly stood up and abruptly said, "Well, you would know about that! Heil Hitler!"

I wasn't surprised to receive a letter from him shortly thereafter. What had not been said during the interview was now laid out in writing. The *Reichssportführer* wrote that he had seen the shameful and scandalous pictures of the Jew Joe Jacobs's appearance in the ring. The *Reichsminister* for Public Enlightenment and Propaganda was also highly indignant over the affair. Further, I was the only German athlete who worked with a Jew. He was most urgently bringing to my attention that the matter must be immediately dealt with.

But I didn't think for even a moment of breaking with Joe Jacobs. In my anger at the arrogantly presented demand of the *Reichssportführer,* I did something, which, in retrospect, now strikes me as rather comical and almost insane—I sought help in the Joe Jacobs matter from none other than Hitler himself.

Through Wilhelm Brückner I once again requested an appointment in the Reich Chancellory and received an invitation to tea for the very next day. Then Brückner mentioned immediately that Hitler requested that I bring my wife as well.

Anny had no idea what she should wear, so I called Heinrich Hoffmann for a consultation. He put his wife on, who told Anny to wear something neither too ordinary nor too sporty or businesslike. The Führer preferred women to be dressed stylishly and elegantly.

We had barely entered the large fireplaced room of the Reich Chancellory when Hitler appeared from another room. He came to us smiling and politely kissed Anny's hand. A uniformed servant led us into the next room where we took places at a table set for three. With the manners of the perfect host, Hitler turned to Anny and asked, "Would the gracious lady prefer coffee or tea?" To Anny's request for tea, he nodded and joyously agreed: "Tea, how nice, Frau Schmeling. I also drink only tea. But it can't be too strong!"

I disturbed this mood of agreement with, "I'm a passionate coffee drinker!" Then a servant rolled in the pastry cart offering all kinds of cake. Hitler grabbed the cake fork and turned to Anny. "Which of the sorts of cake would you like, gracious lady?" Anny pointed to the cake generally called *Napfkuchen:* "Guglhupf," she said. Hitler was delighted: *"Du lieber Himmel, Guglhupf!* How long has it been since I have heard that word!" he cried. "Imagine that! *Guglhupf!"*

Anny seemed to be getting all of Hitler's attention, and then the conversation turned to whether she came from Vienna. "No, I'm from Prague," she replied, which excited him even more. "Prague, beautiful old German Prague!" He raved about the city, about its having the oldest German university, that it had been many years the official residence of the Hapsburgs, and that really Bohemia was the true heart and treasure of Germany: "Ah yes, golden Prague!" he repeated, lost in his thoughts.

Somewhat angered, I sat there while the conversation revolved around *Guglhupf,* Prague, and Bohemia. Lord knows there were more important things to discuss—like the Joe Jacobs matter, for which I had come.

At the first small break in the conversation, I sat forward in my chair. "I received a letter from the Reich Ministry of Sports," I began. "They want me to split from Joe Jacobs, my manager since 1928." I explained that Joe Jacobs was a Jew, but that between him and me it had never been a question of Protestant or Catholic, Jew or American, only of boxing.

Hitler's face showed displeasure. Instead of giving an answer, he lifted his teacup and loudly slurped his tea. "I really need Joe Jacobs," I continued. "I owe all my success in America to him." But Hitler said nothing. In the pause that followed I added, "Mr. Jacobs is competent, he is respectable and correct. And beyond that, you can't get anywhere in New York without a local manager." Unsettled by the still mute Hitler, I persisted somewhat senselessly with: "Besides, loyalty is a German virtue."

Hitler made an angry gesture, then he again stared absently into space. Finally, smiling at Anny without looking at me, he abruptly said, *"Guglhupf!* I had almost forgotten that word." Pleased, he shook his head. "It's good of you to have reminded me of it again!"

Then he stood up somewhat hesitantly and shook Anny's hand, "It was so pleasant seeing you again. How is the film business? Have you been getting good roles?" Without waiting for an answer, he shook my hand and gestured for an orderly to come in. A young man in a white vest with the SS insignia led us out.

Hitler's message had been clear, and I understood its meaning. And just as he had refused to discuss the matter with me, I decided to let the letter from the *Reichssportführer* go unanswered. Tschammer heard nothing more from me, although he would later get his revenge.

We had always called the Roxy Bar the "Missing Persons Bureau." Whenever one of us couldn't be found at home, then chances were very good that that person would be found sitting in the red velvet room on Joachimstaler Strasse, a stone's throw from the Kurfürstendamm. But now that name had come to take on a new meaning. Now for the first time we really were missing one or the other of us from the group of actors and artists, and we got our information here from Heinz Ditgens at the Roxy Bar. Now it was: Alfred Flechtheim left for London last week and his gallery is to be sold; Heinrich Mann* is said to have left Amsterdam for southern France; or Ossietsky* is in a *KZ*, as concentration camps were called at that time; Tucholsky* committed suicide in Sweden. Now it really was a missing persons bureau.

The whole world still met at the Roxy Bar, but now the whole world was only half the world. We could still speak freely and openly—Ditgens knew how to cultivate and hold together a circle of friends among whom caution wasn't necessary. Not that there were particularly inflammatory conversations at the Roxy; many of us, and in some ways I was among them, were impressed by the new optimism in Germany as well as by the successes of the new regime.

But in our sphere we came to know this regime's other face soon enough. Each of us had at least one person we were close to who had been forced to leave the country; others had been forced out of a profession or simply made to live in fear. And we all knew—or at least knew of—persons who had already been arrested.

After the war, many, perhaps hoping to fool themselves, claimed to have had no knowledge of what went on. In truth we all knew. It was no secret that there were concentration camps in Germany; it was openly discussed in the Roxy Bar.

At this time, on March 19 and 21, 1935, the first air-raid drills were held for the Berlin area. There was something both surprising and almost absurd in the sight of this cosmopolitan city blacked out while grown people ran to their posts with fire apparatus in hand. We went out on the street, and many of us laughed. But at the same time, we felt that something strange was happening.

⮮⮯⮮

13

The Joe Louis Myth and My Strategy

My victory over Steve Hamas had inspired Walter Rothenburg to try to match the American promoters. Even at the early stages of the Hamas negotiations, Rothenburg had spoken of his dream match, a heavyweight championship bout in Germany between Max Baer and me. Baer had even indicated his willingness to take an Amsterdam fight for $300,000. But those plans ended with Baer's loss to Jimmy Braddock.

The Boxing Commission could hardly have prohibited a Baer fight; after all, it wasn't only a title fight but also a rematch that had been promised to me. But there was now another "next-in-line" for the new champion: Joe Louis, son of a poor Alabama cotton-picker named Mumm Barrow. Thanks to his many victories—short fights, no facial expression, no emotion—it had become difficult for him to find opponents. No one doubted that he would soon defeat the current titleholder as well. This was the way things stood, such that everything started to point to a showdown between Joe Louis and me.

While Joe Jacobs was in America putting out the first feelers for this bout, I accepted an offer, partly just to stay in shape, to meet Paolino in Berlin. This would be our third bout—the first one I had barely won, the second being a questionable draw. I wanted finally to remove any doubt as to which of us was better; I wanted to knock him out.

The fight took place in Berlin on July 7, 1935. Since promoter Fritz Rolauf couldn't meet Paolino's last-minute demand to be paid in full before the fight, the city of Berlin took on the liability of guaranteeing our purses. Immediately before the fight, Berlin *Stadtpräsident* Dr. Lippert paid Paolino the agreed-upon 35,000 marks; my share, also 35,000 marks, was to be paid on the evening after the fight. Surprisingly, however, there was a paid attendance of only 30,000. Apparently few fans expected much of a fight from the old Spanish warhorse.

In fact, from the first round on, Paolino's only intention really did seem to be nothing more than to finish the fight standing. He covered up from the first round on and never came out, whatever I tried, and I never succeeded in breaking through his cover. It wasn't a very pretty fight, although I won on points by a wide margin. But I was just as disappointed as the fans.

When Max Machon went to the promoter for our payment as we had agreed, it turned out that the gate hadn't covered my purse; Fritz Rolauf shrugged his shoulders and referred us to the City of Berlin for payment. And for the next fourteen days we tried in vain—by telephone and letter—to reach someone in city hall. With ever-changing excuses, however, we were kept at bay. First, the person responsible was on vacation, then the appropriate signatures were missing, then Dr. Lippert wasn't available. We never got beyond an outer waiting room. It was a farce.

Machon and some other friends advised me to just let it go: "You'll never get anywhere with that bunch!" But I was determined. Fourteen days after the fight I filed suit against the City of Berlin and the State of Prussia (which were represented by none other than Hermann Göring and the Minister of the Interior Wilhelm Frick*). My friends simply shook their heads.

But it didn't come to a trial. When they finally realized that I wasn't afraid of creating a scandal, the city decided to pay me in full the purse that I was owed. Since the Joe Jacobs affair, my reputation in offical circles had suffered considerably. The alleged impudence with which I had conducted myself was thrown back at me for years in the form of harmless inuendos, the cause of which, I knew, was dead serious.

During this time in the States, Joe Louis's string of wins continued. Since Paolino had gone the distance with me, Mike Jacobs was able to get him a fight with Joe Louis. The bout was set for December 1935 in Madison Square Garden.

The news of this matchup had barely hit the presses when Max Machon and I decided to go to New York to see the fight. I wanted not only to study Joe Louis, but also to see whether he could succeed in doing what I never had—stopping the tough master of defense Paolino before the fight went the distance.

As we were packing, preparations for the XI Olympic Games were well underway in both Berlin and Garmish-Partenkirchen. The foundation for a stadium of classical style and proportions was already being laid in Berlin, while outside the city the construction corps of the *Wehrmacht* [army] was putting up the Olympic Village, which would house athletes from around the world.

༺༻

The racial policy of the regime, the boycotts and abuses against Jewish citizens, the continuing wave of emigration from Germany—all that had started people thinking, especially in America, that it might be better to stay home. The refusal of a sports power like America to participate would not only devalue the Olympic Games, but would also mean a serious loss of face for the regime.

At that time I was the best-known German athlete internationally, and certainly in America. It was, therefore, interesting that just before leaving for America I got a call, not from the *Reichssportführer* himself but from his assistant, Arno Breithaupt. After some well-rehearsed friendly chitchat he got to the heart of the matter. He explained that America's hesitation to participate in the upcoming Games was being followed in Berlin with great distress. Then he came right out and asked, "You know America well. Could you go over there and exert a positive influence on the right people?"

I asked if that was an official request. Without answering the question directly, Breithaupt let it be known that this request for mediation had come from higher up. I explained to him that I was leaving for America anyway and that I would of course be willing to speak with officials of the American Olympic Committee.

A few days later I received a call from the president of the German Olympic Committee, the old state secretary, Dr. Theodor von Lewald. He had heard about Breithaupt's conversation with me and asked me if I would personally deliver a letter from him to his American friend and colleague, Avery Brundage. Von Lewald, who was half Jewish himself, read the letter to me over the phone; in it he tried to disperse any reservations and promised fairness and hospitality for all the participating athletes.

By coincidence, the American Olympic Committee was meeting to make its final decision at my usual New York hotel, the Commodore, just a few days after my arrival. I contacted Mr. Brundage regarding Herr von Lewald's letter, and he came up to my room on the twelfth floor to get the letter in person. He was both friendly and concerned at the same time. His concern was expressed in the form of newsclippings which he took from a small leather folio; they were articles by American correspondents reporting on disturbances in Germany—some of the photos showed the arresting of Communists and harrassment of Jews, one of the reports told of Jews being prohibited from using the public swimming pools in Stettin.

"What do you have to say about this, Max?" asked Brundage seriously. "A good number of black and Jewish athletes will be on the American team. Who's going to guarantee us that they won't be abused in Germany?" My reply was that all of the German athletes would guarantee the integrity of the Games and would not allow any discrimination for whatever reason.

∽∼∾

In retrospect, it was incredibly naive of me to guarantee things that were completely beyond my control, especially given my knowledge and personal experience of the situation in Germany. No assurance or promise of mine would keep Hitler—to the extent that he would even know of it—from doing whatever he pleased. And in fact Hitler did refuse the customary congratulation to the black star of the Games, Jesse Owens, and the Jewish fencing medalists. Whenever a black or Jewish athlete won, Hitler would leave the stadium early.

My intervention did have some impact, however, and the American Committee voted by a slim margin to attend the games.

Ten days before Christmas I was sitting ringside at Madison Square Garden with Max Machon and Joe Jacobs. All around us were past and present champions, everyone eager to see the fight between "The Brown Bomber" and Paolino.

That evening I saw Joe Louis for the first time. His face showed no emotion as he entered the ring, and he seemed calm almost to the point of indifference. His cornermen worked quietly, barely speaking a word. Only his trainer, Jack Blackburn, would occasionally speak to him. Everything about Louis's corner was precise, supremely confident, unsettling.

Each of the first three rounds showed me that the fascination which the twenty-one-year-old boxer drew from all quarters was more than justified. He threw almost exclusively lefts, but his left was the hardest and most versatile that I had ever seen. Again and again that left was rammed into the Spaniard's face—it didn't matter to Louis if he sometimes only hit Paolino's cover. The effect of his lethal punches was such that the cover would inevitably fall.

Between rounds Louis would easily stride back to his corner and sit there silently, almost bored, as his trainer spoke only a few quiet words to him.

Then came the bell for the fourth round. In a few quick steps Louis was on his opponent with hard, lightning-fast lefts that visibly rocked Paolino. And when the Spaniard's guard fell for only a second, Louis's rights followed, landing with devastating effect. The full power of a natural talent—a boxing genius—was behind these blows.

Instinct alone got Paolino to his feet again, only to run into a blitzing combination. It literally ripped Paolino off his feet and put him down for well beyond the count—the same Paolino Uzcudun that I had yet to put down for a nine-count.

While a badly beaten Paolino was being tended in the ring, reporters surrounded me and asked, "So, what do you have to say now?"

"Joe Louis is the hardest puncher that I've ever seen," I answered. "He's a good man. Anyone who plans on beating him had better know what they're doing." And when one of the reporters came out with, "No one stands between him and the championship, not you either, Max!" I answered, "Joe Louis still has a lot to learn! Sometimes he looks like an amateur and makes mistakes that he couldn't afford to make against me." That provoked another to ask, "Do you really think you'd stand a chance against him?" I answered only, "I don't think it's impossible to beat Joe Louis."

This remark really set them off. "Did you hear this?" one of them yelled over his shoulder to the others, "Schmeling thinks he can beat Joe Louis!" I heard a few laughs in back and saw expressions of shock and disbelief. Then one asked, almost taunting, if I had a plan: "Tell us, Max, how you intend to do this!" Amid all the chaos, I only said, "I saw something." "What was it?" they asked almost as one voice. Now I was looking at microphones coming from everywhere: "What did you see, Max?"

But I only repeated what I had said, "I saw something." I didn't reveal anything more than that, but the words became part of boxing's lore.

The morning papers played it up big: "Max has seen something!" And it wasn't long before Mike Jacobs came to the Commodore Hotel to get my signature on a contract to fight Joe Louis. The winner would meet Jimmy Braddock in a title bout. Needless to say, I signed.

A few days later Max Machon and I left for Europe in order to be home in time for the holidays. My contract for the Louis fight, set for June 1936, wasn't the only thing in my luggage; one whole suitcase held nothing but film. Machon had managed to get copies of all the films of earlier Louis fights. Once we were back home, I wanted to have slow-motion copies made in order to study, in as minute detail as possible, every aspect of every fight, backwards and forwards. I had to prepare myself for the Louis fight with military precision, or I didn't have a chance. Machon and I agreed to tell no one about the films. I didn't even tell my close friends who drove to meet us in Cherbourg.

But the peace of the holidays was interrupted by a call from Munich. I had barely arrived when I was summoned by Hitler to come to him that same day. He wanted a personal report on how it had gone with the American Olympic Committee. Heinrich Hoffmann was at the Munich train station waiting for me. We drove directly to the restaurant Osteria Bavaria for lunch. Hitler was waiting in a private side room with a small group.

At lunch I mentioned that I had signed to fight Joe Louis in the coming year. Hitler seemed disturbed and somewhat angry that I would put German honor on the line against a black man, especially one against whom I appeared to have so little chance of winning.

After lunch we drove to Hitler's private residence on the first floor of a large house on Prinzregenten Platz. His housekeeper, a Frau Winter, met us at the door. In the way that little things often strike us first, I was taken aback by the relaxed, homey atmosphere and the way Frau Winter easily spoke with Herr Hitler about everyday household matters. Frau Winter led us from the hall to the living room, where we all took places at a small table.

It wasn't until tea that Hitler asked for my impression of where the American Olympic Committee stood. "Herr Reichskanzler," I said, "the vote was very close. Mr. Brundage told me that it was a margin of only one or two votes. Certain incidents have left a bad impression among Americans—the major concern is for the safety of black and Jewish visitors."

Hitler had been listening with visibly increasing annoyance. At one point he interrupted me with, "It's no wonder that there's so much uproar, where the press is so completely controlled by Jews!"

I had barely finished when a clearly disturbed Hitler stood up, shook my hand with a brusque word of thanks, and left the room. Those of us left in the room looked at each other disconcertedly, while one said to me, "You really shouldn't have said that, Herr Schmeling. He just can't tolerate that sort of thing!" To everyone's surprise, Hitler returned in a few minutes as if nothing had happened and gave me a signed picture of himself.

Seven weeks before the fight, which was set for June 18, 1936, I set up training camp with Max Machon in Napanoch, about ninety-five miles outside of New York City. At the same time Joe Louis moved into his training headquarters in Lakewood, New Jersey. I worked harder than ever before, because I knew the monumental challenge that lay before me. The American press didn't give me a chance; Louis was a ten-to-one favorite. "The man who beats Joe Louis will be the boxer of all time," wrote one newspaper, while another asked me with phony concern whether I had considered the risk that I was taking. Newspaper cartoons showed me on a guillotine or as a helpless victim of Joe Louis's cannon-fists.

But none of that bothered me, and, to the chagrin of the reporters, I limited my pre-fight ballyhoo to the one sentence that I had been saying all along: "I saw something." Privately I was hoping that this cryptic statement would have a more powerful psychological effect than the usual hype that Joe Jacobs put out before a fight.

Joe Louis didn't do much for the press either. As was his natural style, he appeared to be totally disinterested. But the journalists who had been in Louis's camp told us that he was putting down sparring partners like bowling pins. Most of them were refusing to go back into the ring with him.

The latest odds in the newspapers still had Louis a ten-to-one favorite. Only one reporter, Bill Farnsworth, remained immune to the "Louis euphoria" and said that Louis was overtrained. And while Farnsworth was only a third-string reporter for the Hearst Corporation, his father was the head of the Hearst sports division, and this gave Farnsworth, Jr. a license to publish his apparently ridiculous theory. Farnsworth, Sr. was putting his money on Louis; maybe he wanted to add a dissenting voice to the prevailing opinion, or maybe he wanted to give his son a chance to play the interesting outsider; either way, the lone crazy voice of Farnsworth, Jr. kept popping up until the day of the fight.

And then Marlene Dietrich was to be heard from as well. During an interview she predicted—to everyone's amusement—a KO victory for me. Serious discussion of the fight, however, revolved around two questions: (1) in which round I would be knocked out, and (2) whether I was afraid to go up against the boxing genius with the murderous punching power.

The latter question made no sense to me, because Joe Louis was just another human being and, like me, had only two fists. If I hadn't learned how to defend myself in the course of my career, I wouldn't have gotten this far. "Of course," I told myself, "if I get hit hard and accurately enough, I get knocked out. That's pretty simple, what is there to fear? It's part of my profession." But I also told myself and others that I had a chance to beat Louis. No matter how great a boxer might be, there's a chance that a good man can take him. Even the greatest boxer has some weakness. Absolute perfection doesn't exist in the ring any more than it does elsewhere.

What I had seen, but hadn't told either the press or my friends, was a just barely noticeable mistake that Louis made in every fight. In the film room in Berlin we replayed—over and over again, frame by frame—slow-motion films of Louis's fights with Baer, Carnera, and many others; in thirty or forty separate sequences we watched for that instant when Louis would throw his right—his stance, how he set his feet, his favorite distance for throwing his power punch.

In analyzing a boxer's style, the distance from which he throws his most dangerous punches is really *the* critical variable. Once this is known, he can be outmaneuvered by staying out of that range. We sat in that dark room for hours trying to get as detailed and precise a picture as possible of Louis's style. In the process we discovered that the point of origin for a punch is more precisely determined by running the film backwards frame by frame, following the punch in reverse from its impact to its origin.

During those weeks I think I learned more than I had in my entire career up to that point. And this theoretical preparation was every bit as important as the actual training. By the time I had finished, I was pretty sure that I knew Joe Louis the boxer better than he knew himself. Joe Louis's advantages were physical and tactical gifts beyond compare. My advantage was that I knew precisely how he functioned in the ring.

∽∾∽

In the course of our analysis we had paid particular attention to the tiny flaw that I had noticed during the Louis-Paolino fight. Every time after Joe had thrown his short, dangerous left hooks, often in rapid succession, he would then drop his left. It was a barely noticeable, unconscious reaction, which was detectable only if one studied the boxer with the thorough, systematic observation of a scientist. This habit meant that for a split second, the left side of Louis's face was open to a straight right.

I knew that my right could put down even Joe Louis. I threw it as a straight right over the shortest distance possible between two points. I didn't need to pull it back before I let it fly. I held it next to my chest right under my chin and threw it with my entire body weight behind it.

It was the punch with which I had won a lot of fights. But these previous opponents could have been beaten by other boxers with other punches, with a left hook or an uppercut. Louis's vulnerable moment, if I had calculated correctly, could be exploited with only one punch—the shortest possible straight right, because this is the only punch that can be aimed and fired as accurately as a gunshot.

To this extent, Louis's one weakness matched perfectly my greatest strength, the one with which I had made my career since Tex Rickards's "what a right hand!" Louis and I were, so to say, "made for each other." And I had known that as early as the Louis-Paolino fight, even before studying the films.

But I not only had to know how to hit Louis, I also, especially as a slow starter, had to be able to avoid his devastating punches. As the films had shown me, he possessed two exceptionally dangerous weapons.

First there was his lethal right, but this could be dealt with. Steve Hamas had driven me crazy in Philadelphia by using an outstanding eye to pull away from my right—accurate but ineffective—the second it was thrown. Even though I hit him countless times, the effect of the punches was diminished. So I had to use a similar move to try to neutralize some of the deadly impact of the Brown Bomber's powerful rights.

The other dangerous punch was his left hook. In order to avoid it, I had to do everything possible to duck under it. I could only do that by getting in close as quickly as I could; and to do that, I would have to take some left jabs. But the jab is one punch that no boxer who wants to get at close range can avoid. And this left jab, as dangerous at it was, was the one Joe Louis punch that didn't have quite the same devastating effect as all the others.

And I had to be in peak condition. Only that would enable me to carry through with my strategy regardless of any nasty surprises or setbacks. I figured that I would have to take one of Louis's heavy lefts around ten or fifteen times per round. At the same time, I had to be in the kind of shape to throw my own punches and be able to get off my right as quickly and accurately in the last round as I did in the first.

Above all, my legs had to be at their peak if I wanted to slip punches, move in fast, or make Louis miss by sidestepping. If my legs gave out, the fight was lost. Only the legs could enable the most critical aspect of my fight plan —to always be at optimal range. In Napanoch I began a completely new running regimen. I had always felt that extensive roadwork wasn't necessary for me to get in top condition. Now I would make up for what I had neglected for so long. Machon estimated that during those weeks I put in about 1,000 kilometers on the roads.

I only threw my right with full force twice during sparring sessions at training camp. Neither the spectators nor the ever-present press noticed these punches, but I did, and I was satisfied.

In the meantime the fight date was getting closer and closer, and the press was now making the odds eighteen-to-one in favor of Louis. No one gave me a chance to last beyond five rounds. Dempsey said that he was glad that he never had to face Louis, and Tunney not only predicted my early knockout, but also that no one in the forseeable future could take Louis, who would remain champion until around 1950.

On the other hand, only two experts gave me any kind of a chance. One was my countryman Gustav Eder who, on his own mission to win the welterweight title, spent a few days at my training camp. "Don't be so sure," he kept telling the reporters, "you've all been bitten by the 'Louis bug.' As far as I'm concerned, the fight's up for grabs. I've visited the camps at Napanoch and Lakewood. If you ask me, Max is going to land his right a lot more often than Louis and his corner would like. And how the Bomber will react when he's hit by a Schmeling right is still an open question." Eder always got a big laugh with that one.

Ten days before the fight, the promoter, Mike Jacobs, paid a surprise visit to my camp. He silently watched me work for about an hour. Then he came up to me and offered me a contract in the event that I beat Louis. He didn't say a word about my chances, but he was no fool; and for a moment it seemed to me that he was no longer so sure about the fight's outcome. That gave me a tremendous boost.

In order to stay completely focused on the work at hand, we rented a cabin off in the woods, some miles from camp. This was where I resided with Max Machon and our two detectives, because Joe Jacobs's constant upbeat chatter only made me nervous. One of his jobs was to look after the reporters staying at the camp, and he often came home at night singing or making a racket.

At our cabin, on the other hand, there was no noise or hubub. When we sat outside after training, Machon and I didn't say a word about the upcoming fight. These were, strangely enough, quiet and very peaceful evenings; we sat on the rough-hewn wood benches with our legs stretched out, looking out over a field and into the woods beyond. Now and then one of us would say something unimportant; we paged through magazines and sometimes played cards.

The closer it got to fight day, the calmer I became. I had the feeling that I was completely ready. Nothing had been neglected; I had done everything that was in my power. Rarely have I slept so well as in the night before the fight.

The next morning I drove into the city for the weighin. Smiling, I made my way through the reporters, doctors, and officials. I had made up my mind to keep my nerve when meeting Joe Louis, because I knew that many of his opponents had already lost the fight at the weighin, beaten by the myth of Joe Louis. Levinsky, for example, hadn't been able to get on the scales without help. The gargantuan Carnera had gone pale on meeting Louis, and Paolino, I was told, had trembled. Even Max Baer had reportedly had to be physically forced to leave his dressing room before his bout with Louis. World-class boxers came completely undone in the presence of the Brown Bomber.

I approached Joe Louis with exaggerated cordiality. In contrast to his usual poker face, he looked at me with a mixture of curiosity and surprise. "Hello, Joe, how do you do?" I said. And he greeted me similarly. He outweighed me by about five pounds. As we left the scales I said, "Good luck this evening, Joe!" Then we posed together for the photographers. Eight hours later we would be facing each other in the ring.

But around noon we were informed that a storm was approaching and that the fight would have to be postponed for twenty-four hours. And, in fact, a downpour did let loose over New York.

I didn't drive back to camp but decided instead to settle in at the Plaza for the next twenty-four hours; from my windows I could see New York's skyline, including Yankee Stadium. I lay down and tried to get some rest. In the next room Max Machon, Doc Casey, and Otto Petri were whispering and walking on tiptoes; but that made me more nervous than if they had just gone about their business. From time to time Machon looked in on me and repeated what we had already said a thousand times before: "Leave your calling card right after the first bell," he said. "The kid has to know who he's dealing with." The mood was different than before any other fight. The larger-than-life shadow of Joe Louis was everywhere.

At a quarter to eight Joe Jacobs came up to our suite. "The car's wait-ing below," he said. "We've got to get going." In the elevator no one said any-thing. The lobby was a ghost town. Only the desk clerk yelled after me, "Good luck, Max!" A radio sat on the counter in front of him.

The streets to Yankee Stadium were already hopelessly clogged. But a police escort of motorcycles with howling sirens cleared the way for us.

In the locker room there was a constant coming and going. Every time the door opened you could hear the rumble of the over 46,000 fans. The ex-citement of the crowd washed over us like a wave.

Shortly before ten o'clock there was a knock at the door. But it wasn't a boxing commission official coming to lead us to the ring, but rather the eighty-three-year-old Tom O'Rourke, one of America's most respected boxing experts. Sitting down on the rubdown table next to me, he asked me how I felt. Then, without waiting for an answer, he said, "I know you can win, Max. You've just got to be careful and use your head."

Then he leaned back and sat quietly next to me. Suddenly he slid soundlessly to the floor. A couple of my people quickly picked him up and car-ried him into the next room. When they returned they said casually that the old man had fainted. But I knew that he had passed on.

Then the commission official came into the room. "Are you ready?" Police cleared a way for us through the churning crowd. A spotlight's harsh finger of light accompanied us into the ring. Shortly after Joe Louis, I climbed through the ropes. Our glances crossed for only a second as we went to our corners. Joe Louis's face was as expressionless as a mask.

14
The Fight

As he was putting on my gloves, Machon said, "Max, you've done all the right things—now show me what you've got!" We both smiled. Then three men came out of the crowd into the ring, they were announced, and each shook my hand. And each one of them caused me to think.

First came Dempsey. I looked at him and thought: you were a great champion, and you were beaten; you weren't able to win back the title. Next, Tunney was introduced: yes, I thought, you were unique; you're the only champion who retired undefeated. And then came Jimmy Braddock, the current heavyweight champion: from you, I thought, I want the title.

The introductions were over. Referee Arthur Donovan called Louis and me to the middle of the ring and gave us the usual instructions. Then he solemnly said the well-known, "Now go back to your corners and come out fighting!" In Germany it was 3:06 in the morning.

As I went back to my corner, I felt for a few seconds that I was totally surrounded by darkness. The stadium, in which I could sense more than see the crowd, loomed up against the nighttime sky which was itself illuminated by the arc lights. It appeared as though the spotlights had cut the ring and the first few rows of seats out from the darkness; everything else fell abruptly into the blackness. The noise had dropped off, and only a dull rumbling could be heard, every now and then broken by a shrill cry.

The press people, too, whose eyes lined the edges of the ring, had fallen into a nervous silence. Some were just chewing their gum; others arranged their papers or checked their telephone connections. One of them was Arno Hellmis, who would broadcast the fight to Germany. The seconds seemed to me to be an eternity.

Then Max Machon shoved in the mouthguard. Leaning back against the ropes, I scuffed my shoes on the canvas to check for traction. Then came the bell.

The start was different than I had expected. In contrast to his usual fight, Joe began very cautiously. We felt each other out. But suddenly I felt his fist under my left eye. I hadn't seen the painful jab coming. I answered with my right, but it was short.

Louis worked superbly. His movements were fast, cool, harmonius: left jab once, twice. Now I had to re-study him, because up until now I had only seen him from a spectator's perspective. This was a lot different.

I couldn't lose my concentration. I remembered Max Machon's repeated reminder: "Give him your calling card as quickly as possible!" My right was at my chest, cocked and ready. I kept my left stretched out, trying to keep Louis off. But he still landed a left hook with full impact. For the first time I realized the power behind the punches that had finished so many world-class boxers.

Louis kept it up and began to force the pace. I wasn't doing that well, but I wasn't disgracing myself either. Counterpunching was Joe's strength too, but as early as the first round he went on the offensive. I retreated and he followed. Then I tried a few lefts for the first time. Louis answered immediately with a right uppercut-hook to my chest, then two left jabs in quick succession. I would have to take a lot of those jabs if I wanted to get close to him.

There it was for the first time—the opening I had been waiting for. For a split second the coast was clear and I fired a short right to his head, catching him above the chin in the middle of his face. Louis showed some surprise, but didn't seem to be particularly impressed. Immediately he went on the attack and forced me back into the ropes. I took some of the punches on the shoulders. Then came the bell.

"You're still alive!" laughed Machon as I sat on the stool. "Louis can punch," was all I could manage in return. But Machon came back with, "Yeah, so? And you can't?!"

The first round went to Louis, and I lost the second one, too; he opened it with a short punch to the mouth, and for a moment I had the sweet taste of blood on my tongue. To get a little respect, I threw my right a couple of times and landed. But at the same time I was learning what a brilliant boxer this man was. Only a few times was I able to avoid his skillfully set-up attacks. Again and again he caught me with his strong left. It flashed out with lightning speed, and I experienced the cold precision with which he had dismantled Carnera and Baer.

After Louis nailed my left eye in the first round, he kept working on it. I could have avoided those punches, but that would have meant moving out of the range from which I could land my right.

⌒⌒⌒

In this moment he landed for the first time with his full power, and I felt the force of the punch down to my toes. At the same time, however, I discovered something that I hadn't noticed in the films. Louis "set" himself before throwing his punches. Outside the ring you couldn't detect this minimal hint of a movement. It wasn't anything more than planting one of his feet. But for me this was a tiny signal, and whenever I saw it, I pulled back. That seemed to confuse and bother him. Now he had to keep chasing me and reposition himself for punching. I only had to change my range a little bit to upset his fight strategy.

Again Louis fired one of his left hooks. But this time I saw it coming and was able to move with it, robbing the punch of its full effect; I took it only partially on the right side of my face. Then I saw another opening for my right, and this time he had to take it on the chin.

For the first time I had caught Louis squarely. He staggered and went immediately into a clinch. But he was far from done. Coming out of the clinch and switching over to infighting, he drummed on my head with five fast jabs, and my left eye began to close.

Somewhat surprised by the bell, we separated. But Donovan signalled for us to keep fighting. It hadn't been the bell at all, but rather a woman's shrill yell which had fooled us both. Still on the retreat, I took a hard left hook to the body, but I noticed that it hadn't done any damage. The work of all those weeks had paid off; I was in peak condition.

"Five jabs in a row without a single counterpunch! What's that all about?" was Machon's greeting between rounds. I didn't answer, but I thought about it. Then Machon lightened up a bit and sent me into the next round with, "Don't get impatient, Max!"

The third round was my worst. I took heavy punches, and Louis seemed now to be hitting his stride. But it was the round in which I won the fight! The round had begun well. I landed a right to Louis's head, but his response was incredible. I took more jabs or hooks to my head and body than ever before in my career. Thank God I was at least able to avoid the rights that he threw a few times.

But then I saw for the first time what I had been waiting for. Louis threw two short lefts, then pulled his left back to throw another jab. That was the split second that I had studied for weeks and played over and over on our films. In that split second Louis dropped his left. In that same instant I hit him with a hard right to the chin.

The punch wasn't the most precise, and the timing wasn't quite right either. And right after I had thrown it, I had to take a bunch of hard counterpunches. My left eye was now closed. But none of that bothered me anymore. I knew now that my plan was right—Joe belonged to me.

❧

With all this, I hadn't noticed how hard Louis had been hit by me. He was in such incredible shape that he showed no effect and seemed to continue the fight with the same sharpness and intensity as before. But after the fight he told his handlers that he remembered nothing after that punch.

Outside the ring no one had noticed anything. The spectators only saw that I had a swollen face with one eye closed, that I had lost every round and looked particularly bad in the third. Most experts had predicted that I would go in the fourth, and it appeared that they were going to be right.

Even Joe Jacobs started in on me at the end of the third. "Shut up!" I yelled. My cutman Doc Casey was there to work on my body and close the cuts between rounds; Joe Jacobs was my manager and as such belonged in my corner; but Max Machon was the only one who could talk to me and give me advice during a fight.

And Machon said nothing more than, "You caught him with a good one!" He was the only one who had seen it. I answered, "I think I have him where we wanted him now! Just watch!" In the meantime the reporters were at their microphones broadcasting that Louis, as expected, was winning easily. One of them even reported that the "execution" was about to take place. I, on the other hand, now had the confidence that I needed—Joe Louis really could be hurt.

As the fourth round began, things had changed considerably. I now could lure Louis into the distance that I wanted—and it was working. When Louis threw one of his dangerous left hooks, now I was inside the punch and countered with my right to his chin. I hoped that he would think that it was safer for him to throw his left as a jab, which I now *wanted* him to throw.

In that same moment he doubled up on his jab. And again I caught him immediately with a right cross. It wasn't the best punch; once again I had missed the timing by a split second. But it bothered him and he again fell into a clinch.

We were separated, and then suddenly came the jab from precisely the right distance. And that was also the moment in which he dropped his left just a few centimeters in order to throw it again—and now, for the first time, my right landed exactly where I wanted it. I had thrown my entire body weight behind it, and it was hard and sharp.

Joe was staggered. A barely visible shudder went through his body as he danced backwards. And as I went after him, I heard the surprised crowd come to life. Louis instinctively tried to stop me with a left hook, but I was again "inside" the punch and landed another right to the chin with full impact. The power of the punch rocked his head back, he seemed to reel for a moment, and then he fell sideways to the canvas.

⌒⌒

America's "Shoe King," Walter Johnson, opened his estate in Endicott, Massachusetts, to us as a training camp for the Sharkey fight.

Since Gene Tunney retired unbeaten in 1928, everyone was anxious to see who would be the new champion, Sharkey or Schmeling.

Friends and backers visited me at my Endicott training camp in 1930.

Clearly looking for a quick end to the fight,
Sharkey went all out from the opening bell.

It happened in the fourth round: I was paralysed by a low blow, and Sharkey was disqualified. I was the new world champion. There was little protest regarding the decision, even from Sharkey himself.

The newspaper *Tempo* covered the fight. My mother was extremely worried about the low blow.

The pain was soon forgotten — I had achieved my goal, but my crown was tarnished.

My friends in Germany were surprised to hear my voice coming from America over the new medium of radio.

Young Stribling, who had never been knocked out, was TKO'd in the fifteenth round of my first title defense in 1931.

During training for the Stribling fight, the "Sea Devil," Count Luckner, invited me aboard his three-masted boat, *Mopelia*.

Lufthansa sent a plane to pick me up in Bremen and take me to Berlin.

My mother and I were driven from the airport in an open limo.

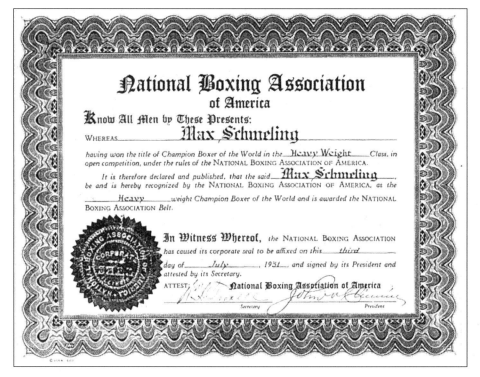

National Boxing Association
of America

Know All Men by These Presents:

WHEREAS _____ **Max Schmeling** _____

having won the title of Champion Boxer of the World in the **Heavy Weight** *Class, in open competition, under the rules of the* NATIONAL BOXING ASSOCIATION OF AMERICA.

It is therefore declared and published, that the said **Max Schmeling** *be and is hereby recognized by the* NATIONAL BOXING ASSOCIATION OF AMERICA, *as the* _____ **Heavy** _____ *weight Champion Boxer of the World and is awarded the* NATIONAL BOXING ASSOCIATION *Belt.*

In Witness Whereof, *the* NATIONAL BOXING ASSOCIATION *has caused its corporate seal to be affixed on this* _____ *third* _____ *day of* _____ *July* _____ *, 1931, and signed by its President and attested by its Secretary.*

ATTEST; _____ **National Boxing Association of America** ;
_____ Secretary _____ President

Only with my victory over Stribling was I recognized as the true world heavyweight champion.

Finally, I was also recognized as champion by the German Boxing Authority, and a reception was given in my honor.

After my victory over Stribling I received a lot of attention. Here I am presenting the prize to the winning jockey at a horserace run in my honor.

Since his loss, Sharkey had worked his way back to a rematch.

Other individual sportsmen were celebrated in those days, such as the pilots Ernst Udet, Freiherr von Gromau, Prince Friedrich von Hohenzollern, and Captain Koehl.

I made golf into part of my training routine (facing page).

One day Franklin Delano Roosevelt, who at the time was a candidate for president, visited my training camp. His visit gave the fight publicity that money couldn't buy.

Although he was on the brink of being knocked out from round ten on, Sharkey was awarded a controversial decision.

I never faced the gargantuan Carnera in the ring; he knocked out Sharkey in the sixth round to bring the heavyweight title back to Europe.

In 1932 Anny and I had a beautiful wedding, and the celebration lasted into the wee hours of the morning.

Articles and cartoons appeared concerning my relationship with Anny.

We bought our home at Saarow–Pieskow in the late twenties. It was an idyllic location on the Scharmützelsee.

In the same year we acquired an apartment in Berlin-Dahlem.

Anny Ondra, Czech
by birth, was already
a successful actress
when I met her.

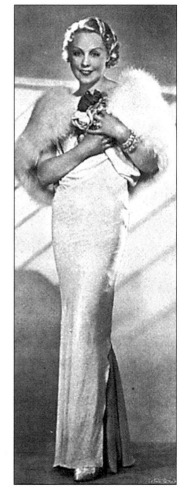

In 1934 Anny and I did
a film together called
Knockout.

Whenever we could,
we drove out to
Saarow-Pieskow to
escape the chaos of
the city.

My co-star in the film *Love in the Ring* was the well-known actress Frieda Richard (above).

A prominent couple, seen often at Berlin's meeting spots, were the tubercular poet, Klabund, and his wife, the celebrated beauty Carola Neher.

Josef Thorak also did
a sculpture of me.

I posed for the painter,
sculptor, and bon
vivant, Ernesto de Fiori
(left).

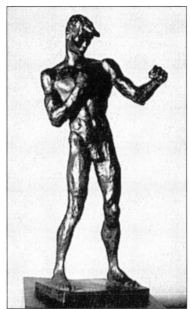

Rudolf Belling
(far left) and
Renée Sintenis did
sculptures of me.

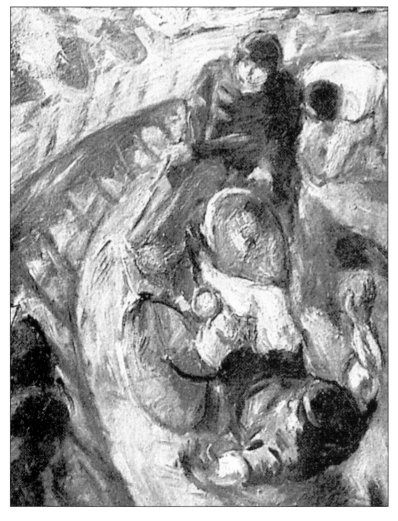

Max Beckmann's
Bicycle Race reflects
the revival of
artistic interest
in sports and
competition.

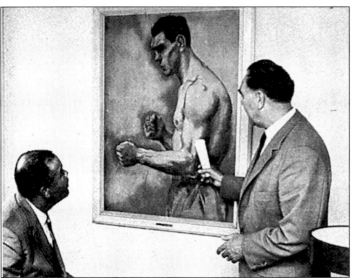

I didn't know what to make of George Grosz's art at first, but I agreed to pose for him.

Many years later I showed Grosz's portrait of me to Joe Louis.

Joe Louis—a boxing genius
such as comes along only
once in every few generations.

In 1934 I TKO'd Walter Neusel; the referee stopped the fight at the start of the ninth round.

Walter Rothenburg managed to bring the American Steve Hamas to Germany for a rematch in 1935. My victory over Hamas paved the way for my comeback to American boxing.

In the U.S. Joe Louis had become one of the most
feared boxers. Right after the contract-signing, I began

a hard training regimen, which included studying films
of his earlier fights. The results are shown above.

This picture was transmitted back to Germany as the fight took place.

My heart was in my throat as I watched referee Donovan's hand rhythmically rise and fall: "Seven-eight-nine!" Then he spread his arms wide — Joe Louis had been knocked out.

Directly after the fight, the ring was flooded with people. Amidst the storm of flashbulbs, I heard Joe Jacobs yelling to the reporters, "What did I tell you?! What do you say now?! We beat him!"

In the other corner,
Louis's seconds worked
on him.

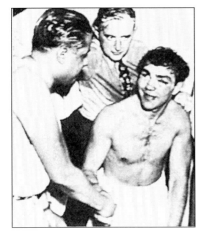

Well-wishers stormed my
dressing room.

I had beaten the myth of Joe Louis. Could I beat
Braddock as well? The press asked this question.

Two days after the Louis fight I was on my way
home. An officer of the sold-out Zeppelin, *Hindenberg*,
let me have his cabin. After more than fifty hours,
we set down in Frankfurt. The landing area was
black with people as far as the eye could see.

othandschuhe aus den Kämpfen
of the fights
iginals de Max Schmeling dans ses match
Stribling | Schmeling-Louis
1931   19. 6. 1936

On the day of my arrival in Berlin, I received an invitation to the Reich Chancellory. My mother is on Hitler's right, Josef Goebbels is directly to her right, and Anny is the blond woman facing the camera.

At the 1936 Olympics everything possible was done to impress foreign visitors. The parade of athletes from fifty-two nations followed Hitler's entrance through the stadium's Marathon Gate.

Berlin's days of pomp and peaceful competition were soon at an end. In the years that followed, the city became more and more the show place for military parades.

I had never before heard such an explosion—the 40,000 jumped onto their seats, and Yankee Stadium seemed ready to burst. Up until then the crowd had been unanimously behind Louis and had cheered every time he landed. Now I sensed that the crowd was swinging over to me. Even before I reached a neutral corner Louis was back on his feet. Clearly he wanted to show no weakness and got up by the count of four.

But now I knew for sure that Louis wasn't the unbeatable boxing wonder that everyone had raved about. Any experienced boxer would have stayed down until eight to recover as much as possible. But Louis was now a badly shaken, confused kid who had just lost his bearings. It was his first knockdown, and maybe a lack of experience that had made him get up too quickly.

In the break between rounds my corner went nuts. Joe Jacobs inundated me with words, and even Doc Casey was bubbling over. But I only listened to Machon, who calmly said, "Now be careful, Max!"

Joe Louis looked recovered and fresh as he came out for the fifth round. I hit him immediately with a right, followed by a left hook that visibly shook him up again. I wanted to keep him from getting too used to my right and let him know that my left was dangerous as well.

From this point on, Louis retreated while I aggressively pursued him. But I still wasn't hitting him as squarely as I wanted. I kept getting the left side of his face, which had begun to redden and swell.

In the middle of the fifth round Louis landed a textbook left hook to my head, and as I went over to infighting, he started to make the same fatal mistake—after his jabs he let his left drop just a few inches. By the second or third time, I started landing again with a hard, accurate right. In the same moment the bell rang, and I turned to go to my corner, not seeing the effect that the last punch had had. Louis weaved back to his corner on heavy legs. As I sat down, Machon said, "Joe's on rubber legs now! Patience! He can't last much longer!"

The sixth round was bad for Louis. I hit him so often with my right that it was tiring me out. But I wasn't able to put him away; as groggy as he was, he still instinctively protected his chin. So I only kept catching the left side of his face, deciding that I would hammer away at it until he weakened to the point of dropping his guard.

As I came back to my corner at the end of the sixth I was breathing heavily. The assault on Louis had tired me out, which Machon saw with concern: "Max, take it easy in the next round! You've got to pace yourself."

The seventh round almost reversed the tide. Louis roared out of his corner at the bell and seemed as fresh as at the beginning of the fight. Raging, he landed a powerful right hook to my body, followed by a barrage of punches, and for a moment I almost lost it; it took everything I had to weather that storm.

It appeared that Louis's corner had come up with a new strategy, because now he was no longer punching to the head, and practically all of his blows were to the body. Suddenly I felt one of his punches go below the belt. The referee jumped in immediately and warned Louis to keep his punches up. Joe then put his arms on my shoulders and shook his head apologetically. He clearly wanted me to know that the low blow wasn't intentional.

As I came back to my corner, Joe Jacobs looked concerned. "Louis still hits like a bull," I groaned. Machon replied, "You've got to keep it together! Next round you have to go back on the attack." "I took a low blow," I gasped. "Pay attention!" said Machon. "For God's sake, you've got to watch out!"

None of us heard the crowd anymore. Since early on I was only aware of our own hot breath, the scuffing of our feet on the canvas, the gasping, and the dull thud of our punches.

A few seconds after the start of the eighth round I caught Louis again with a full-impact right hand that buckled his knees. "Thank God," went through my mind, "his attack in the seventh round cost him. Now he's back to where he was in the sixth!" That thought brought me back to life. And as the crowd rhythmically chanted, "Kill him! Kill him!" my only thought was to hold to my fight plan, to stay cool amid all this hysteria. Not until seeing the film after the fight could I count the number of rights that I had landed to the left side of Louis's face.

But the ninth, tenth, and eleventh rounds weren't decisive either. Louis threw almost exclusively left hooks to the body, and I would usually come on at the end of the round with my straight rights. Each time he was groggy at the bell but would recover between rounds.

Louis was young and in tremendous shape; I just couldn't seem to put him away. At the same time, however, I could feel that he was wearing down, and his punches, even when they landed squarely, didn't have the same devastating power—they didn't hurt anymore.

Now I was able to land my right pretty much when I wanted. But Louis just wouldn't go down. It was unbelieveable how much punishment he could take. In each of these three rounds he was hit dozens of times, but he stood up to those punches, any one of which would have finished most of my previous opponents. I still remember what was written in the *New York Daily News* the next morning: "I can't remember ever having seen a boxer so completely knocked out yet still standing and still trying to turn the fight around. Joe Louis kept fighting when the odds were one thousand to one that he wouldn't make it to the final bell."

I had decided that in the twelfth round I would turn his head around with a left hook to finally set up a clean shot for my right. I was determined to do whatever it took not to give him another between-round-break in which to recover.

But I was overeager. My left hook was off, and I completely missed with my right. We both went into a clinch. We were both drained. But when we broke from the clinch, Louis dropped his shoulders and fired a hook way below the beltline. Even though I was wearing a protector, for a second I felt paralyzed. And in that same second I realized the danger that I still faced in this man. Louis was close to the end and didn't know where his punches were landing anymore. This low blow was a warning for me. I wasn't going to let this kind of accidental blow rob me of a fight that I had won. I decided that whatever it took, I was going to get off a shot that would end the fight.

In the span of a few seconds my right hit home three times, and each punch was fired with all the precision and power that I had left. The lefts with which Louis countered were only reflex actions. Then I threw another right cross, and Louis fell into me and held on. Donovan had to pull him off of me. I forced him into the ropes and crashed another right to his chin.

In this moment his arms fall. Joe Louis is finished and is giving me the clear shot that I've been waiting twelve rounds for. This is it. Finally I don't have to get my right over his left arm; I can fire from the inside with everything I've got and there's nothing in the way. This is it—all or nothing.

The punch turns Louis around. Astonished, he looks at me with eyes that no longer see anything. He turns 180 degrees and falls into the ropes and then down to his knees. His arms go back. Referee Donovan sends me to a neutral corner and starts his count. Louis tries to use the ropes to get back up. He holds himself in this position for a second or two, his face surprisingly calm. Then his head falls forward, his shoulder slides along the ropes, and then, as if his will has finally given in, he collapses. He lies there stretched out on the canvas. He seems to be trying in one last desperate effort to get up. He actually does manage to get his shoulders a few inches off the canvas but then suddenly collapses completely. Joe Louis rolls over and lies face down, stretched out and motionless.

My heart is in my throat as I watch referee Donovan's hand rhythmically rise and fall: "Seven—eight—nine!" Then he spreads his arms wide—Joe Louis has been knocked out.

As I watched the film afterwards I discovered that I raised my arms in this moment. Then I raced over to the fallen Louis and helped his handlers carry him to his corner. He was still out a minute later; I could feel it in the leaden weight of his body.

Suddenly the ring was flooded with people. I was being slapped on the shoulders and embraced. Standing in the lightning storm of flashbulbs, I heard Joe Jacobs yelling at the reporters, "So what did I tell you?! Didn't I tell you that we'd beat him?! What do you say now?! We beat him!"

One of the first to congratulate me was Jimmy Braddock, "Great fight, Max! You've earned a title shot!" Mike Jacobs congratulated me, as did Madison Square Garden president, Colonel Kilpatrick. All this time I was being hugged by Joe Jacobs and Max Machon, who were out of their minds.

Only with great effort could I make my way to the locker room, through the cheering crowd of happily distorted faces and deafening noise. Some people reached out from the crowd as if they just wanted to touch me, while others tore at my hand wraps as if they were sacred relics.

Looking back now with the perspective of many decades and experiences, I realize that I was nothing more than a boxer in his moment of triumph. The people needed a reason to let loose, and I was it—I was the idol around which they gathered in those few minutes.

On the opposite side of the ring Joe Louis was leaving the arena. His handlers had draped some towels over his head, and, though he had barely regained consciousness, they were leading him out of the ring. Hardly anyone took notice. Only a few remaining fans caught furtive or astonished glimpses of yesterday's hero, his head bowed and covered with towels as he disappeared into the dark exit.

The New York Herald Tribune wrote the next day: "The 'Brown Bomber' staggered to his dressing room. They laid him carefully on the rubdown table, massaged him, gave him smelling salts, and, after fifteen minutes, got him into the shower. But he was still groggy. His eyes were closed and he groaned on trying to make a fist. Dr. Walker and Dr. Nardiello examined him and found that he had sprained both thumbs. Louis, still in a trance, mumbled a few words, 'I just couldn't get at him. There was no way. Schmeling danced in front of me, and then he was gone. Oh God, my face!'"

While Louis turned to the wall, as if he finally wanted to be alone, tears ran down Jack Blackburn's face. "What happened?" asked Louis when he noticed. The gray-haired black man patted him on the shoulder and, through his tears, answered, "Nothing tragic, son; you just got knocked out."

In my dressing room there was absolute chaos—loud and wild. The congratulations continued, and Arno Hellmis had all he could do to get me to the microphone. I had barely gotten out a few words when Jack Blackburn, his face serious, came into the room and elbowed his way over to me. He was very down about his man losing, but he shook my hand and said, "You were great, Max!"

∽∾∾

The ride from Yankee Stadium took us from the Bronx, through Harlem, to Manhattan. In Harlem there was hysteria and despair. Cars heading downtown were spit on and hit with bricks and boards. We picked up speed down Lenox Avenue and took some shortcuts to the Plaza. Only the next morning did I read that hundreds had been injured in the rioting; *The New York Times* reported that it had been even worse in Chicago. Joe Louis's defeat was felt deeply in black America, experienced in that moment as a loss of hope and pride.

Hundreds of people were gathered before the hotel. As I appeared they began to applaud, and it took some doing to get to the elevators. Reporters came at me from every side: "Max, tell us what it was that you saw!" I explained about Louis dropping his left after jabbing. Suddenly they seemed to get what I was saying, and somebody said, "Blackburn should have known that, especially since you're a counterpuncher! Don't you think?"

I didn't know. Films of later fights showed me that Louis never quite broke that one bad habit. But the fact that he remained heavyweight champion longer than anyone else proved his incomparable skills.

My hotel room was drowning in flowers. There wasn't any point in thinking about sleep on this night. New crowds of people kept arriving at our suite, and the bellhops came every few minutes with baskets of congratulatory telegrams.

Herbert Ritze sat on the sofa and tore open the telegrams. In the din of voices he would call out names from time to time: Heinrich Schlusnus, Hans Albers, Primo Carnera, Viktor Schwannecke; then some unknown names from America, France, and all over the world; then Ernst Lubitsch, Hugo Abels, Marlene Dietrich, Aenne Maenz, George Grosz—for a moment it was as if my old, half-lost world were coming to me again. Then he yelled, "Douglas Fairbanks" and then "Adolf Hitler."

We sat together as it started to get light outside and the morning papers were brought in. Paul Gallico wrote in *The Daily News:* "Millions were lost and Harlem mourned as Max Schmeling, old man Schmeling, sent the unbeatable Joe Louis to the canvas for the full count. I think we journalists (myself included) owe Max an apology. He was the first of Joe's opponents (with the exception of the courageous Paolino) to face him without fear from the opening bell."

And Dan Parker, senior reporter for *The Daily Mirror,* wrote: "Max Schmeling, who was given no chance, knocked out Joe Louis, the boxing wonder of our era, in the twelfth round of a brutal match in Yankee Stadium and thereby pulled off the biggest upset in boxing history since Corbett demolished Sullivan in New Orleans. Before he collapsed on the ropes in the twelfth round, Louis had taken enough punishment to finish four ordinary fighters." Other papers wrote of "The Fight of the Century," "The End of a Legend," and asked whether Louis would ever return to the ring.

Then I was put through to Anny. The transatlantic long distance operators had cleared the lines and gotten a connection to Berlin in a few minutes. Anny had listened to the fight on the radio. She only asked, "When are you coming home?"

An officer of the *Hindenburg* let me have his cabin on the sold-out Zeppelin so that I could head home only two days after the fight. We flew over Ireland and Holland and on to Frankfurt. On July 26, after about fifty hours in the air, we passed over Doorn, the residence of the former Kaiser. We dipped several times and flew very low. From the gondola we could see Wilhelm II as he stood on his grounds and waved his hat.

That afternoon the *Hindenburg* landed at the Frankfurt airport. The ground was covered with cheering people as far as you could see.

15

In the Maelstrom of Politics

On the day of my arrival in Berlin I received an invitation to the Reich Chancellory. Hitler made sure that I was told to bring my friends and relatives as well. Aside from my wife and mother I also invited a director and a composer and their wives. As I entered the Old Palace, the guards and orderlies looked at my still swollen face with respectful amazement. Then Brückner came out and led us into the familiar reception hall; Hitler was waiting for us along with Goebbels, Heinrich Hoffmann and another aide, Philipp Bouhler.*

Hitler was introduced to my friends and greeted them cordially. After we had stood around chatting for a while, Hitler came up to me and in a formal, almost ceremonial manner expressed his thanks and those of the German people. Although he only spoke two sentences, it sounded like a formal speech and made me feel embarassed. After I had managed to thank him, the atmosphere again became relaxed. Hitler also lightened up and invited us to sit around the big table, where he assigned each of us our seat. Then he turned galantly to Anny with, "Certainly you want to have your husband next to you on this day," and led her to one of the deep armchairs. Then he said to my mother, "You have, gracious lady, truly every reason to be proud!" Then he added by way of confirmation, "Every German does!"

After the servants had served the cake, Hitler wanted to be told of the fight in full detail. It was clear that he had already been well informed by the press accounts. For example, he asked me if I had known even before the fourth round whether I would "beat the Negro."

I had brought a few American press clippings, which he and Goebbels looked at with interest. It appeared to me that he couldn't read the English text, but he looked carefully at the photos and observed, "It's too bad that we can't see a film of this!" I explained to him that I had brought back a film which was still in customs at the airport. Hitler was surprised and extremely interested. "That's fabulous!" he shouted. Then he turned to one of his adjutants and told him to send someone to Tempelhof Airport to pick up the film.

While we waited for the driver to return, Goebbels asked me whether it was a film of the entire fight or just selected outtakes. I explained to him that I had gotten the entire film as one of the conditions of my contract. When Goebbels asked whether the film was just for my private use, I told him that the promoters had offered me the film with the expectation that the fight would be over in a few minutes. For a small fee they had sold me everything. When the fight took another course and the film went to almost an hour, it was already too late to talk about charging me for world rights as well.

The conversation turned to the imminent Olympic Games, and Goebbels reported that every hotel in Berlin and the surrounding area had been booked-out for the duration of the Games. Hitler nodded with satisfaction. "Yes," he said, "you see! When I wanted to have the Olympic Stadium built, the 'experts' came to me and warned that we couldn't spend seventy-one million marks for a sports stadium. But I told them: either we build it right or not at all. The ludicrous seventy million we will make back several times over! I guarantee you!" In fact the German Reich did take in over five hundred million marks with the 1936 Olympic Games.

At this moment one of the adjutants came in and reported that the film had arrived and was ready to be shown in the film room. We all walked over to the film room together, and Hitler invited a few of the orderlies we met along the way to join us. The film was played in the unedited form in which it had been shot, and there were still some rough spots.

At the start, the camera swept over the massive arena and the crowds of people streaming in. Hitler was captivated. This was the kind of atmosphere that he knew from his own experiences and that he clearly enjoyed. Even the first couple of fight sequences seemed to put him in a state of feverish excitement. He gave a running commentary and every time I landed a punch he slapped his thigh with delight. "Schmeling," he suddenly directed at me, "have you read what I wrote in *Mein Kampf* about the educational value of boxing? Boxing is a manly sport. That's why I tell everyone, Schirach* and Tschammer, that boxing should be introduced into the public school curriculum."

Then he went back to watching. "Alright," he called out suddenly, "Goebbels, listen—this isn't going to be used as part of the *Wochenschau* [weekly newsreel]! This film is going to be shown as a main feature. Throughout the entire Reich!" he added emphatically.

As a new reel was being mounted, Goebbels assigned my director friend Zerlett the task of turning the film into a documentary feature film. Clips of my training as well as my reception in Frankfurt were added. The film

≈≈≈

was released under the title *Max Schmeling's Victory—A German Victory* and ran for weeks in every movie theater.

As we walked back to the reception room, Hitler turned to me and said, "You look quite banged up!" and, looking at my swollen face and eye, added, "Are you getting good medical attention?" I replied casually that I had been so happy and excited that even directly after the fight I hadn't felt the injuries. Now I felt completely recovered. "Except," I corrected myself, "for my throat. Even before my return I saw a doctor about some hoarseness and coughing."

Then I told him of a Berlin doctor whose simple method of treatment could cure symptoms that other doctors labored over in vain. Hitler asked for the name of this doctor, and I said "Theo Morell! You must know of him, *Herr Reichskanzler.* Hasn't Heinrich Hoffmann ever mentioned him? He's used him for years."

When we were back in the reception hall Hitler turned to Hoffmann and, seemingly annoyed, asked, "Why didn't you tell me that you knew an outstanding ear-nose-and-throat specialist?" Hoffmann, visibly somewhat embarassed, replied that Dr. Morell wasn't an ear-nose-and-throat specialist. He was primarily a dermatologist but took interest in areas beyond his specialty. He added that Morell was more of a trendy society doctor and not a leading specialist in any field.

A short time later Hoffmann told me the reason for Hitler's particular interest in Morell. Hitler had frequent problems with his throat and even feared that he might have throat cancer. Shortly after that afternoon, Hitler sent for Morell and came to trust him. A few months after that, Morell became Hitler's personal physician.

But this trust turned into a kind of dependency. With an array of nebulous drugs and injections, Morell kept Hitler running, especially towards the end of the war. Not until a few days before his suicide in the bunker of the Reich Chancellory did Hitler dismiss him. "Now even you can't help me, Morell!" he is supposed to have said as he took leave of his personal physicain.

I had met Morell in 1927, shortly after my move to Berlin. Wolfgang Fischer, an amusing party animal of those times, asked me if I would like to go for a drink at the fashion designer Max Brüning's place. Fisher had made a name for himself through his annual parties for the rich and famous in Westerland on the island of Sylt; the biggest names from theater, film, and sports came together on the yet-to-be-discovered island. To be a member of his "Westerlanders' Club" was a status symbol.

As an artist, Brüning had a somewhat questionable reputation: his favorite subjects were young women in scanty shorts and sweaters. Even knowing this, we were still surprised when a completely naked young woman answered the door at his apartment.

Assuming that we had come to the wrong apartment, I mumbled an apology and turned to go. "No, no, you're at the right apartment!" said the lanky, boyish young woman with a violet shawl thrown casually around her neck. "Come on in!" she smiled without embarassment. She seemed totally unaware of the strangeness of the situation.

Embarassed and with Fischer poking me in the ribs, I followed her through the dimly lit hallway to a living room. Sitting there around a brightly polished samovar were seven people, four men and three young women all sitting on large leather cushions and in animated conversation.

I couldn't believe my eyes. The four gentlemen were well-dressed in somewhat sporty clothes, while the ladies were stark naked. The whole scene had an unreal, slightly grotesque feel to it, because, despite the unusual dress code, everyone behaved according to normal social etiquette. After kissing each girl's hand with exaggerated politeness, Fischer introduced me to the gathering, and the host bid us take our places.

The conversation touched on the last auto race at Avus and the premiere of some revue. One of the ladies seemed to be the girlfriend of an Avus driver, because she dominated the conversation with her knowledge of technical jargon. Then some of the latest affairs—just begun or dramatically ending—were gossiped about. And finally one of the gentlemen began a vivid telling of his experiences as a ship's doctor. That was Dr. Morell.

After we had met a few more times, Morell treated me and actually did help me on a number of occasions; I believe that he was a competent physician. But I still never really understood why Hitler, to whom the most prominent specialists were available, would have made him his personal physician after so short a time. All of Morell's devotion to his profession, however, could not quite remove the hint of quackerie that stuck to him and that was particularly evident in his ongoing attempts to develop the most varied assortment of powders and medicines. And maybe that was exactly what drew Hitler to him; after all, there was something of the dilettante about him, too, and he never really trusted the experts.

We had been at the Reich Chancellory with Hitler for about three hours when Göring was announced. In his usual way, he burst through the door and stood there. In an expansive mood, he greeted Hitler and then turned to me: "So, Schmeling, with the fat eye—that will last a while! But for hunting you don't need your left eye—you close that one anyway when you aim!"

Göring looked around as if expecting applause then bellowed out a laugh. Finally he leaned over to Hitler and whispered something to him. Then

⌒⌒⌒

he turned to the group and said, "You'll excuse us, ladies and gentlemen!" Hitler stared straight ahead, momentarily lost in thought. Suddenly he stood and gestured that it was time to go. While he took leave of me, my mother, and the rest of the group with formal politeness, he smiled at Anny and said, "You see, gracious lady, yet another delightful afternoon!" Then he jokingly added, "Make sure that your husband wins a lot, so that we can see each other more often!" Then he left.

Max Machon arrived by ship a few days after me. He brought with him a gift for me from Joe Jacobs—an American sports car called the Cord, which was all the rage in the States. Its most celebrated feature was its retractable headlights. Whenever I returned to the parked car, it was always surrounded by crowds of teenagers.

Otherwise, however, Machon seemed uneasy. "There's something rotten about the Braddock fight," he said. "I have a bad feeling." But I dismissed this with, "After the victory over Louis, no one can deny me a title fight, not even the American Boxing Commission!"

But I was a little worried too. In order to nail down the fight as quickly as possible I decided to return to America by the beginning of August, because I really had nothing more than Braddock's verbal agreement. So Machon and I reserved seats on the *Hindenburg*.

During the hottest days of summer, Anny and I were glad to be able to flee the sizzling heat of the city. We wanted to spend the next fourteen days out in Saarow-Pieskow on the lake and in the forest. Evenings we sat outside in the cool summer breeze.

One day, as we sought refuge from the blistering sun in the swimming pool, heavy sulfur-colored clouds gathered over the pines and quickly changed over to blue-black in color. While we continued to watch nature's show, hot gusts of wind would start and then suddenly stop. Soon the first heavy drops of rain started, and Anny ran to the house to bring blankets and pillows inside. I stayed in the water and watched as the first flashes of lightning came from the black clouds.

As kids we had counted the seconds between the lightning and following thunder to tell how far off the storm was; lost in my thoughts while splashing around in the water, I gave myself over to that same game. Suddenly it was bright as day all around me and in the same instant came the thunder—first dry and crackling and then a deafening crash. As I looked up I saw the first flames jumping from the straw gable of the house. Paralyzed for a second by shock, I wasn't out of the pool before half of the roof was engulfed in flames. In the same instant Anny came running out of the house.

～～～

It was never a question of extinguishing the fire, which in minutes had spread to the whole house. So I ran in to save at least the few things I could grab on the run. As I came back out the door Anny was standing there out of her mind. "Max, let it be!" she cried. But I just dropped what I had and ran back to get some more. "Max, I beg you!" screamed Anny again. "It's burning like kindling!"

But I was already back in the house. As I came back out she was still standing on the lawn wringing her hands in panic. "Leave it! Those things aren't worth anything! Don't do this to me!" As the thick, acrid smoke began to come from the windows and I again ran by the screaming Anny, she suddenly sank to the ground with a final shrill, "Max!"

In a second I was at her side, lifting her and carrying her across the lawn. I carefully laid her on the ground near the swimming pool, but she was still unconscious. I grabbed a watering can, filled it in the pool, and threw it in her face. Then I ran once again past a shocked Anny to get a few more things from the burning building. Minutes later the roof collapsed. Our neighbors arrived shortly, but there was nothing that could be done. The women looked after Anny while the men helped me to move the few articles I'd been able to save away from the smoke.

Only that evening, after things had calmed down a bit, did Anny admit that she had faked the fainting spell. Acting furious, she scolded me for my roughness. "A whole watering can! At least twenty liters, and right in the face!" she yelled again and again. I acted contrite. But since she had only been putting on an act, my regret—as often as the subject came up in the following years—was also a put-on.

For Anny, the loss of the house that had held so many of our personal memories wouldn't be the only blow of that time.

We had been looking forward to the Olympic Games for months. We wanted to attend all the important events together, and for this reason Anny had postponed some of her filming dates. But my decision to leave for America on the second day of the Games changed all that. Now we could only be at the opening ceremonies and the first day of competition. The invitations to the numerous receptions, premieres, and gala evenings had to be regretfully thrown into the wastebasket.

For weeks Berlin had been in a frenzy of bustling anticipation. Films, posters, press releases in fourteen languages, flyers, hit songs—everything pointed towards the coming celebration. By mid-July the first visitors were already arriving, and the officials had gone all out to impress the foreign guests.

In the trains that arrived before and during the games from every possible direction, workers from the Travel and Tourism Bureau went from compartment to compartment with information for travellers who had yet to find lodging. The leading tourism experts had been retained months before the Games to work through any possible problems. A completely new subway line was built to bring spectators directly to the front gates of the stadium. Trains of the *S-Bahn* and *U-Bahn* [subway] now arrived and departed every ninety seconds. Although 510,000 international guests poured into a city of four million, all of the arrivals and departures came off without a hitch.

In Zeesen, just outside of Berlin, the world's largest short-wave transmitter went online, providing twenty-four-hour service. Twenty-five hundred journalists had come, and for the first time a public event was carried on about two hundred television sets.

In order to show the regime in the best possible light, Goebbels proposed a "world-press-amnesty" and actually took some measures to make it happen. Foreign visitors found at newspaper stands every imaginable newspaper, while the anti-Semitic paper *Der Stürmer* disappeared; also during this time you saw no political slogans, no anti-Semitic placards, none of the usual signs saying "No Jews Allowed."

I also noticed, to my amazement, that bookstores were once again carrying books by Thomas Mann,* Hermann Hesse,* Klabund,* and Stefan Zweig,* all of which had been banned since the book burnings at German universities in May of 1933.

I was also told by a journalist friend that nothing was to be written about the "plutocratic democracies" or the "decadent twenties," while Teddy Stauffer appeared at the Delphi offering the latest in swing music; all of Berlin was lined up outside, and those who were lucky enough to get in danced until the wee hours of the morning.

I don't remember if anyone actually said it, but in those days Berlin regained its uniquely cosmopolitan atmosphere—the bustle and urban splendor of years gone by. This was to be our farewell to that Berlin.

On the afternoon of the following day, August 1, 1936, we attended the opening ceremonies. When Hitler came through the Marathon Gate into the stadium, he was followed by the parade of 4,269 athletes from 250 nations; only the Soviet Union and Spain (where the Spanish Civil War had recently broken out) did not participate. The Spanish equestrian team, which had already arrived in Berlin, was called back to Madrid.

Behind Greece, the traditional parade leader, came all the other teams in alphabetical order. Except for the Japanese and English athletes, all of the teams greeted Hitler with a raised right hand. And each time a team passed the German war memorial and lowered its flag, it only increased the excitement in the stands. When even the French saluted Hitler with outstretched hand, the stadium went wild.

♁

I still remember how Anny and I were moved by this ceremony and the spirit of reconciliation that was everywhere. Then the flag-bearers formed a semi-circle and repeated the Olympic Oath; when they sang Handel's "Halleluja Chorus," many of us had tears in our eyes.

Even the first days brought some important results. At the center of attention was the "Wonder Runner" from the USA, Jesse Owens, who easily won the 100-meter sprint in the then-incredible time of 10.3 seconds. As winner of the 200-meter dash and the long jump, as well as a member of the winning relay team, he was the most successful athlete of the Games and the true star.

Hitler, who had personally congratulated all the winners before Owens, left the stadium directly after Owens won. Everyone noticed this, but most took it for a coincidence. I also wasn't sure whether Hitler had intentionally avoided the black athlete. Only later, when someone told me of similar incidents with Hitler, did I realize that despite all promises, he had intentionally snubbed the black and Jewish athletes.

Brundage, whom I saw again later, never mentioned the guarantee that I had given him at the Commodore Hotel on behalf of the German athletes. But I personally felt somewhat betrayed. In any case, I drove out to the Olympic Village in the early evening of August 2 to visit the American team. I had a long, friendly conversation with Jesse Owens, and we were friends from that day on.

Despite these repeated affronts, which were noticed by relatively few people, by the end of the Games, Hitler appeared to the world to be some kind of "Prince of Peace." The journalists who had painted such ominous pictures of Germany for the previous three years appeared to have been exaggerating. But the Polish ambassador said to a French colleague, "We must be wary of a people with such organizational ability. It would be just as easy for the German military to mobilize."

The last visitor had barely left before Berlin returned to its pre-Games state. *Der Stürmer* was again to be found at newspaper stands, and the foreign newspapers disappeared overnight. Jazz and six-day bicycle races were again forbidden, and Alfred Flechtheim's *Querschnitt* was again shut down. At this same time my friend Ernesto de Fiori, depressed and alone, left the country. Shortly before, he had done a sculpture of a sad young boy entitled *In Despair.*

On August 8, 1936 the *Hindenburg* was again secured at Lakehurst, New Jersey. Still uneasy, I had my luggage brought to the hotel, while I drove directly to the Boxing Commission.

The atmosphere was friendly and cordial. I was told to return in four days for the official contract signing with Jimmy Braddock. The ceremony was recorded by numerous photographers and camerapeople. "There we have it!" said Braddock as he gave me a friendly slap on the shoulder. I had heard that he had already started training. I had to get started as well. The fight was set for the middle of September, so only four weeks remained.

I felt relieved as we drove to the hotel. "You see, Joe," I said, "once again you've played the pessimist. Everything's falling into place!" But Joe remained skeptical. "Just wait!" he said. "I don't think I'm wrong—something stinks!"

Even before we set up training camp there was a rumor that Braddock had injured the little finger of his left hand. The next day, the rumor was that the finger was broken and Braddock had shut down his training camp. After visiting Braddock's training camp, a reporter from *Paris Soir* wrote: "Braddock won't be in a position to defend his title. His manager, Joe Gould, informed me that Jimmy had broken a finger on his left hand and was suffering neuroparalysis up to his elbow. He must undergo an immediate operation."

This statement seemed to alarm the New York Boxing Commission, because Joe Gould added that the doctor had said that Braddock must stay out of the ring for four months. In order to verify this diagnosis, the New York Boxing Commission had Braddock examined by a second physician, whose surprising finding was that Braddock was suffering from mild rheumatism in both elbows. This doctor said only that the fight should, if possible, be postponed for fourteen days. But Joe Gould persisted: "You can say what you want. My man's not going to fight in this condition!"

None of us believed the sudden rash of new ailments that seemed to attack Braddock daily. But since we had no choice, Machon was forced to say that I had no interest in fighting a world champion who wasn't completely healthy. The commission accepted this statement with apparent relief; the press praised my fairness. Then a new date was set—June 8, 1937. The parties declared themselves in agreement, and the awkward ceremony of signing the contracts was undertaken once again.

Not only had I wasted a week sitting around New York, I was also losing ten months with this rescheduling. Other fights were offered to me for this waiting period. In London they put together a deal whereby I would fight British Empire Champion Tommy Farr, and the winner—thanks to the intrigues of the American boxing business—would be declared the "alternative world champion." The contracts were already signed when the Americans, whom we were trying to outmaneuver, bought out Tommy Farr's contract.

Joe Louis's manager also put out feelers, but I was only interested in the title. I wanted to be the first former heavyweight champion to break the adage "they never come back." That was my only thought. I turned down the Louis rematch with the explanation that I wasn't looking for a big payday, but rather for the world championship: "I want my title back and nothing else."

Then I shipped out for Europe. But restlessness and frustration wouldn't let go of me. In the next few months I travelled back and forth to America several times.

In late April 1937 I began training again. But the rumors persisted that Braddock had no intention of fighting me. Yes, he had resumed training too, but they were whispering that his training was for a completely different fight. I couldn't and wouldn't believe that, but early in May Gene Tunney paid a visit to my training camp. He encouraged me to keep training, but with the warning, "Be ready for anything, Max! You don't know what's possible in this country."

Ten hours before the fight I appeared at the weighin. In the narrow, bare room sat the officials with their air of propriety. The president, General Phelan, stood and greeted me with a formal statement. Then came the doctor, who quickly examined me. After a few minutes he turned to the Boxing Commission and said, "Gentlemen, this man is alright!'

Braddock was nowhere to be seen. General Phelan played out the farce to the hilt. He stood up behind his desk, turned to the commissioners and said, "Gentlemen, you've seen what happened here. Mr. Schmeling has, as per regulation, been weighed and declared fit. His opponent, Mr. Braddock, however, has not appeared. Therefore the Boxing Commission declares that the current world champion may not participate in this match and is further fined $1,000."

I almost felt like laughing. The comedy of this past year seemed to have reached its finale. From the first rumors of Jimmy's injured finger right up to today, everything had been a setup: the doctor's diagnosis, the signing of the contracts, the promotion (including posters that were hanging even as we stood there), right up to the ludicrous fine for Jimmy Braddock.

And at that point I didn't even know the half of it. I learned the *whole* scandal a few days later. The "sick" Jimmy Braddock had some time before signed a contract for a title fight with Joe Louis, which in fact took place in Chicago a few weeks later. A secret clause of that contract was that Braddock would receive 10 percent of Louis's earnings for the next ten years. Joe defended his title twenty-five times in that decade. By not fighting me, James Braddock became a wealthy man.

Let me make it clear that Joe Louis had nothing to do with it. He and I were both pawns in a game between other, more powerful players.

When I came back to Berlin at the end of August 1936, the Olympic Games had just come to an end, and Germany had done extremely well. Since Count Coubertin had re-initiated the Games in 1896, Germany had usually only gotten a few medals here and there. This time it had the highest medal count with thirty-three gold, twenty-six silver, and thirty-six bronze medals.

The regime saw in this athletic success a political validation. And in a sense it could point to a revitalization of what had been a country plagued by unemployment and misery. It is only natural that a nation feel pride over the victories of its athletes. But it had never before occurred to a state, a monarchy, or a republic to justify its form of government based on the success of a long jumper.[1] Now the victories on the field of sport were being converted into political currency.

Without wanting it, I, too, was being pulled into this political aspect. A few days after the reception with Hitler, our maid came running and said, "There's an SA man at the door! Should I let him in?" When she turned around, however, he was already standing behind her. Clicking his heels together, he announced in a military voice: "Heil Hitler, Herr Schmeling! I am here at the command of *Obergruppenführer* von Jagow, and I have the honor of presenting you with the Dagger of Honor and the honorary title of *Ehrensturmführer* [Honorary Commander in the SA]."

I was rather taken aback for a moment, and my somewhat confused answer wasn't only a means of stalling for time: "Thank you very much! But please, *Herr SA-Führer,* sit down! You'll understand, this is such a surprise! I'm not very political. I have to be honest, I don't know the difference between *SA* and *SS*.[2] Could you possibly give me twenty-four hours to think it over?" The man looked at me with surprise. Then he stood up and said, "I shall return tomorrow at the same time! Heil Hitler!" Then he disappeared.

I had gotten myself into a difficult situation, and both the refusal and the acceptance would have their consequences. In this dilemma I called Heinrich Hoffmann in Munich, but I was told that he was with Hitler in Obersalzburg. Since I had no time to lose, I called Obersalzburg directly and got through to Hoffmann.

At first Hoffmann couldn't understand the problem. Race drivers Caracciola, Brauchitsch, or Rosemeyer wore the pin of the Dagger of Honor, and a good number of other athletes did as well. He only understood after I explained to him that I boxed mostly in America and would encounter considerable problems there as an *SA-Führer.* Hoffmann was silent for a moment and then said, "Max, wait a minute!" Then he put the receiver down and returned after about two minutes. "Your decision is right. Do whatever you feel! You can simply refuse it!"

I was very relieved, and, although Hoffmann and I never discussed it, I'm sure that he had spoken to Hitler. I had heard often enough that Hitler thought it was a nuisance, trying to get "his" athletes to join the Party:

"Politically they are nothing but children. What good is an opera singer to me who wears a Party pin but has no voice?"

The next day I answered the door when the SA man returned. "Come in!" I said cordially. He looked at me in surprise and expectation. After we sat down I began, "I hope you will understand that, unfortunately, I can't accept this honor." The *SA-Führer* looked at me with surprise. "Yes," I said, "as a sportsman who is very often in America—I ask you to see my position. I will tell your *Obergruppenführer* myself in a letter that I'm now writing. I can also tell him that this decision was made with approval from the highest level!"

I left it with this implication. My visitor gave me one more dazed look, took the package which presumably held the Dagger of Honor, put it under his arm, and wordlessly stood to leave. At the door he gave the Hitler salute and brusquely said, "Heil Hitler!"

A few years later, sometime in the summer of 1943, I was sitting in a train bound for Pomerania when the door to my compartment opened and in walked a ranking naval officer. When he saw me, he stopped short and introduced himself: "Herr Schmeling?" Then he bowed slightly and said, "von Jagow!"

We got to talking, and I said to him, "You remember? I hope you didn't hold it against me." He barely smiled. "I have to tell you, Herr Schmeling," he replied, "I understood completely. That's all so long ago now."

And as we rode through the monotonous Pomeranian landscape we spoke of the coming harvest, forestry, and the weather. I had the impression that for von Jagow, the illusions of that earlier time had long since died.

But it wasn't only in Germany that sports began to serve a different function. After the Braddock fiasco it was finally clear to me—a German world champion could be tolerated in 1931, but one coming from Hitler's Germany was acceptable to no one.

I could, however, understand this reaction. When I returned to Germany after the Louis fight, I saw the bout characterized in headlines and newspaper cartoons as a "Battle of the Races," and my victory had been turned into a "German victory." Congratulatory telegrams and occasional contact with those in power was now being held against me. I was a young man then, whose sole thought was to get a title shot. I had tried to convince Hitler of the merits of my Jewish manager, Joe Jacobs, and I wanted to convince the Americans of my right to a title bout. Both attempts were equally naive.

Once I had gotten the true picture of what had happened with the Braddock affair, I was reminded of something that had happened a few months earlier. I had been in London to sign the contract for fighting British

Empire Champion Tommy Farr. As always, I was staying in the old Savoy Hotel. Shortly after my arrival a bellhop brought me a small envelope on a tray: "Dear Max," was written on the small stationary, "I have just read that you're in London, and that we're both staying in the same hotel. I would be frightfully pleased to see you again after all these years. This evening I'm giving a cocktail party in my suite. Will you come? Yours, Marlene Dietrich."

I was glad; we hadn't seen each other in about five years. Only once, for my fight against Sharkey, did she fly from Los Angeles to New York, and we nodded to each other as I stood in the ring before the fight. Then before the Louis fight she had put the experts to shame with her gutsy prediction of my KO victory.

I wrote a word of thanks back to her and asked if it would be alright for me to bring a few German friends. There was no reply. When I returned to the hotel late that afternoon there was still no word from her. No one at the reception desk knew anything. In order not to offend Max Machon and Walter Rothenburg, who were with me, I decided to forego the reunion. Instead we went to a small seafood restaurant in Soho.

At first I hadn't thought too much about Marlene's silence. She may have just forgotten to reply, perhaps she was reluctant to meet new people, or maybe there were already too many people.

But now it seemed to me that her silence had spoken volumes. I hadn't said whom I wanted to bring, and she may have thought that I would bring some kind of Nazi sports official. That's all years ago, and I never saw Marlene Dietrich again. Time has a way of breaking up friendships. Soon I would have experiences that were not only disappointing but also threatening.

---

[1] The long jumper in question was Lutz Lang, whom Hitler had expected would win at the 1936 Olympics, but who was beaten by Jesse Owens.

[2] The *SA* or *Sturmabteilung* were the paramilitary Brown Shirts/Storm Troopers, which began in 1921 and which supplied the force for Hitler to gain and maintain power in the early thirties; their importance was drastically reduced after the so-called "Röhm-Putsch" in 1934. The *SS* or *Schutzstaffel* was considedred to be an elite unit which had been subservient to the *SA* from 1926 to 1934, but which, under Heinrich Himmler, became independent and predominant after the "Röhm-Putsch."

16
Nothing but Farewells

In the weeks after the fire at Saarow-Pieskow, Anny and I, sometimes with friends, had often discussed rebuilding the house. Soon we were sitting over plans for reconstruction and even enlarging the house, which at times had seemed too small.

It was Anny who suddenly looked up from the plans one afternoon and said, "Is this really what we want?" I didn't understand what she meant until she said that maybe the misfortune of the fire had been a sign. After all, Saarow-Pieskow had only been a getaway house for weekends and summer vacation. "Can you really see us getting old there, Max?"

I had no illusions that my boxing career could go on much longer. I was thirty-one years old, and even my victory over Louis had been heralded by the critics as doubly amazing given the ten-year age difference between us. I was determined to win back the world championship and then retire unbeaten as Gene Tunney had done. It was time to make plans as to what I wanted to do with the next few years.

Again, it was Anny who made me see that I was happiest when either hiking or hunting in the forest. "You're from the country, Max" she said. "The Schmelings have peasant blood. You're still a boy from Uckermark.*" And sometimes in my dreams I did see my life the other way around—not as a city-dweller with a weekend place in the country, but rather as a farmer or forester who from time to time visited the city.

So we began at this time to drive around the countryside, seeing where we might want to live—perhaps Mecklenburg with its forests and many lakes, perhaps the broad open expanses of Pomerania, or maybe Mark Brandenburg with its sandy paths among the melancholy birches and dark stretches of forest.

❧

And there was another reason why Saarow-Pieskow had become somewhat tarnished for us. One day, some time before the fire at Saarow-Pieskow, Frau Grumbkow, the wife of our gardner, came pedalling across the field on her bike, probably to check on the garden as she sometimes did. Her good heart and cheerful manner were always welcome.

But on this day she was visibly disturbed. "My God!" she said softly, "what's going on here?" It turned out that the area had been surrounded by the Gestapo during the night, and that the reason was our friend Josef Thorak.

Thorak had already remarried after the death of his first wife. Although many were a little put off that he hadn't waited the year of mourning, everyone was impressed when the artist introduced his new wife. The new Frau Thorak came from an old Jewish family and was not only beautiful but also an excellent cook, whose *Kaiserschmarrn* [a sugared pancake with raisins] was known far and wide. Highly educated, she was fluent in a half dozen languages. When Hitler came to power she had seen before any of us the direction in which things were going. Even then she had told her husband that she did not want to hurt him in this new situation and that it might be better to separate. Thorak was probably bothered by this at first. But then his ambition got the better of him, and a short time later they divorced, with the secret intention of staying together. In appearance, nothing had changed. As before, they still lived together next door to us.

The Nuremberg Laws of 1935 then created a new and threatening situation—where the Thoraks had formerly been freely living together, now they were committing the punishable crime of *Rassenschande* [race-mixing] between unmarried persons. The separation, which was supposed to have made everything easier, now only made things worse. Without the divorce they could have stayed together. "Mixed marriages" were still allowed at first.

We never found out who had been the informer. By watching the house, the authorities wanted to determine whether Thorak and his wife were still living together and who came and went at Thorak's house. That is how we got involved.

While Frau Grumbkow was still wringing her hands, I went next door to Frau Thorak. She was alone, her three children in school. "Oh, Max!" she greeted me "it's only the beginning! I've always said this was coming." She had no illusions. When I asked her why Josef hadn't used his good connections, she only smiled and replied, "Oh, you know Josef!" She sat quietly at the kitchen table. She didn't seem to be in despair or even upset. Outside the Gestapo had surrounded her house, and she smiled.

The next morning I decided to do what I could. I drove to Berlin and went straight to Goebbels. When I told him why, he told me that it would be better to speak in his home than at the ministry. At his ministry villa near

Brandenburg Gate, Goebbels received me in the presence of his wife. Without much discussion he came right to the point: "What's wrong, Herr Schmeling?" I told him what had happened, that Frau Thorak was a thoroughly apolitical woman and an exemplary mother; further, that she didn't try to influence her children against the regime and that she had voluntarily released her husband. Goebbels listened attentively, but when I had finished he only said, "But she is a Jew, isn't she?" I replied, "Of course she is, Herr Minister—she's a tremendous woman!"

Goebbels looked at me silently for a moment. Then he repeated, "But she's still a Jew!" I tried a different tack and told him how Frau Thorak even encouraged her children to listen to Hitler's speeches on the radio, how I had personally witnessed her explaining the speeches to them so that they could discuss them in school. As I explained this to Goebbels, his wife added, "Yes, Josef, there are such cases!"

Goebbels himself sat there silently for another moment, and I didn't know what more to say. Staring into space, I focused vacantly on a sculpture that was on top of the radio. Just as Goebbels began to speak again, I realized that the sculpture wasn't by one of the currently approved sculptors, but rather by the banned Ernst Barlach.[*1] "Yes, Herr Schmeling, what do you really want me to do?" he asked helplessly but not without a sharp edge. Without much reflection I replied, "Herr Minister, could you at least speak to her and make up your own mind?" Goebbels was dumbfounded. "I'm sorry, Herr Schmeling, but you actually expect me to receive a Jew?" He shook his head almost amusedly. "Maybe I've misspoken, Herr Minister," I corrected myself, "I only meant that *someone* could speak to Frau Thorak." Goebbels looked over to his wife and then at me and then finally said, "Hanke will do it!" Hanke was at that time state secretary in the Ministry of Propaganda.

In leaving, greatly relieved, I said to Goebbels, "Please understand, I see it purely in human terms." For a second it appeared as if he even understood what I meant; maybe his wife's being there had made my mission easier. In any case, he replied, "I accept that!"

Next weekend Frau Thorak sent Frau Grumbkow over to get me. She didn't come over herself anymore because she didn't want to cause us any problems. She told me of her meeting with Hanke, who had invited her to the Ministry of Propaganda. Hanke had been charming and suggested that she remain living in Saarow-Pieskow with the understanding that she not have contact with her husband. Finally, he said that laws are, after all, laws, and no one can go against them.

In fact, the Gestapo people left a few days later. Thorak finally did separate from his wife and soon had the career success that he wanted so badly —he became, along with Arno Breker,[*] the official sculptor of the Third Reich, and his enormous statues graced Albert Speer's* German Pavillion at the Paris World's Fair. Just as Breker was Hitler's favorite sculptor, so Speer chose Thorak to design the sculptures for the Nazi Party Parade Grounds at Nuremberg.

Whatever feelings Frau Thorak might have had regarding her husband's unencumbered success, she kept them to herself. One day, it must have been late 1939, Frau Thorak came to say good-bye to us before emigrating. Some time after that we heard that she was supposed to have been a secretary for the Duke of Windsor, who later abdicated as King of England. Shortly before the war I met her in Paris. Just before the German invasion of France she left for England.

In the summer of 1937 I was, thanks to so many fight projects falling through, mostly sitting inactive when Gustav Eder invited me to come to Rotterdam to watch him defend his European championship title against the Dutchman Beb van Klaveren. It was an exciting fight, which Eder won by KO in the eighth round.

After the fight a bunch of us joined to celebrate the victory, when someone mentioned that some old friends of mine were currently appearing at a cabaret in nearby Scheveningen. The very next day I drove with Max Machon to the seaside resort where we met Willi Rosen, Siegfried Arno, and Otto Wallburg—all old friends of mine who had also done films with Anny.

The get-together, however, took an unsettling turn. Even from the stage the three had recognized us and as a kind of greeting did songs and bits from our old Berlin days. They seemed to be very pleased with the unexpected reunion, and I had never seen them so witty, energetic, or funny.

As we sat at dinner afterwards, they wanted to know all about Berlin: how was Aenne Maenz and who hung out at Schlichter's. They asked about old friends, about Anny, and they couldn't believe that Hitler had chopped down the trees along Unter den Linden. What moved me most was how they still thought fondly of the country which had forced them into exile. It was with a feeling of secret pride that they viewed from afar the recovery that Germany was experiencing.

The longer the evening went on, the more sentimental they became, until Otto Wallburg suddenly began to cry. We all tried to console him, but he continued. "It just can't be!" he sobbed with head in hands. "In the First World War I earned the Iron Cross, and my family . . . we all grew up there! It just can't be that we'll never be allowed to return to our fatherland!" Willi Rosen and Siegfried Arno also had tears in their eyes. It was heartbreaking to see those grown men crying in a nightclub in Scheveningen. They still hoped to return one day.

Otto Wallburg and Willi Rosen did return. At the beginning of the forties they were captured in a police raid, and sent back to Germany, and were
gassed to death a short time later in Auschwitz. Only Siegfried Arno was luckier; shortly before the German invasion he escaped to America.

At some point that evening the restaurant owner came over to our
table and asked me if it would be alright if he took a picture of us; pleased to
have a souvenir of the evening, I said yes. But when I arrived back in Berlin
two days later, I was immediately greeted by a call from the Ministry of
Propaganda. On the other end was *Reichspropagandaleiter* Hinkel.

In a very casual tone I said, "Hello, Herr Hinkel! How's it going?"
Hinkel didn't answer except to say "How was it, then, in Holland, Herr
Schmeling?" It became immediately clear to me what this was all about, and I
answered "Oh, so you mean my get-together with Arno and Wallburg?" In a
friendly, almost concerned manner he continued, "Yes, that's already on the
Minister's desk."

The reunion with old friends had really had an effect on me, so I answered somewhat angrily, "I want to tell you something, Herr Hinkel! I really
don't care if it's lying on the Minister's desk. I conduct myself abroad as would
any good German. Those are my old friends and I won't be told how I should
treat them!"

Hinkel was clearly taken aback by my outburst, and I got the feeling
that he would rather drop the matter than pursue it. Anyway, he said, "Calm
down, Herr Schmeling!" and then continued "Did you have to have your picture taken?" So I asked Hinkel what he would do upon seeing old friends
again for the first time in years.

I only vaguely remember the rest of the conversation. Finally Hinkel
laughed and said something to the effect that he himself didn't know anything
about politics and that I really shouldn't be allowed to go abroad alone.

Some time later I ran into Goebbels by chance. In passing he softly
hissed, "What are you thinking, Herr Schmeling? You just go ahead and do
whatever you please! You don't concern yourself with laws! You come to the
Führer, you come to me, and still you continue to socialize with Jews." Then
he kept walking.

In America Joe Louis had taken the heavyweight championship from
Jimmy Braddock, and if I ever wanted to win it back, I had to get it from Joe
Louis. For that whole year Joe Jacobs had been trying in vain to get me into
the title picture. And just as Louis had replaced me in the Braddock title fight,
now Tommy Farr got a fight with Louis instead of honoring his contract to
fight me—once again I had been outmaneuvered.

☙☙☙

Still, I didn't give up on the idea of meeting the winner of the Louis-Farr match. In order to study both of them, I travelled to the States and saw the fight on August 30. Joe Louis was booed by the fans when he only managed to win on points.

The next day Mike Jacobs offered me a title fight with Joe Louis. There was, however, one condition attached—I first had to face the extremely strong Harry Thomas. That fight would put me back in the public eye and serve as ballyhoo for the title match with Louis. I was in no position to refuse, so I accepted the condition and signed the contract.

On December 13 I knocked out Harry Thomas in the eighth round of an unexpectedly tough fight. I could have just as easily become a stepping stone for Thomas, and I suspect that that had been the intent. Directly after that, however, I got the contract for a title fight against Joe Louis. The matchup would take place on June 22, 1938 in New York.

Since the late twenties I had scarcely missed any of the important auto races in Germany. I knew a lot of the drivers of those years, from Rudolf Caracciola to Hermann Lang to Hans Stuck; but I was only really close to one—the youthful and carefree Bernd Rosemeyer.

Rosemeyer was the "Wunderkind" of the German race drivers. In a single season he had made the jump from motorcycle racing to the top of the auto-racing world, and the races of recent years had always been a duel between Mercedes star Caracciola and Rosemeyer, the ace of Auto-Union.

But while Caracciola was the cool-headed tactician behind the wheel, Rosemeyer seemed to drive with the facility of a natural genius. His style was incomparable. Everything seemed almost playful, a foregone conclusion, yet behind all that was a no-holds-barred will to win. When he married the attractive stunt pilot Elly Beinhorn, it was a dream wedding. More than any of us, he embodied the modern gladiator—an existence between risk and victory. He was the idol of the masses.

On January 28, 1938 on the test track from Frankfurt to Darmstadt, a duel was supposed to take place between Rosemeyer and Caracciola for the world speed record. I would have loved to be there, but I had been in training for weeks, secluded at a cabin in the forest out in Sachsenwald. In two days I was to fight the new British Empire champion, the South African Ben Foord, in Hamburg. I regarded this fight, as well as the subsequent bout with the American Steve Dudas, as a warm-up for the Joe Louis fight. I won both.

It was only the early afternoon of January 28 when I received a call from the auto race—Bernd Rosemeyer was dead.

The chase for the record had started promisingly. Even in the first run, Rudolf Caracciola had topped Bernd Rosemeyer's world record by reaching

432.7 kilometers per hour. As Rosemeyer's Auto-Union car was rolled to the start, the wind conditions had become less favorable. Caracciola advised his friend Rosemeyer to postpone his run for the record. But Rosemeyer, unconcerned as he always was, simply laughed as he waved off the warning.

In his first test run, Rosemeyer came close to Caracciola's record, and he was sure that he would top it now that his engine had warmed up. But at the 9.2 kilometer-marker a gust of wind swept down and lifted the car from the track. None of us could believe it. A few days later, tens of thousands—friends and admirers—paid their last respects to Bernd Rosemeyer.

[Here Schmeling tells of selling the Saarow-Pieskow property and acquiring a large old farm-estate in eastern Pomerania on the then-border with Poland; the estate was called Ponickel.]

After we had acquired Ponickel we decided to sell Saarow-Pieskow. Whenever I came home in the evening, having been out hunting in the forest with my dogs while Anny was at work in her herb garden—I knew that this would be my life. I had no fear of that day when I would have to hang up my boxing gloves. In fact, I was even looking forward to it. I only wanted that one last fight.

[1]Goebbels' ownership of a piece by Expressionist sculptor Ernst Barlach demonstrates the hypocrisy of Nazi cultural policy. Expressionist and avant-garde works were publicly condemned as "degenerate art," while collectors such as Goebbels secretly hoarded many of the banned and confiscated works, which they knew to be of great and ever-increasing value.

17

The Second Time
Against Joe Louis

Early 1938 saw Hitler at the height of his popularity. In the second week of March, Germany and Austria united, thereby "realizing an old longing of the Germans." But as great as was the celebration in both countries, so was the rest of the world put ill at ease. Concerned and upset, people wondered what Hitler would do next.

I felt the shift in public opinion when I arrived in New York in early spring to start training for the Louis fight. Even as the *Bremen* pulled into New York harbor, there were people yelling and carrying signs, apparently waiting for none other than myself. The posters that they held over their heads called me an "Aryan Show Horse" and a representative of the "master race," while they shook their fists at me. In order to avoid any incidents, the harbor police escorted me through the crowd and brought me to the hotel via back streets. But at the hotel was the same scene. Protesters marched back and forth in front of the hotel carrying signs saying "BOYCOTT NAZI SCHMELING!"

Whenever I went out to Broadway or Fifth Avenue, people would stop and taunt me with an outraised arm. In small groups I would try to explain—to no avail—that I would hardly have Joe Jacobs as my manager if I were a Nazi. At this point, friends would suggest that I stay in the country and become an American—that I could only be unhappy in Hitler's Germany. "Everything would be much easier," they said.

For the previous ten years New York had practically been my home, so of course I was bothered and hurt by all of this. But whomever I spoke with, they always told me that I had to understand how it was. There was Hitler, who was filling the world with hate and fear; among the demonstrators were surely many who had been forced to emigrate; and no one wanted to see me win the title because, whether I had wanted it or not, I was a showpiece for the Nazis. Up to the day of the fight I received thousands of hate-letters signed "Heil Hitler" or "Hit Hitler." I didn't know what to do—only two years earlier this same city had cheered me wildly.

Joe Louis, who had yesterday been celebrated by Harlem as a hero of the underclass, was now suddenly transformed into the symbol of freedom and equality for all people and races against the Nazi threat. Pretty soon I was hearing that people had convinced Louis that with this fight I was hoping to prove the superiority of whites over blacks. Joe, the black man, found himself cast in the unexpected role of national hero for all Americans. There was a daily stream of visitors to my camp who had seen Louis training at Pompton Lake, all reporting that Louis had worked himself into a rage of retribution.

These visitors also reported that Louis was training harder and more intensely than ever before. His trainer Jack Blackburn was working hardest on eliminating the defensive flaw that had cost Louis the last time. In Nat Fleischer's *Ring* we read that the champion had learned how to defend against my "devasting right." There was no doubt that I was facing one of, if not *the* toughest fight of my career.

The experts almost unanimously favored Louis, despite my knockout of him and my subsequent victories. Yes, *Ring Magazine* conceded me the psychological edge, but practically all of the physical advantages, especially youth, were seen as being on Louis's side—Nat Fleischer predicted a Louis victory by the twelfth round. Past champions such as Willard and Jeffries, Sharkey, Baer, and Braddock also expected a victory inside the distance. Dempsey and Tunney changed their predictions from day to day. Still, the betting odds this time weren't 10:1 or 20:1 as they had been for the last fight but only 2:1 for Louis.

Not only New York, but the whole world eagerly awaited the fight. Days before the fight, people were arriving from all over. All of Hollywood came, from Clark Gable to Douglas Fairbanks to Gary Cooper to a young Gregory Peck—they were all there. Roosevelt's sons sat at ringside, along with Postmaster General Farley, the governors of several states, most of New York society, J. Edgar Hoover, and the German Ambassador Dieckhoff. It was the second fight in history, behind the legendary Dempsey-Tunney fight, to have a gate exceeding one million dollars. A seat in the fiftieth row went for $30, while something closer cost between $100 and $200. The cheapest bleacher seats were sold on the morning of the fight for $5.75 and $11.50. Two hours before the fight the stadium was sold out—75,000 spectators awaited our entrance into the ring.

As we drove to Yankee Stadium accompanied by a large police escort, I noticed that the area around the stadium was cordoned off by hundreds of police; Max Machon and I entered the stadium under their watch.

In the locker room I noticed for the first time that the tension of the last weeks had taken its toll. I was nervous. A few days earlier the Boxing Commission had declared Joe Jacobs ineligible to work in my corner. Once again, he had had one of his public relations inspirations, when he had one of his other fighters, "Two Ton" Tony Galento (a.k.a. "The Walking Beer Barrel"), photographed in the ring with a keg of beer. What the commission would have normally accepted as a harmless gag was now grounds for punishment. They banned Joe Jacobs not only from my corner but also, to my amazement, from the locker room.

Even Doc Casey, who had been in my corner so many times, wasn't there. The general hysteria and flood of threatening letters had both shocked and scared him. I had never before felt so alone before a fight. In the critical last few minutes even Max Machon was missing, as he had to go and observe the wrapping of Joe Louis's hands. So I was actually relieved when the door opened and an official came to bring me to the ring.

Surrounded by a wall of policemen, I walked to the ring. As I became visible to the crowd, all hell broke loose. Of course there were some cheers as well—I had fought in the States often enough that I did have my fans—but they were drowned out by the others. It was like walking a gauntlet. Even though I was flanked by twenty-five police officers, I was still hit by cigarette butts, banana peels, and paper cups, so that I had to pull a towel over my head just to reach the ring safely.

Amid the deafening noise I climbed through the ropes. Shortly after me came Joe Louis. Once we were in the ring, it was surrounded by police. They stood facing the crowd as a barrier against thrown objects.

The next few minutes were given over to the introduction of former world champions. As Sharkey, Braddock, and Baer were announced there was a round of boos. In an effort to focus, I watched Joe Louis. He had his poker face on again and seemed to be oblivious to everything going on around him. After what seemed like an eternity came the bell for the first round.

Contrary to what I had expected, Louis came right after me, and before I knew what had happened I was hit with three hard lefts to the face. I retreated two steps, but Louis came right after me with a hail of head and body shots. From below I heard Max Machon desperately yelling, "Move, Max, move!" yet I just couldn't get away and tried to save myself in a clinch. But in a second Louis pushed me away and caught me with a short, hard left to the head. Once again on the retreat, I tried to stop this raging fighting machine with a hard right. But Louis showed absolutely no effect and came at me again with a tornado of lefts and rights.

In this moment I lost it. One reporter described the rest as follows:

Again Louis swarms over his opponent with a volley of blows, first landing to the head, then moving in the next split second to Schmeling's unprotected body, even as the challenger tries to cover his head. It's obvious that Schmeling has already lost his legs; he just can't escape Louis and stands like lead amidst the storm of punches. Then a murderous left hook right to the point of the chin, and in the same moment a short, powerful uppercut tears Schmeling's head back. Max staggers, raises his arms mechanically, falls again into the ropes, sinks halfway to the canvas, takes another hard shot to the mouth, and, half turning as he falls, has to take an incredibly hard left hook to the left side of his body. Still on the ropes, Schmeling goes to one knee.

Donovan, the one cool head amidst this noise and frenzy, jumps between the fighters. He didn't even get to "two" before a badly battered Schmeling rises and staggers toward Louis. A left and a right to Schmeling's chin and he goes down again. And again he rises too quickly instead of using a nine-count to recover.

It's clear: only the last desperate sparks of a fighter's instinct bring the nearly paralyzed body to its feet. Reeling, a defenseless target for the titleholder, Schmeling falls into yet another annihilating volley of head and body shots. A left hook to the chin, a right to the heart, two more crashing lefts to the head of the reeling challenger . . . and Schmeling goes down hard. Once again he tries to get to his feet. By Donovan's three-count a glassy-eyed Schmeling is once again standing. . . . Then Machon finally throws in the towel.

The clock shows 124 seconds into the first round.

Max Machon later described the end of the fight to me: "After the third knockdown I thought, 'now it's enough,' and I threw in the towel. But Donovan just calmly picked it up and tossed it aside. Apparently he wanted to show that it was his decision as to when the fight should be stopped. In the meantime the Bomber was all over you again.

"I'd had enough by then. Ready to do whatever it took, I climbed through the ropes. The others behind me jumped up and tried to hold me back, practically tearing off my pants. 'What do you want?' hissed Donovan as I came up next to him. 'Get out! Get the hell out of the ring!' I shouted back at him 'I'm not letting my man get beaten to death. Don't you have eyes? He's had enough!'

"The seconds from Louis's corner stormed into the ring as well, and in the general confusion Donovan had to stop the fight. At that point you were conscious, but you couldn't get up. The four of us lifted you, and the first thing you said was, 'My back! Something's wrong with my back!' Then we dragged you over to Louis, and with a painful smile you shook his hand. That was it!"

As for myself, I experienced the end in a semi-conscious state. But as the towel flew into the ring, I sensed the stadium go completely silent. Then Max Machon was next to me; and in the same moment the stadium broke into deafening noise. As if looking through a veil, I saw Donovan go over to Louis and lift his arm. . . .

Some time later I must have been led out of the ring. I really don't remember. In any case, suddenly I was lying in my dressing room with the ring doctor bent over me. Then I was in an ambulance, being taken to the hospital.

As we drove through Harlem there were noisy, dancing crowds. Bands had left the nightclubs and bars and were playing and dancing on the sidewalks and streets. The whole area was filled with celebration, noise, and saxophones, continuously punctuated by the calling of Joe Louis's name. Then I found myself in the emergency room being x-rayed.

I remained in the hospital wearing a Thomas collar for ten days before I could be moved. One of my first visitors had been General Phelan, president of the New York Boxing Commission. He wanted to know if I had been hit with a kidney punch. The doctor showed him an x-ray and said, "You decide for yourself; here the vertebra is split in two places. The punch that did that must have been directly to the kidney. Whether that's a kidney punch according to the rules of boxing I can't say."

Phelan was clearly not there to express his sympathy. He then left, his manner cool and businesslike. He needed the doctor's opinion in order to determine whether my purse should be held up for failure to continue the fight.

Otherwise, I wasn't allowed to have visitors—no reporters, no friends, not even Joe Louis. When he tried to visit me, Joe Jacobs and Max Machon wouldn't allow it, as there were still some bitter feelings regarding fight-related circumstances. I was too out of it to get involved.

Only the German ambassador managed to get in to ask me whether the punch in the back had been an illegal blow. He knew nothing about boxing, so I explained to him how I had grabbed the ropes and turned during the rain of punches. As I turned, Louis threw that devastating right that had probably been aimed at my heart. It was too late to stop the punch, so I took it in the back.

"But objectively speaking, that was an illegal kidney punch," the ambassador persisted. I explained to him that according to the American rules, any punch above the beltline was legal. And since I couldn't see the punch, I really couldn't tell if he could have stopped it or not. In any case, it wasn't a question of a foul. It had been my mistake to turn, which only shows how far gone I was at that point.

Herr Dieckhoff didn't seem to want to let go of the idea that my defeat was the result of foul play. "Don't you want to file a protest? You should really consider it, Herr Schmeling!" I didn't need to consider it: "Herr Ambassador, in sports a protest isn't going to matter. I had known that I was fighting under American, not European rules. Aside from that, I would only make myself look bad!"

∾∾∾

Herr Dieckhoff seemed taken aback that the question of an illegal blow wouldn't be pursued—he had apparently been sent to me as an official duty. But at the same time he seemed relieved. "Well, as you wish!" he said as he departed, wishing me the best.

In Germany, however, even as I was confined to my bed on the homeward-bound *Bremen,* slanderous rumors were being circulated. Goebbels was spreading the story that Louis had not only intentionally hit me with an illegal blow, but that he had also hidden lead in his handwraps. What they were really thinking, however, was something that I already knew—after this defeat, I no longer existed for Hitler and Goebbels. The time for receptions in the Reich Chancellory and Daggers of Honor was over. For quite a while my name simply disappeared from the newspapers.

The experiences of the foregoing few years helped me handle these humiliations a lot better than would have normally been the case. June 22, 1938 had not only brought me the bitterest and most painful defeat of my career, it had also destroyed my dream of ending my career on a winning note. But from the distanced perspective of age, I have to believe that the defeat had its positive side as well. A victory over Joe Louis would have made me forever the "Aryan Show Horse" of the Third Reich.

On that same night after the fight, Anny reached me by telephone in the hospital. She was beside herself, and in a voice filled with despair she stammered, "Max, dear, good Max! I'm coming over on the next ship." I tried to calm her and told her that in a few days I would be back on my feet and heading back to her as soon as possible.

But the doctors determined that the vertebra had been cracked in three places. I was told that I should remain in bed for six weeks, and at first I wasn't allowed to move at all.

My room quickly became a sea of flowers. Messages came in from everywhere, from friends and strangers alike. Rumors were circulating to the effect that I had been partially paralyzed and would never fully recover.

Despite the numerous get-well wishes, there was a conspicuous silence from official circles—nothing from the Reich Ministry of Sport or the Reich Chancellory. But there was one notable exception. It was Albert Speer,* whom I had only met briefly at a couple of receptions. He called me while I was still in the hospital: "So, Herr Schmeling, it's Speer—I just wanted to call to see how you are doing." I told him that I would soon be released from the hospital and planned to return home to rest for a while. He invited me to visit him after my return, out at his place on Schlachtensee.

It must have been September when the four of us sat together on the terrace of Speer's newly built, surprisingly modest little house. Speer and I were both in our early thirties, and in the previous year the seemingly bashful archi-tect had been named head building inspector for the Reich capital of Berlin. In January the new Reich Chancellory of his design had been dedicated and her-alded as a trend-setting work of architectural genius. It was said that he was Hitler's true favorite and confidant. As we parted at the end of the afternoon, I thanked Speer for the invitation and conversation, which seemed to take him aback. I didn't tell him how isolated I had felt since my return from New York.

The loss of "official" contacts really didn't hurt that much. Since my loss to Louis, I had had my eyes opened in both Berlin and New York. More and more I felt myself wanting to pull back from public life. During this time I sold my large apartment in Berlin's Dahlem section and bought something much smaller for the increasingly infrequent trips to Berlin.

The times were taking their toll on old friendships as well. At the high point of the second crisis in Czechoslovakia in early 1939, a bunch of us were gathered at the Roxy Bar in a much smaller circle of friends. A few days earlier German troops had marched into Prague, and we all felt that the time of "peaceful conquest" was coming to an end. The threat of war was now clearly in the air.

But you could still speak freely at Ditgens's Roxy Bar. On that evening, which would take such a dramatic turn, I was sitting together with Ditgens, the director Rolf von Goth, and Michael Bohnen. We had all been shocked by the events of the past days. Ditgens complained about Hitler's gambling with peace, and von Goth said that the man had to disappear or we would certainly end up in a war.

In that moment Bohnen abruptly jumped to his feet and stood stiffly before us. "I would send my own son if need be!" he said excitedly, and then added, "I won't tolerate this type of conversation in my presence!"

We were all flabbergasted but assumed at first that he couldn't be se-rious. "Michael, come on!" I said. "Sit down and take it easy! Have a drink!" But Bohnen was transformed and wouldn't listen. Half to calm and half to pro-voke Bohnen, von Goth said, "Don't go making any promises—in case it *does* come to that."

That was too much for Bohnen. Turning to Ditgens, he said brusquely, "Heinz, I'll pay tomorrow!" Then he took his hat, threw his gloves down on the table in a strange, furious gesture, and stormed out of the bar. The remaining friends sat there, speechless. Dazed, we asked ourselves what had gotten into our friend Michael. But soon other friends arrived and we changed the subject.

An hour and a half later the door opened abruptly and two men came in, looked over the clientel, and then came over to our table. Ditgens said, "Gentlemen, take off your coats and hats and stay a while." But instead of

☙☙☙

answering they flashed identification. Bohnen had left us and gone straight to the Gestapo; he had reported his old friends. After the officials had taken down our information, they turned again and disappeared into the night.

A few days later Rolf von Goth was picked up, and Heinz Ditgens was told not to leave town. No one approached me. But Ditgens phoned me and said, "Max, you've got to do something!" I told him that I no longer had any connections; but finally I called Heinrich Hoffmann and told him what had happened. Hoffmann reacted angrily, but again showed himself willing to help. "Man," he said, "what kind of crap were you guys up to there? You're beyond help!" Then he asked me if Hinkel weren't also a regular at the Roxy Bar. When I said yes, he said that he would do everything he could to settle the matter.

In fact, Hoffmann and Hinkel did then smooth things over; von Goth was to certify that he had had a great deal to drink that evening. In a few weeks he was released. But our friendship with Michael Bohnen was over forever.

After the war, Bohnen experienced a good deal of ill will because of what he had done and was even prohibited from performing for a while.

In the weeks after my defeat at the hands of Joe Louis I had now and then considered giving up boxing. But we had negotiated a return-bout clause in the contract, and, besides that, I didn't want to leave the boxing stage with such a crushing defeat. Maybe the "Tunney Dream" still haunted me—regaining the title and then retiring as champion.

Anyway, I travelled to New York in early 1939 to see how things looked. Mike Jacobs, with whom we had negotiated the return fight, suggested that I first get a few European fights under my belt, just as Louis had had to come back from our first fight with a series of victories. "In Summer 1940, I think, you could get another shot."

At that time in Europe Adolf Heuser was the man to beat. Powerful and stocky, the "Bonn Tornado" was one of those offensively minded fighters whose style had always been just right for me. On August 2, 1939 in the Stuttgart-Neckar Stadium—called Adolf Hitler Stadium at the time—the eagerly awaited showdown took place before over 60,000 fans.

I wasn't the favorite in this fight. In the eyes of the experts, Heuser's toughness and punching power cancelled out my experience. Also, there was the defeat by Louis, and many wondered if that had marked the end of my career. In any case, the betting before the fight was about even money.

The fight lasted only seventy-one seconds. Right after the opening bell Heuser was all over me, like Joe Louis, landing a few hard right hooks in a row. But I had learned my lesson from the Louis fight. The punches landed harmlessly on my cover.

∽∼∾

At that moment Heuser went on the attack again, when I hit him with a hard right counterpunch exactly on the point of his chin. The punch was so hard that it tore Heuser's legs out from under him. With his arms spread wide, he toppled forward.

Long after the referee had counted ten, Heuser was still unconscious. After we had taken him to his corner, he still hadn't come to. Everyone was panic-stricken. As a doctor was being summoned, a screaming woman—Frau Heuser—came running to the ring. In tears, she threw herself down next to her husband and stroked him with helpless gestures. After a while the doctors succeeded in bringing him around by means of artificial respiration.

I stayed in the ring during those minutes. Any joy over the win was already gone. But I visited him that evening in his hotel. He had somewhat recovered and through a painful smile said, "If you had caught Joe Louis with that punch, the fight in New York would have turned out differently."

Willy Fritsch, one of my oldest friends from my early Berlin days, had come with me to the hotel. At this point he asked, "Which one of you is going to pay for my ticket. I came all the way from Berlin just to see this fight and bought the most expensive ticket. And then I didn't see a single punch!"

To my question of whether my right hadn't been worth something, he answered, "I didn't see it!" My friend's hat had fallen off right after the fight started, and he was bending down to get it. When he sat back up, Heuser was lying unconscious on the canvas.

I still remember an amusing episode connected with that Stuttgart fight. Because of the interest in the fight, several local newspapers had come out with special editions that could be printed and distributed quickly. In the haste to print this edition, one typesetter had made quite a mistake. The headline, which wasn't corrected until the second edition, read:

MAX SCHMELING KO'S ADOLF HITLER
IN ADOLF HEUSER STADIUM

A few weeks later I happened to run into Adolf Hitler in the foyer of the Deutsches Theater in Munich. He nodded in passing, saying only, "We're still getting by, are we?"

The next stop on the road to New York was to be a return bout with Walter Neusel. The fight was set for September 1939 in Dortmund. I had asked for a postponement from the earlier August date so that I could get the harvest in at Ponickel. Gradually my second life was beginning to push my first life aside.

The autumn of that year was unforgetable. The sky had never seemed so big. I can still see the clouds before me, looking like huge pillows over

Ponickel. The fields were bearing the harvest that I had planted myself and which I now intended to gather in.

Shortly before that we had observed an old Pomeranian custom of celebrating with our farm workers the anniversary of our settling in at Ponickel; it was a moving experience for all of us as we toasted in celebration. Trucks were now coming into the barn loaded down with the harvest. Every evening I walked across the threshing floor and looked proudly at the rising mountains of grain.

The Czech crisis of earlier in the year had once again passed without breaking out into war. But no sooner had that gone by than Hitler was making new territorial demands. First he occupied Memel, on the northeast border of Prussia, which had been annexed by Lithuania in 1919. Then he started making claims on parts of Poland. The relations that had been peaceful until then were becoming more and more strained. Autumn 1939 marked the first time that Polish harvest workers didn't come to work on the farms of eastern Pomerania.

The crises of the past few years and months had happened a great distance way from our idyllic Ponickel. But in the summer of 1939 trenches were being dug, barbed-wire barricades were being set up, and farm workers were being drafted into building an "Eastern Wall." I was forced to supply a tractor and a few workers. Many farms were forced to give up horses.

In August, Germans fleeing Poland started pouring over the border. In panic and fear they had abandoned their farms. The "Polish Crisis," intentionally promoted by Hitler for weeks, was now having its effect on the other side of the border. In the last days of August long lines of motorized *Wehrmacht* [army] troops sent up huge clouds of dust as they drove through our district, setting up headquarters just this side of the German-Polish border. We were used to this, however, and didn't assume that it meant war.

I too must have been oblivious, despite the growing tension. But on the evening of August 31, the calm seemed to be breaking. As it became dark, motors could be heard off in the distance. I stayed outside, watching, and the feeling that something was about to happen kept me at my watch throughout the night.

Towards five in the morning a dull roar filled the air, and I could just make out a squadron of bombers to the south, flying over Neu-Stettin heading east. As I headed home between six and seven, I ran into Roni, a Swiss worker on our farm. Instead of "good-morning," he said, "Well, Herr Schmeling, this is it. Now it's war."

It was war, and for me and many others it signalled more than just the end of peace.

∽∾∽

18
In the War

To my surprise, I received shortly thereafter a notice to report for an induction physical exam at the *Wehrmacht* district headquarters. No one had expected that. Not only were prominent artists, actors, and athletes usually exempt, but I was also, at thirty-five, well over draft age. Outside the examination room stood mostly eighteen-to-twenty-year-olds, and I felt that I belonged to another generation.

Even this first morning gave me a foretaste of the soldier's life. Hour after hour we stood around, crowded into a corridor through which ran busy orderlies. Now and then one of the many doors along the corridor would open and a name would be yelled into the crowd.

After a good four hours it was my turn. I undressed in a waiting room, and as I stood there buck naked, an equally naked gentleman whom I didn't recognize at first came out of the examination room; but his face was somehow familiar. Then he came up to me with an actor's slightly exaggerated sparkle and said, "Hello, Herr Schmeling. My name is Minetti.* We met once at George's place."

As we stood there naked chatting, observing all the social amenities, a young bespectacled assistant physician shouted through the door, "Please, no private conversations here, gentlemen!" And then to me, "Come!" But in the same moment I heard the slightly reproaching voice of someone who was apparently the young doctor's superior: "There's no need for that!" And then to me through the half-open door, "Herr Schmeling, if you would be so kind!"

The commission consisted of three physicians, but the snappish young assistant performed the actual examination. At a table sat a second young doctor, to whom the first doctor called out height, weight, and other

〜〜〜

information, while the physician in charge, who had called me in, oversaw the whole procedure.

"What brings you to us, Herr Schmeling?" he asked, staring up at me with small, darting eyes from a round, reddish face. For all his pompous geniality, he was somehow likeable. "Such prominence here. . . ." And instead of finishing the sentence, he slapped his knee and roared, "A state actor and a world champion! And one right after the other!"

He could hardly contain himself, having me standing there before him. "Well, my good man, you must *really* have some connections!" he shouted, shaking his head. And as I bent and had my knee hammered, he chattered on. He had the congenial manner of many doctors who seem to relate to their patients in the plural: "Now let's see how our reflexes are!" and "How tall are we, then?" as he provided his assistants with running commentary. "Yes indeed," he said, satisfied with the results, "we seem to be quite fit!" I tried to point out to him my various sports injuries, but he shook his head, his considerable jowls jiggling, "Don't worry, by the time you're inducted it will all be over!"

Outside in the corridor I met Minetti again. "Why us two oldtimers, anyway?" I asked him. But he only laughed. "They can't get me. I'm getting out of it. I have it straight from Göring that the state actors are being classified as 'indispensable.'"

The chief doctor had been mistaken and given me false hope. A few weeks later the order to report for induction was on my desk. All my efforts to mobilize anyone I knew who had influence came to nothing. And I soon learned that my induction hadn't been a random mistake. *Reichssportführer* von Tschammer und Osten had not forgotten our various run-ins; he had personally arranged—with Hitler's support and approval—my induction into the *Wehrmacht* [army].

I had been assigned to an anti-aircraft unit in East Prussia. My inclination toward the military had always been limited. And now that I knew that my enlistment was part of a personal vendetta, I kept looking for a way out.

A slight crook in the ring finger of my right hand had given me problems since my youth. Now I asked my old friend Professor Gohrbandt to operate on it. I had barely come from the clinic with a temporary release from service when I received a notice that I would be well advised to report to my unit immediately. But the invasion of Poland was now over, and it looked as if the war might soon be at an end. So I decided, despite the warning, to see how things would play out.

To this day I'm still not sure whether it was by chance or a carefully planned intrigue, but in the next few weeks I finally was—in a very unusual fashion—drawn into the military.

An editor of the *Berlin Twelve O'Clock Gazette* invited me to accompany him on a visit to the paratroop unit in Wittstock an der Dosse. We observed instruction, ate with the recruits in the canteen, and that afternoon I was invited to observe a practice jump from the plane. While we were still on the ground, the commander of the training unit asked me if I would be ready to undertake such a test of courage. The question was apparently just hypothetical, and, laughing, I replied that I had lived through worse. That evening I drove back to Berlin.

It must have been around this time that the Berlin office of the Associated Press called me. Louis P. Lochner was on the other end: "Hello, Max," he said, "I have some sad news for you. Joe Jacobs died last night. We just got the news. It was a heart attack."

The news was a shock. Joe Jacobs had been only forty-one years old. Others might say that he died from cigars, whiskey, and all-night partying. But I knew better. It wasn't his lifestyle that had killed him but his temperament —the way he totally threw himself into everything, never relaxed, never at a distance. This was the personality to which he owed his success and to which I owed mine.

How often had he made us laugh with his constant state of excitement—gesticulating, voice cracking, never finishing a sentence, working on his cigar, gasping for breath. That's what Joe Jacobs died of. First politics had complicated our working relationship, then war had separated us, and now death.

A few months later—my military status was still somewhat unclear—a general of the *Luftwaffe* [air force] whom I met at a reception asked me if I wouldn't want to fulfill my military service with the paratroopers. "No, no!" he assured me, "You don't want to be a regular soldier at your age." He said that he was thinking more of my testing young recruits on their physical and sports aptitude.

Since it appeared that I wasn't going to be able to avoid some kind of military service, this seemed like an acceptable solution—I would be fulfilling the requirement without having to serve as a soldier. And soon after that—the summer of 1940—I did receive another notice to report for duty. So I gathered together my last gasoline-ration coupons and was driven to the paratroop training batallion in Stendal. My appearance before the post sentry had the desired effect—he clicked his heels together, saluted, and called a comrade, who in a very unmilitary fashion took my suitcase for me. Then I was led to the post commander, Colonel von Kummer.

The batallion commander greeted me very cordially. "Please, Herr Schmeling, have a seat!" he said. "I've been fully informed." We chatted a bit, and when he said that the recruit training program would be easy for an athlete such as myself, I said, somewhat put off, "Herr Colonel, nobody said anything about being a soldier—I was only told that I would be testing recruits." The Colonel reassured me, "Yes, yes, of course, you're entirely correct," he said, "but you're a kind of supervisor and you have to learn the training program. Just do the basic training and then we'll see!"

On that same afternoon I was assigned to a company and got my equipment. During the next weeks I learned how to drill, make a bed, and give a military salute. Only in the company of Colonel von Kummer could I let down. Our communication had taken on a more or less civilian tone. Sometimes I visited him, and he would ask me with extreme courtesy what brought me to him, to which I would reply, "Herr Colonel, I have come once again to pay my respects." Kummer laughed heartily, "Ach, Herr Schmeling, you are already the archetype of a Prussian soldier!"

The Colonel soon invited me to take my meals in the officers' mess, and from that I inferred that my soldiering wasn't to be taken all that seriously. But since I slept in the barracks and didn't want any special treatment, I declined the offer.

I bunked with three recruits who were all in their mid-twenties. First there was a young publisher with already somewhat sparse blond hair and an intelligent, rather melancholy face, who spent every spare minute replaying historical chess moves from a book that he carried. Then there was a not unlikeable, always somewhat overexcited journalist who had been working in the Ministry of Propaganda and who was now attempting to fulfill the regime's slogans with his soldierly ambition. The third was a Herr Leibrand, a German national from the Transvaal who had taken it into his head to win over South Africa for National Socialism; despite his fixation, which he preached with his concerned, messianic expression to anyone who would listen, I found him likeable—helpful, modest, and somewhat awkward. Only von Kummer became indignant when at inspection, our "Afrikaner," standing at attention before his locker, tried to report to him on the successes of the Transvaal regiment. The three chose me to be senior soldier of our barracks room.

The unit had been at camp for about eight weeks. They had already finished with weapons training, so I never did learn how to handle a *Karabiner 98*. When the others went for arms drills, von Kummer usually pulled me out on one excuse or another and had me do "reconnaissance." What that meant was that I would lay down in a sand trench somewhere, squinting into the sun as I observed jays and rabbits while the others gasped their way through open terrain maneuvers. After a few weeks I was promoted to corporal.

Soon thereafter I began actual paratroop training. In the beginning there were the so-called "courage checks," which consisted of a series of jumps into a six-meter-deep trench. Thanks to my conditioning, the jumping wasn't hard for me, but when our platoon leader, a sergeant, jumped, he landed so badly that he lay there unconscious. Concerned, I jumped back into the trench, but in that moment the sergeant came to, got up, and we collided; I came away with a meniscus injury. When von Kummer wanted to have me taken to the infirmiry, I requested that I be treated by Professor Gohrbandt, who had since been made a physician general in the *Luftwaffe*.

I remained laid up in the clinic on Augsburger Strasse for about six weeks and started hoping once again that the war might be over for me. But the man behind the scenes, whether it was Tschammer or someone else, still had his eye on me. I was barely able to hobble around again when I got my marching orders to report to the jump school at Wittstock. Although I still didn't have any real basic training, I completed the jump course and was assigned immediately to a combat unit stationed at Wolfenbüttel.

I don't have any concrete memory of the weeks that followed. In the morning we would march out of the barracks, march singing through the town, drill some on the parade grounds, march back through the town, sleep, eat, march. It was a strange, pointless monotony. Only a particular maneuver on the edge of the Lüneburger Heide* has stayed in my mind.

We made our jump under combat conditions and I landed successfully. But then I didn't have a clue as to what I should do next and just stood around on the field. When others began to run in formation, I followed at the rear, when they threw themselves to the ground, I did that too; when they jumped up again I followed, and when they started to dig foxholes, I got out my spade. That evening we sat around together in high spirits—it was a funny, senseless experience.

In early May 1941 we were sent to Greece. This again seemed to me to be a sign that I wasn't in for any serious war adventure, and I consoled an upset Anny accordingly. She, however, had none of my illusions and laid it out for me plain and simple: "Max, you've been had! Nobody's talking about testing recruits anymore! Stop kidding yourself! You're a regular soldier now!" When I countered that I hadn't even been trained in how to use a rifle or hand grenade yet, she laughed ironically, "I'm sure that Herr von Tschammer would be glad to know that!"

She was right. In the night of May 20 we set out marching to the small airport of Torpolia. On the following day our unit was to be the first wave to jump over the defending English emplacements south of Chania on the island of Crete.

Wearing heavy equipment, we climbed into the JU52 planes—waiting at the end of the runway with motors running—shortly after midnight.

Heading south, we flew low over the Greek islands to avoid enemy radar. The dimly lit interior of the plane was filled with the constant drone of engines, mixed now and then with the somewhat tinny sound of the fighter planes that escorted us. Using a flashlight, our platoon leader tried to follow our course on a map.

Outside, a pale dawn was coming up on the horizon behind us, as the outline of the island began to take shape. The first thing that could be seen was the bright hem of surf that skirted the island. The ridges and peaks of the mountains arose out of the haze.

In this moment came the command to prepare to jump; and as we were lining up, we heard a flat, popping noise, which was the start of heavy flak fire. The hatch was then opened and we got ready to jump.

As I looked out, the air was already filled with parachutes. From the ground, defending fire showed reddish through the morning gray. When we got to our jump target we were flying at an altitude of only about 150 meters; that was to minimize the amount of time that we would be hanging in the air as defenseless targets.

But we still had heavy casualities. Floating down like dandelions, the parachutes showed up in stark relief against the pale sky. We literally jumped into enemy fire. I could see how some parachutes didn't open and bodies smashed into the ground; other chutes were torn to shreds by machine gun fire; here and there a plane would start to falter, come apart, and plunge to the earth with a banner of smoke training behind it.

As for myself, I had both good and bad luck. I landed in the middle of a vineyard. The hard vines, however, prevented the rolling landing that we had so often practiced, so I landed on the ground such that the meniscus injury was reaggravated. And I suddenly became painfully aware of the vertebra which had been injured in the Louis fight. I could barely move.

As I crawled the approximately 150 meters to my supply container, a white barrel with red stripes, I came under furious English fire. Slowly I inched forward. Several times I blacked out from pain and fatigue, and by the time I finally reached the container, I had lost contact with my unit.

It wasn't until the following night that I found my outfit. Since I could only move with great effort, I was taken to a field hospital that had been set up about three kilometers south of Chania. A couple of buddies made me two canes, but just as I was leaving a sergeant came and gave me a prisoner to take to Chania. He gave me strict orders not to talk to the wounded Englishman. Both limping, we hobbled on our way.

When we had gotten around a bend in the road, out of sight of the German command post, we joined arms to give each other some support. We still hadn't exchanged a word, but I noticed how he kept looking at me curiously. Finally he got up his courage and said, "You look familiar. Are you a fighter?" Then, suddenly sure, he turned to me and said, "Yes, you're Max Schmeling!" It turned out that he was an avid boxing fan and a good friend of Tommy Farr; both came from Brighton.

I was barely managing to drag myself forward, half supported by my cane and half by my prisoner. Finally we decided to take a break and set down in an overgrown olive grove. I gave him a cigarette and he took out an orange, which we shared.

In the distance the fighting became louder, and we both tried our best to make out the front lines, which were somewhere out there on the plain between hilly vineyards and burning villages. In the meantime the English had apparently brought in heavy artillery, because now, larger caliber shells were landing at a short distance, sending debris and yellowish-gray smoke into the air. We both flattened ourselves against the ground. As the noise began to subside, my Englishman said that his guys were pulling back. He felt bad to be losing contact with them, but I told him that the war was probably over for him. "The war's over," he said, "when you're home again."

After about an hour we set out again. The going was hard, and because of the low-flying planes we stayed on the edge of the road. It took us several hours to cover the short stretch, and it wasn't until evening that we arrived at the field hospital, which had been set up in what had been a jail.

After his wound had been treated, my travelling companion was taken to a stockade with other prisoners. As we parted he said, "When I see Tommy Farr again, I'll tell him about our meeting." Then we wished each other good luck.

Even before the invasion I had started to show signs of dysentery, but I hadn't said anything. Now the symptoms were back in full force, and the doctors separated me from the other wounded for fear of infecting them. Orderlies took me out to a nearby vineyard and set up temporary quarters.

I spent the night in the open with severe stomach cramps. As the gray morning dawned, *Stukas* [dive bombers] flew over and dove at enemy positions in the distance. At some point in the morning, orderlies came and took me away on a stretcher. Soon after that I was taken to a hospital in Athens. A few days later I was promoted to non-commissioned officer of the Iron Cross, Second Class.

German soldiers on Crete who had been captured by the English told their interrogators that I had been wounded in the fighting. In a short time that report became "severely wounded," and on May 28, 1941 Reuters reported that "the former World Heavyweight Champion Max Schmeling has fallen in the fighting on Crete." The report was picked up by practically all English and American newspapers and by some German papers as well.

Goebbels immediately used this as an opportunity to demonstrate the unreliability of enemy news reporting. Berlin sent word to Athens that a meeting with American journalists should be arranged. Since the Americans weren't yet at war with Germany, American papers were still represented by correspondents throughout occupied Europe.

In early June the American journalist Bill Flannery from the International News Service looked me up in the Athens field hospital. The interview went differently, however, than the Propaganda Minister had expected. After a few pleasantries Flannery came right to the subject of reported English infractions of international conventions of war. But I objected—perhaps they had decoyed German paratroopers by displaying German flags on the ground, but during the actual fighting they had fought fairly. When asked about excessive cruelty toward the Germans, I replied that I hadn't heard of it. I told him that local Greek villagers, incensed over the destruction of their homeland, might have taken out their anger on some captured Germans, but I didn't believe that the English were engaged in needless cruelty.

Finally Flannery asked me about the possibility of war between Germany and America, and I said, "For me that would be a tragedy. I have always seen America as my second home."

The interview received a great deal of positive attention abroad. In Germany, on the other hand, the candor with which I had spoken put Goebbels in a blind rage, and for a time he tried to have me brought before the *Volksgerichtshof* [National Socialist People's Court]. But as a soldier of the *Wehrmacht* I was subject only to the military court, so the worst he could do was a regular military court action.

After my recovery I was sent to Berlin, where I soon received my court summons. Heinz Ditgens, whose Roxy Bar had closed down in the meantime, accompanied me to the trial. Civilian lawyers weren't allowed. We had arranged, however, that Ditgens would notify the defense attorney Dr. Reinhold Walch if I weren't out in three hours.

It really didn't come to an actual trial. After I had been interrogated, the court found that there was no cause to embark on a criminal trial. There was no criminal action in my statement of favoring a neutral America, and members of my company had confirmed that they hadn't witnessed any English atrocities—more than that I hadn't said.

Having failed at the legal approach, Goebbels tried another avenue. During one of the confidential ministry meetings at which the press received its official directives, Goebbels ordered that the name "Schmeling" never appear again in a German newspaper. In the official record of the meeting held on June 7, 1941 it said: "The interview with Max Schmeling is not to be printed. The Schmeling matter will disappear from the German press (good boxer, bad politician)."

Since my enlistment I had been asked many times if I planned on returning to the ring; even my English prisoner had asked. But the war had put an end to my dream of regaining the championship and retiring. Still, the victory over Adolf Heuser had given me back the European title, and, though it wasn't a world title, I could at least give up that belt unbeaten.

But my ring farewell happened differently than I had imagined. The war had broken out when Walter Neusel had challenged me to a European title fight in Summer 1939. In the course of the year 1940 our managers agreed on a new fight date. Then I received from the Ministry of Sports an official ban from fighting. The intent of this intervention was even clearer when Neusel received permission to fight another opponent shortly after that.

After all the intrigues and plots by von Tschammer, this was the final straw. I wanted to make the break complete. On the same day I gave up my title to the European Boxing Union in Rome, at which time I announced that I wouldn't box again.

So this was the end of the boxing career that had meant so much to me and given me so much. I had imagined it differently. I was now thirty-seven years old, there was still no end to the war in sight, Joe Jacobs was dead, and my thoughts were more and more on my farm at Ponickel rather than in the ring.

But I stayed close to boxing through numerous friendships. While I was lying around in barracks and hospitals, Heinz Lazek from Vienna was the German heavyweight champion, although he lost it two years later to Adolf Heuser. And it was Lazek's manager who came to me one day, very upset, to ask if I could help him. His fighter was at his wits' end—he was desperately in love with a young Viennese woman of Jewish descent. Every petition for permission to marry had been in vain, and because the young woman had recently had Lazek's child, she had been arrested by the authorities for *Rassenschande.* Heinz Lazek was facing the same charge.

Although I had long since fallen into disfavor, I was still believed to be someone with influential connections; that is why Lazek had sent his manager, Heinz Rudolf, and his lawyer to ask me for help. Since my previous connections were now of little or no use, I came up with the idea of contacting Philipp Bouhler,* whom I had met years ago at Hitler's country outing at Tegernsee. Bouhler was the person in Hitler's Chancellory responsible for clemency petitions. When I explained the situation to him, he reacted angrily.

"Whenever anyone hears from you, it's always about Jews!" he said sharply. "As if there weren't more important matters at the moment."

But as narrow-minded and pedantic as Bouhler was, he eventually softened a bit. Presumably he got in contact with Baldur von Schirach,* who at that time was *Gauleiter* [district commander] of Vienna. In any case, the proceeding was soon dropped and Lazek's girlfriend was released from prison. Lazek, however, was drafted into the *Luftwaffe* and stationed in Vienna.

A few months later, I had to intercede again on behalf of a friend. This time it was not as serious, but it looked bad for a while. The German lightweight champion Paul Noack, who had since been drafted into the navy, had sought shelter with his wife under an *S-Bahn* bridge during an air raid. When his wife said that she had been molested by someone in the crowd, Noack beat up the real or presemed perpetrator. Now he was facing a criminal complaint.

Given Bouhler's reaction the last time I had approached him, I decided to try another avenue. Years ago I had met Count Helldorf,* who in the interim had become police commissioner of Berlin. I asked him if he could put in a word for the young athlete who had overreacted in defending the honor of his wife. Helldorf was able to help, but it gave me an idea of the regime's communications network when, a few days later, I was called by an official of the Ministry of the Interior. He reproached me with threatening remarks to the effect that I only used my name to help criminals and Jews; that official later became state secretary in the Ministry of the Interior and president of the German Red Cross. Count Helldorf, however, was hanged as one of the conspirators in the July 20, 1944 plot to assassinate Hitler.

Just as unexpectedly as I had been drafted by the *Wehrmacht,* so was I discharged. My stint in the military ended on Easter Sunday 1943. I had been a soldier for three and a half years. Of that time I had spent two days at the front.

19

Return and Escape

When I returned in April 1943, Ponickel was almost unchanged. The war, which had taken a decisive turn [for the worse] during the winter, seemed far away and unreal. The only thing missing were the men. Some women wore black, and the farmwork was done by the old people and a few prisoners of war. The sons from neighboring farms had also gone into the army, and the rural delivery brought letters from posts at every corner of Europe.

With the start and rapid escalation of bombing, we at Ponickel had taken in the children of some friends as well as two little girls from Kiel, so that the house was filled with noise and children's screeching for the first time. For several months we watched the hubbub with a mixture of joy and sorrow. Anny was especially happy in her new role. Some time before the war she had herself expected a child, but an auto accident had led to a miscarriage and destroyed all our hopes.

The only evidence of my absence could be seen in some small things that had been left undone. During the first weeks I had my hands full with repairing rusted locks, fixing the stall door, putting up fallen fences, and painting sheds and walls with whatever paint I could get my hands on.

Planting had already begun by the time I arrived. Wildlife in the forests had greatly multiplied, and it was hard to keep deer and rabbits away from the seedlings. It was strange to drive through the area now, as there was no longer a Polish border. West Prussia, which had gone to Poland in 1918 was once again part of the German Reich, and Baltic Germans had repopulated the area. A severely wounded soldier who had been awarded the Knight's Cross was now working on an estate just on the other side of what had been the border; we learned that the farm had belonged to a Polish family of lower nobility that had been driven off.

᧞᧞᧞

The Germans were now retreating on every front. The Russians were pushing ahead in powerful offensives, an English-American expeditionary force had landed in Sicily, and the submarine war that had seriously threatened England had finally collapsed. But that was all far from Ponickel, and an unreal peace lay across the Pomeranian landscape.

Even as early as my time in the Berlin military hospital, I had been engaged in working for the Red Cross, with permission from the *Wehrmacht,* helping with prisoners-of-war. My job was simple. I was to visit *Stalags* [prisoner-of-war camps] from time to time and talk to the prisoners, find out how they were doing, and add a little diversion to the monotonous life of the POW. It was, if I'm not mistaken, a kind of a gesture by the *Wehrmacht* to try to demonstrate humane treatment of the enemy in a war that was going increasingly badly.

So I would come to a *Stalag* and sit around the barracks for an afternoon surrounded by a circle of twenty or thirty prisoners, telling them of my American fights. I heard later that Joe Louis had done the same for German prisoners of war. One of the prisoners told me of how he had been there when Joe Louis beat Max Baer's younger brother, Buddy. Again and again I was asked if I had access to some special information as to when the war would end, and I became used to repeating the same phrase: "I hope very soon; and I wish I could go with you."

One day I received a call asking whether I would be willing to meet with a delegation of prisoner-of-war officers who had been chosen by their men to discuss their complaints with me. Since our little house in Dahlem had been confiscated and given to the family of Field Marshall Keitel, my old friend John Jahr offered his house at Roseneck as a meeting place.

The spokesmen for the group of American and British officers were General Vaneman and Colonel Spiway. Surprisingly, they all appeared in full uniform, but with a Red Cross armband on their left arms. After we had discussed my upcoming visits to English and American *Stalags,* Colonel Spiway pulled me aside and asked me in a hushed voice if I could do him a personal favor. One of his closest friends, a Colonel Spicer, had been sentenced to death by a German military court for attempting an armed escape; now he was waiting for the sentence to be carried out. I wasn't sure whether I would be allowed access to the condemned man, but I promised the Colonel that I would do everything humanly possible to see his friend and give him any messages or letters.

Indeed, I was only able to locate the prisoner after going through a great deal of bureaucratic red tape. The commandant of the camp had been informed of my visit and greeted me very cordially, yet he was not quite ready to let me meet with the prisoner without obtaining additional permission.

Only after waiting for hours did the call from Berlin come through. Then the call seemed to take an unexpected turn. In any case, the tall, one-armed major made his request, but then kept asking, "Are you absolutely sure? Really?" With the receiver pressed between his tilted head and shoulder, he fished out a cigarette, then waved off the light that I offered him. "Yes sir, Herr Colonel! Then it's official?" he finally said. On edge, I sat listening.

As he hung up the receiver, he looked at me for a moment in silence and then said "Uff!" He was visibly relieved. "They told me you have clearance to visit the prisoner. But more importantly, I was told that Colonel Spicer has been pardoned. Since written confirmation hasn't yet been sent, I have to request that you don't yet tell the prisoner."

A sergeant led me to the cell. Colonel Spicer sat motionlessly at a table, his back to the door. He seemed totally apathetic and remained sitting as I entered the cell. Not until I had spoken to him did he slowly turn around and hesitatingly stand. "Hello, Colonel," I said, "my name is Max Schmeling, and I bring you the regards of Colonel Spiway."

Only on hearing this did any movement come into the stiff, expressionless figure standing before me. While he asked me about Spiway and some of his other buddies, I asked the sergeant if I could speak to the Colonel alone for a moment. He went out and locked the door behind him.

Spicer looked at me with surprise, but before he could say a word I whispered to him, "Colonel, your sentence has been lifted. You've been pardoned!" For a moment the Colonel seemed dazed. He stared at me, white as a ghost, and then managed to stammer, "Is that true? Who told you? Were you sent here to tell me?" I told him that I had happened to overhear a phone conversation, that the confirmation hadn't yet come but would arrive shortly.

The Colonel had seemed totally composed up to that moment. But now a twitching ran over his face, and I could see that he was trying to hide his emotions. Finally he turned his head to the side and, as if totally exhausted, fell back onto the chair. He sat there for a few moments, hunched over, wordless. I could almost feel the tension of the last few weeks going out of him. I too said nothing.

Then Colonel Spicer stood up, went around the table as if to get a running start, came to me and took my right hand in both of his. "Mr. Schmeling," he said, "I don't have to tell you what I'm now feeling." He spoke in a clipped, dry, almost military tone. And as he spoke, tears ran down his face.

About five years later, at the time of the Berlin Blockade,[1] Colonel Spicer, in the interim promoted to General, sent his greetings to me via the Commandant of Tempelhof Airport.

∽∾∾

In occupied Paris there were boxing matches from time to time for the troops there. I was able to get travel permission for one of these, a fight between Walter Neusel and Jakob Schönrath. I have practically forgotten the fight itself, but the days in Paris brought a memorable reunion with two friends from the old days.

One was Andre Routis, who had brought me together with Joe Jacobs back in the days of Madame Bey's Camp Summit in New Jersey. He invited me to his Sports Bistro, where I was surprised to find a large photo of myself hanging over the bar. Routis had also invited Georges Carpentier, the idol of my boyhood, who now also had his own cafe and managed the Lido. I was glad that I could congratulate my old friend on the occasion of his fiftieth birthday.

We traded stories until curfew and then went to Georges' apartment. When I asked him if he would be willing to do a radio interview with me for Occupied Paris Radio, he agreed, with the condition that politics be kept out of the conversation.

On the following day we sat before the microphones and had a lively ten or twenty-minute conversation about his fight with Jack Dempsey. I added that as a boy I had, with my father, seen a film of the fight and decided to make a career of boxing.

On the way home, however, the reality of the present crept into the conversation. Georges and also Andre, who had come along, told me of numerous problems. One had had his large American car confiscated by the occupation authorities, while the other was being threatened with the closing of his restaurant.

I cautiously told them that I was having problems myself, that I had been officially prohibited from boxing. They could hardly believe it. "But you are the leading German athlete!" said Georges, but I told him that those days were long past. Together we complained about the war, and I still remember Andre saying, "Max, if it were up to us athletes, we would have peace tomorrow!"

At least I was able to help them out a little. Through friends in the command post I was able to get Georges a used motorcycle, and Andre's bistro wasn't closed. But my visit only created problems for Georges Carpentier. A little over a year later, after the *Libération,* he was accused of having collaborated with the enemy, the radio interview and the acceptance of the motorcycle both being cited as damaging examples. Andre was left alone.

And during those months of impending German collapse I got together with another friend from the old days in the ring. The BBC had broadcast that the former World Heavyweight Champion Primo Carnera had, as a member of the Italian partisan resistance, been captured during a night skirmish with the Germans and had been summarily put before a firing squad.

An arm of the State Department asked me to go to Italy and find Carnera, who was missing and presumed dead—a photo of us together would serve to document the unreliability of enemy propaganda. So early in 1944 I set out for Italy. The German authorities had tried in vain to learn of Carnera's whereabouts through official Italian channels, but Primo remained among the missing.

For ten days I stayed in Fasano at the residence of Ambassador Rahn, whom I had met years before at the Thorak's in Saarow-Pieskow. I heard nothing of Carnera. Finally I asked an official what kind of information had been obtained from the boxer's family in Undine. And it turned out, to my amazement, that no one had even thought to try asking. Next day I drove to Undine, where I was told that of course Primo would be at home—where else?

The reunion with the giant Carnera—and with the passing years he had become even more gargantuan—was appropriately Italian. Carnera embraced me, and, although we were in the same weight class, I was afraid of being squeezed to death. That same afternoon we drove to Venice, and we spent a long evening reminiscing in the enigmatic city, now more unreal than ever.

Shortly after the war had hit the Italian mainland, Venice had been declared an "open city," off-limits to both the German and Italian military; only wounded soldiers were allowed in the city of lagoons. While the rest of Europe burned to the ground, Venice remained an almost surreal oasis. It had become a refuge for Italy's wealthy upper class, only a few hundred kilometers from an ever-closer front and increasingly severe bombing. Several orchestras played in St. Mark's Square, as they had during peacetime, and only the sandbags before the cathedral brought one back to reality. The cafes were filled to overflowing, and nannies—at an appropriate distance behind their employers—pushed baby carriages across the square. But high over the city, the sky was criss-crossed by the vapor trails of bombers flying northward to Germany.

Carnera was having an easier time of it than my friends in Paris. He spoke openly of the need for Italy to get out of the war—the country was at the end of its rope and Mussolini's reputation was played out. And, he added, Germany should also pack it in, before the entire country was destroyed.

Who didn't know that? But I told him that I could no longer see a way out. Lost in thought, he sat there staring straight ahead. Then, with the characteristic simplicity that caused many to underestimate him, he said, "This terrible war! Everything is going to ruin!" And finally, "What will be left?"

When I returned to Ambassador Rahn in Fasano and told him of my successful mission, he interrupted me at the end as if he had just had a sudden thought. "I have something else for you, Herr Schmeling; another diplomatic mission." As I looked at him, puzzled, he added, "You must go to the Pope. Would you go to Rome for a papal audience?" Then he explained the reason. German relations with the Vatican had been severely strained ever since several officers of the SS had provoked the Pope with an unplanned and unannounced appearance. They had even greeted him with raised arms and a booming, "Heil Hitler, Herr Pope!"

"I would be extremely grateful, Herr Schmeling, if you could somehow put things back in order," explained the ambassador. "You're an apolitical man. If the Pope receives you, at least we have a starting point from which we can gradually begin to normalize relations." He indicated that good relations with the Vatican would be important for the planned talks on making Rome an "open city" in order to protect it from war damage. I told him that under those circumstances I would be willing to make the trip. A few days later, it was either the Tuesday or Wednesday before Easter, I arrived in Rome.

A member of the German Embassy at the Vatican brought me to the Papal Palace. There I was received by a clerical secretary who led me through a long series of rooms, past the colorfully uniformed Swiss Guards and clerics dressed in a variety of cassocks, to the Pope's private chambers. In a room of medium size he asked me to wait for a moment and went into an adjoining room.

I went to the window and looked out. Below me, seeming strangely empty and abandoned, was St. Peter's Square. All that I can remember of the simple room was a crucifix and a portrait of an earlier Pope.

After about ten minutes a bell sounded softly, and shortly thereafter one of the doors opened. A gentleman entered the room bowing and walking backwards, followed by a veiled woman in black. Through the half-opened door I saw the Pope as he bid farewell to the couple. The secretary again asked for my patience as he led the couple out.

When he returned in a few minutes the bell sounded again and Pope Pius XII entered the room. I recognized the Pope from numerous pictures, as he had been the papal nuncio in Germany during the twenties; I knew that he was a dignified and impressive presence. But the dignity that he commanded was even increased by the natural manner with which he approached me. I had inquired earlier as to how I should address the Pope. But before I could say a word, he began in a hearty, if somewhat muted voice, "We are so pleased, Herr Schmeling, that you have come!" and took my hand.

I forgot the greeting that I had rehearsed and said simply, "I thank Your Holiness for receiving me." Then he continued, "We think warmly on Our time in Berlin—the city and the people. Those years were wonderful and exciting, yet in some respects also unhappy."

I told him that I admired his excellent German, and he replied that he enjoyed the opportunity to speak it. Then he told of his years in Berlin, of Stresemann,* Brüning,* and *Reichspräsident* von Hindenburg.* He also told me of how he had followed my career with interest, that he had always been interested in sports, and that he himself had been an avid mountain climber. Then he asked after my wife and mother.

Ambassador Rahn had explained to me on the way that it was not important to speak of politics. The point of my meeting with the Pope was simply to reestablish contact. But Puis XII suddenly said, "The war has brought so much tragedy to people all over the world." And then after a pause, during which we walked back and forth in the small room, he added less as a question than as a statement, "Berlin is probably destroyed. We read all the news of what is happening in Germany—of the countless victims of bombing, the destruction of so many cities. It must be terrible."

I agreed and added that no end was in sight. As we walked, the Pope pressed his hands together and was visibly troubled. "We are certainly prepared to do anything in Our power to alleviate the horrors of war," he said, and asked for details—the housing of those bombed out of their homes, the situation of refugees, the people's state of mind.

After about twenty-five minutes I looked over to the baroque clock hanging on the wall and thanked the Pope for the audience. The Pope took my hand and held it firmly. "We would like to give you a small gift with which to remember this meeting." Then he went to the door, opened it, and said something into the room. Shortly thereafter he came he came back with two small cases. "They are for you and your wife," he said. "They are two rosaries. We know that you are Protestants. But they are only meant to be a remembrance." Finally he gave me a signed picture and said, "My greetings to Berlin! We can do so little. But We pray for a peace soon."

When I returned to Berlin I was immediately called to the Foreign Office. The official with whom I spoke listened in detail to my report of the audience and particularly asked about the Pope's reactions. When I told him of the Pope's parting words, he asked, "Are you sure you heard the Pope correctly?" I didn't understand. "I mean," continued the official, "didn't the Pope say that he was praying for German victory soon?" I told him no and repeated what the Pope had said.

The *Osservatore Romano* reported a few days later of my audience with Pius XII, and newspapers around the world picked it up. Only in the German press was there nothing.

When I returned to Ponickel it was overflowing with refugees. I had already encountered long caravans of them along the roads, with all their possessions piled on handcarts or rickety wagons. They had already gone hundreds of kilometers by then, pushed forward by their fear. Amongst the pillows and trunks, soaked linen, and every sort of bulky item sat the old people and children, while women walked next to the horses. The Russian offensive had already reached East Prussia and set this wave of flight in motion.

The refugees now brought a visible sign of the war to Ponickel. In otherwise half-empty stalls and barns we set up emergency quarters. Anny and the wife of our foreman saw to the needs of the exhausted people as best they could. Usually after a short time these people continued on, without knowing where they were headed. But for every wagon that left Ponickel, two or three new ones would arrive.

For a time our house had been a safe haven. But now we were sending the children of our friends back to Berlin and Schleswig-Holstein as the war moved ever closer to us.

We all still hoped that the Russian tide could be brought to a standstill. Certainly we had all long since stopped believing in a German victory, but there were still vague expectations that perhaps some sort of armistice or partial peace could be reached, or that the Allied coalition might fall apart. When I look back now, I realize that no one dared look reality in the eye. To all of us it was simply unthinkable that we were facing not just a temporary defeat and occupation by a foreign army but rather expulsion from our homes and permanent loss of everything.

At the beginning of 1945 the Russians had surrounded Königsberg and cut off East Prussia, and I decided to bring Anny, my mother, and the two children from Kiel to safety. Then I wanted to return home and wait to see how things played out. If necessary, I would join up with the last German units.

The car was fully packed and stood before the front door as we went through the house one last time. Saying nothing, we walked through the rooms, and as we stood looking at trophies, awards, and medals, we were overcome by dark foreboding.

I lifted my world-championship belt for a moment and then let it fall. It was only a poor, somewhat tarnished piece of a memory. Then I picked up the golden miniature boxing gloves that the great Gene Tunney had given me. As I held them in my hand, Anny must have sensed the thoughts and emotions that filled me at that moment. In any case, she suddenly put her arm around me and simply said, "Max, all that isn't so important. What matters is that we come through this together."

Then we left the house quickly and got into the car. We didn't look around us as we drove down the drive and onto the open road.

⌒⌒⌒

We avoided the congested main roads, taking out-of-the-way back roads in the direction of Berlin. We had decided that once we were in Berlin, we would see how things looked. From Berlin I was able to get the two girls back to their parents. But since the capital was also in great danger, Anny decided to go to friends in Rostock and await the next move. As for myself, I would try to get back to Ponickel as quickly as possible. Once again I set out on back roads, and, a short distance past Stettin, I met up with some *Wehrmacht* trucks. They belonged to an infantry division that was bringing wounded back from the front. A corporal, unshaven and smeared with grease, leaned out of the cab of his truck and asked what I was doing still in this area.

The corporal urgently warned me not to drive any further east; "Ivan" had broken through and had since cut off all of eastern Pomerania. Beyond Rummelsburg it would be impossible to get any further. They had to move fast. After giving me some food they continued on their way.

I hesitated for a bit. The mix of snow and mud on this cold, sunny January day had made the roads very difficult. I broke some branches off of a hedge and laid them in the deep tracks that the truck had made. Then I carefully turned the car around, because if I got stuck now I was as good as gone.

For a while I didn't know what to do. Now Ponickel had already been cut off. Had the last refugees gotten away in time? I imagined how deserted the farm must be now, the doors unlocked and the remaining animals uncared for. In a few days or even hours the Russians would move in. I was somewhat relieved that there would apparently be no fighting there. For a long minute I imagined what the Russians would think when they saw my memorabilia. Perhaps they would destroy the house or burn it down.

But the old walls would remain. And one day I would return and rebuild. I was still young and had time. My second life, which the war had only interrupted, still lay before me. What did it matter that it was different and would start a little harder than we had thought?

I decided to drive to Berlin. I had stored a couple of trunks there, which, along with the car, were all that I owned now. Maybe I could make myself useful in the city. And, finally, this was the only place where I still had somewhere to stay. John Jahr had offered me a bed in his house at Roseneck.

As I approached Berlin, the shimmering reflection of countless fires hung over the city. Even from the *Autobahn* you could see the deep black clouds of smoke that stretched off into the horizon. As evening came, the sky over the city was a dirty red.

Towards morning I neared the outskirts of Berlin; here there were surprisingly few signs of the war. The attacks of recent years had been mostly in the inner-city. As a *Wehrmacht* patrol checked my papers, there appeared to be another air attack taking place over the city, and for a moment I considered whether it might not be better to turn around and try to reach Anny in Rostock. My decision was made more by fatalism, fatigue, and, more than anything else, a lack of gasoline; I continued on into the city.

As I drove through my old West End towards Grunewald you could taste the acrid, burning air. Slowly and laboriously I moved ahead; the streets were clogged by bomb craters, rubble, and trucks, and it took hours to reach the less damaged area around Halensee. At Roseneck I turned onto Hohenzollerndamm. After almost a quarter of a century this was my second "arrival" in Berlin.

During the next few weeks I didn't do much more than survive. After a while you stopped hearing the air-raid sirens; there was always some kind of aircraft over Berlin, and between the continuous "air raid" and "all clear" you started to lose your bearings. After a while you became used to heading for the cellar when the bombing or flak became heavy.

Without letup, there was always work to be done. We cleared rubble, repaired roofs and power lines, nailed up windows with wood and cardboard. Glass in the form of window panes had long since disappeared; rather, it lay everywhere, pulverized by bombs and mines—on chairs and tables, in beds, in our clothes and crunching between our teeth when we ate. From the huge clouds of smoke over the city rained a constant mix of dust, soot, and ashes, which settled on everything in a thick layer. When I think back I can still see women hovering everywhere, brooms, rags, and shovels in hand.

I let the Red Cross know that I was in Berlin. To my amazement there were still prisoners of war in the city, and, to the extent that public transportation still allowed, I made my rounds as before.

Most of my old friends had left the city. But a few were still there, including Max Machon and Heinz Ditgens. We spent a lot of time just sitting around, waiting, gabbing, trading news. We were all just putting in time, and the city had become a waiting room for the final catastrophe.

I put up my car in a cellar garage, removing the tires and battery so that it might still be there when the final collapse came. At that point I wanted to be able to try to get Anny in Rostock.

By the end of March the radius of the functioning city had become considerably smaller. Up until then public transportation had only been shutting down for a matter of hours at a time, then for days, and finally it stopped running altogether. A trip to Tempelhof Airport was a day-long undertaking, a trip to the inner city took hours.

And after there was no more power we received less and less information. The latest information and announcements were rare. Every few days

there were new rumors. Our never-ending source of the latest pronounce-
ments was the air-raid warden at Hohenzollerndamm—a fat, bespectacled
man endlessly running around in a safety helmet too big for his head. One day
it would be secret negotiations with the western allied powers, the next day
it was new weaponry which would turn the war around at the last minute;
then fresh troops were on their way from the west to fight the decisive battle
of the war outside the city. Those who were still sure of a German victory had
convinced themselves that the approach of the Russians was actually the
Führer's final stroke of genius—troops would be pulled from the north and
south and destroy the Russian army in a massive pincer formation. In the
meantime we waited in line, buckets in hand, for drinking water.

In the second week of April I got my car running again. The *Autobahn*
around the city had by then been almost completely shut down, and only in
the northwest was there a narrow opening. At any time the city would be
completely cut off.

It was high time. Telephone lines were still intact so that during the
last few weeks I had been able to speak regularly with Anny. Now she was
waiting impatiently, expecting me to come any day. Once again I tried to call
the friends that remained in the city to say good-bye. But I only reached a few;
most were too busy just staying alive.

At 3 A.M. I pushed my car out of the garage. Those fleeing the city
streamed down Heerstrasse. There were no more air attacks since the
Russians had reached the eastern edge of the city. Behind me lay what was left
of Berlin, burning and in despair.

[1] The Berlin Blockade was a postwar/Cold War attempt by the Soviet Union to force
Allied powers out of West Berlin by blocking off all surface access from West Germany to West
Berlin; the blockade was maintained for nine months in 1948–49 but was eventually rendered
ineffective by the American and English *Luftbrücke* [air bridge], whereby planes kept West
Berlin supplied with necessary provisions.

20

Once Again from the Start

On May 4, 1945 Anny and I heard the news of the partial capitulation of German forces in northwest Germany. On that same day, the English occupied Hamburg.

John Jahr had also managed to escape from Berlin and was presently living not too far from us in Westerland on the island of Sylt. As if by some miracle I was able to reach him by telephone after only a few tries. He didn't have any idea either what he would do next; his Arnim Press had been liquidated by the Nazis in the Fall, so we quickly agreed to meet back in Hamburg in order to be among the first to bring the destroyed city back to life.

On May 6 I picked up John Jahr in my car and in two days we made our way, continuously stopped by British tanks and patrols, back to Hamburg. I brought our most valuable capital—a typewriter; Jahr was determined to resume his old profession.

But he considered it doubtful that the occupying force would allow him to re-open his publishing company. Since I was "untainted," he suggested that we found the enterprise under my name. He was also counting on the English love of sports—hoping that they wouldn't refuse permission to a former boxing champion.

As the third partner we called on a mutual friend from before the war, the young Axel Springer.* His father had been a well-established old Altona publisher, and he himself had been editor-in-chief of the *Altona Nachrichten* until 1941.

We found Axel Springer sitting around doing nothing, and he was easily won over to the idea of starting our own press. His contribution was an ancient Opel P4 which was hidden in a barn under a haystack. We couldn't get

‿᷇᷇᷇‿

it going and finally had to tow it back to Hamburg. So the publishing enterprise now had three directors, a typewriter, and a "motor pool."

After we had rented three rooms in one of the few villas that hadn't been confiscated, we held our first board-of-directors meeting to discuss our publishing program. John Jahr had the most experience. Axel Springer had the "start-up capital" in the form of his parents' bombed-out press. I supplied my unblemished name.

Our first book was to be Robert Louis Stevenson's *Treasure Island* which, for some strange reason, had been banned during the Third Reich. We figured that this choice would also make a good impression on the occupying English. Beyond that, John Jahr had the idea that we should publish school books. But Axel Springer wanted to continue in his father's footsteps with a newspaper and soon applied for a license for an *Abendblatt* [evening newspaper]. Since I was the "name" in our triumvirate, I signed the application along with Axel Springer.

For weeks we sat around waiting. But nothing happened. It was now August, but we still sat and waited. Once in a while we got a printing job, we made calls, dealt with paper and bookbinding companies, but mostly the three of us just sat around the telephone and waited.

In these uneventful weeks filled with pointless busy-work, a piece of property became available to us. I already owned two bombed-out properties in Hamburg in which I had invested years before. But John Jahr convinced me that it would be wisest to invest our [soon-to-be] worthless money in something tangible. So we scraped together our last money and leased it. We drew a line down the middle—he took the left side, I took the right, and we began our building plans.

When the waiting became too long we would undertake new initiatives and call the English occupation officer. But he always had excuses: "I tell you, you have to wait. . . ." At the same time we were starting to hear rumors that one of us three had something in our past that was a problem and was holding up the granting of a license.

In these weeks I was visited by a journalist, an extremely pretty redhead in uniform. Miss Bachelor wanted an interview for the *Daily Express.* When she asked me in the course of our interview about my plans for the future, I told her that I expected shortly to recieve a publishing license from the military government. She seemed surprised and asked how a former boxer came to be in the publishing business. I really didn't want to discuss my present business affairs, so I exaggerated the importance of my apprentice year at Wilkens as a factor in my decision.

Three days after the interview we were sitting around the office, still discussing our plans and waiting for the license, when there came a loud knocking at the door. When Axel Springer opened the door he was greeted by a patrol of English military police. Before I knew what was happening, they grabbed me and ordered me to come along. "You are under arrest!" They were two chubby, baby-faced boys, whose red MP helmets and armbands were the only things giving them a military bearing. They loaded me into the jeep parked before the house and brought me to prison.

Not until a few days later was I told the charge against me. It was "making a false statement regarding a member of the military government." It turned out that the English journalist had written in her article that I had said that the publishing license was a "sure thing;" and this small misrepresentation was enough, given the climate of mistrust, to cause a criminal complaint to be brought.

I had to wait two weeks for my trial. The English military judge, a bald giant with a handlebar mustache and a friendly face, was not oblivious to the bizarre nature of the charge. During the proceedings he said that it had been my American English which had led to the misunderstanding. And on the witness stand the contrite Miss Bachelor stated that she considered such a misunderstanding to have been possible, indeed, even probable. After the mustachioed judge—looking testily over at the plaintiff—pronounced me free to go, I met Miss Bachelor in the hall. Relieved, she ran up to me amidst the popping photo flashes and, despite the ban on fraternization, threw her arms around my neck.

But on the heels of one proceeding there soon followed another. In the interim I had begun with construction on the property we had acquired, but I had neglected to obtain some sort of building permit. So one morning the two baby-faces again stood at my door and ordered me to come with them. This time they brought me directly to the military court, and within a half-hour I had been sentenced to three months in prison and a ten-thousand-mark fine. I was brought from the court straight to prison and served every day of my sentence.

But the string of bad luck didn't end there. On the day of my release Anny and I decided to go to the circus, just to get our minds off of everything. In the course of the performance the circus director, Hans Hasslach, introduced us to the crowd with great fanfare, a spotlight, and a flourish of his top hat. For the first time in years I was feeling the rush of applause around me.

This harmless episode was the beginning of the end for my publishing career. The English saw it as a demonstration for the boxing idol of the Third Reich and claimed that my public appearance revived undesirable memories of the recent past. A few days later I received a terse notification that the publishing firm of Springer, Jahr, and Schmeling would never receive a license as long as I was involved.

∽∼∾

I told my two friends to go ahead without me. And they both said simultaneously that that was out of the question. But I persisted that there *was* no question—it had already been decided. It wouldn't do me any good if all three of us starved. On that same day I officially withdrew from the partnership; and shortly thereafter Axel Springer and John Jahr were granted a license.

So once again I found myself with nothing—my money had gone for building the house, and the edge that the early start in Hamburg was supposed to have given me was long gone. I had wanted to be one of the first to act in the *Stunde Null* ["Zero Hour"], and now, a year later, I hadn't gotten one step further. The prison sentence and fine, the refusal to grant a license, and, most of all, the often-repeated accusation that I was a symbol of the fallen Reich—all these things hurt and depressed me.

For a while I didn't know which way to turn. We lived from hand to mouth and started to consider selling the few things that we had managed to rescue. The only thing of value that we still had was a massive gold plaque from Chicago's Steuben Society, which had been awarded to only six people—the pilots Koehl, Hühnefeld, and Fitzmaurice, the Zeppelin pioneer Dr. Hugo Eckener, and the channel swimmer Gertrude Ederle. Only Anny kept me from selling it. The future looked more uncertain than ever.

The scenario that I had once feared—back in the days of my ice cream enterprise with Hugo Abels—had now come to pass: my boxing career was over, I hadn't learned a profession, and my savings were gone. A lot of boxers, from Jack Dempsey to Georges Carpentier to Gustav Eder, had opened a restaurant or a nightclub when their boxing careers had ended, and I had visited and enjoyed these establishments, but I had never seen myself in that role.

"Would you want to be a boxing referee, Max?" asked the Heidelberg promoter Heinz Schuble. He had heard of my situation and wanted to help. I hesitated in answering, and I think he misunderstood. For whatever reason, he added, "I'm not doing this as a favor. As a referee you would be a big draw." When I finally said OK, we could try it, he immediately had a number of referee jobs for me. Doing this, I could at least keep my head above water.

In the summer of 1946, more than a year since escaping, I returned to Berlin for the first time. Once there, I quickly looked up Max Machon, who had gotten back his license as a manager and trainer.

Berlin, along with Hamburg and the Rhineland, had once again become a center of boxing. There were still some pre-war stars such as Walter Neusel and Gustav Eder, as well as rising talent from the amateur ranks. It seemed that a boxing revival was close at hand, and trainers, managers, and promoters didn't have to worry about the future.

꩜

The Avus was the yearly setting for the great auto races. Among the stars of the famous Berlin race track was the young Bohemian, Prince Georg Christian Lobkowitz, who in 1932 suffered a fatal accident in his Bugatti.

The sport pilot Elly Beinhorn was an attraction in Berlin society and later became the wife of the race car driver Bernd Rosemeyer.

An auto race at the Avus drew hundreds of thousands of fans.

My closest friend among the race drivers was Bernd Rosemeyer, who was killed on January 28, 1938, while trying to set a speed record.

Before there could be a second Louis fight, I had to go against an extremely strong Harry Thomas in 1937. In an unexpectedly tough fight in Madison Square Garden, I knocked Thomas out in the eighth round.

After my victory over Joe Louis, no one could deny my right to a title fight with Jimmy Braddock. We signed a contract for the fight, but it never took place.

MADISON SQUARE GARDEN BOW

45TH ST. & NORTHERN BLVD. — LONG ISLAND CIT

WORLD'S HEAVYWEIGHT CHAMPIONSHIP - 15 ROUNDS

BRADDOCK SCHMELING

CHAMPION HABENGER

Thursday Eve., JUNE 3, 1937

RINGSIDE

Est. Price $20.91
Fed. Tax — 2.10
TOTAL $23.01

REDUCED PRICE $23.0

$23.00

The contract-signing for the Braddock fight was the prelude to a grotesque comedy. Only later did I learn that Braddock had signed another contract and had no intention of fighting me.

Politics also cast its shadow on sports. The new powers in Germany demanded that I drop my Jewish manager, Joe Jacobs.

Many of the friends that I had come to know and admire in Berlin were forced to leave the country after Hitler's takeover. At the seaside resort of Scheveningen in Holland, a reunion with Willi Rosen, Otto Wallburg, and Siegfried Arno had disturbing repercussions.

I had been warned. During training, Gene Tunney (left) visited me and said, "Be ready for anything, Max! You don't know what's possible in this country."

When I arrived in New York for the second fight with Joe Louis in 1938, I found that public opinion in America had turned against me.

In order to find peace, I quickly put the formalities behind me and went to my training camp.

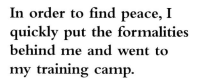

Joe Louis had become the symbol of freedom and equal rights for all races, fighting against the "representative of Nazi Germany," Max Schmeling.

For the first time
before a fight I was
nervous. Louis was
all over me, and
before I knew what
had happened, I was
hit with three sharp
lefts to the face. At
124 seconds into the
first round Machon
threw in the towel.

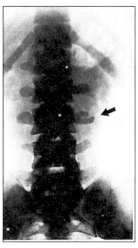

I suffered a spinal injury that took weeks to heal.

In our search to replace Saarow–Pieskow we happened upon a manor called Ponickel in 1936.

It did not take us long to settle in at the estate in eastern Pomerania.

Our enthusiasm for
Ponickel was probably
somewhat of a reflection
of the times — a return
to the simpler life.

I was the only leading German athlete drafted into the army at the outbreak of the war.

After receiving paratroop training, I was sent to Crete in 1941. I was injured during a jump and brought to a military hospital.

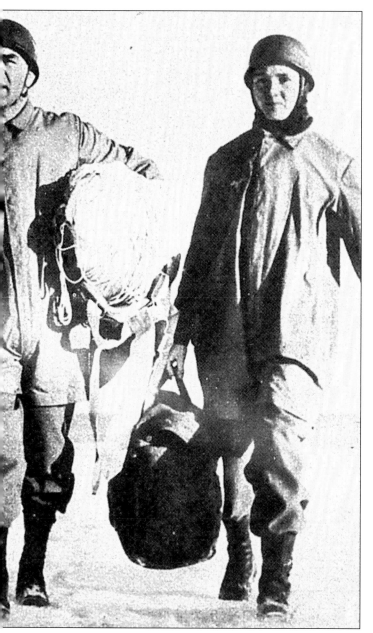

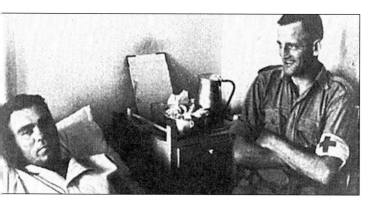

After my release from
the military hospital,
I received permission
to travel to Paris, where
I got together with
Georges Carpentier.

When I returned to Ponickel in 1944, it was overflowing with refugees. With all of their worldly possessions loaded onto wagons, they were fleeing westward. Soon we were all in flight.

As we approached the city, the reflection of countless fires hung over Berlin. The streets were hopelessly clogged.

**Survival was
everyone's priority.**

Any green spot in the
city became a vegetable
garden.

We lost everything in the war. I had begun with the building of a small house in Hamburg, but I had neglected to get a building permit. I was arrested by the military police and sentenced to three months in jail and a 10,000-mark fine.

Before Berlin had been completely surrounded, I managed to leave the city in a rickety old car on the one road that was still open.

Among the old friends whom I saw after the war was Primo Carnera.

In order to improve my financial situation I returned to the ring. I knocked out my first opponent, Werner Vollmer, in the seventh round.

I never lost contact with the sports world. Gustav Jaenecke and I reminisced about the old days.

I soon realized that my fighting days were over. With the Richard Vogt fight I announced my retirement for good.

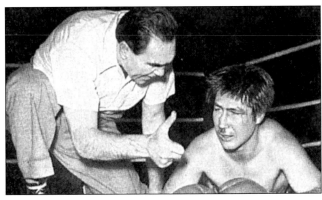

After the war I worked as a referee just to get by.

I barely had my feet back on the ground when I returned to my second home: America. One of my first visits was to my one-time opponent, Joe Louis.

In New York I got together with my boyhood idol, Jack Dempsey and my old friend, Paul Damski, who had "courted" Anny on my behalf.

Anny and I at the
Berlin Film Festival
with Zarah Leander.

When I appeared as a
referee I would often run
into old friends, such as
Andre Picard, the former
matchmaker for the Berlin
Sports Palace (above).

In the mid-fifties I was
invited to Milwaukee to referee the match between the
American Kilgore and the
German Hans Stretz (left).

I had dreamed of a more glorious end to my boxing career, but boxing did give me the means to a new start. With the money from my last purse I was able to buy a piece of land in Hollenstedt, on the edge of the Lüneberger Heide.

Axel Springer and I had wanted to start a publishing firm after the war. It didn't come to that for me, but we remained friends.

I had always imagined that I would spend the rest of my life as a farmer, and in a small way I did, as a breeder, tobacco farmer and hunter.

I have never lost my passion for
hunting; I still look forward to
those hours that are spent afield.

On the evening of our reunion, Max Machon and I spoke about the newly awakened boxing fever. He was of the opinion that whenever a country had been defeated in war, the people were overcome by a sports frenzy. "You know," he said as we reflected on his point, "it occurs to me that it started in 1806 with the father of gymnastics, Jahn,* and then we saw it again in 1918, and now again."

We spoke about this phenomenon for a while and tried to come up with reasons for it. We decided that there had been no such outbreak after the victories of 1870–71 [the Franco-Prussian War], so that there must be a human dynamic whereby the frustration of defeat in war causes overcompensation in sport. But when Machon pointed out that America's boxing heyday came right after a military victory, I suddenly cut him off and said, "Let's forget this nit-picking. Don't call me crazy, but I want to box again!"

Machon looked at me, flabbergasted. Then he laughed in my face, seeming to believe that I was kidding. But when I persisted he said, "Max, you've lost your mind! You haven't boxed in over eight years. In the last few years you've been operated on almost constantly. And you haven't gotten any younger!" Then he tried to convince me that I wouldn't have a chance against the twenty and twenty-five-year-olds.

I conceded that, but I came back with the point that I hadn't lost my technical know-how. My tactical experience would compensate for age, and after a short training period I would regain my punching power.

Unimpressed, Max shook his head. None of that convinced him. He insisted that I would only ruin my good name by attempting a comeback. But he became silent when I said, "Machon, I have no choice. I don't know what else to do. Tell me what we're supposed to live on!"

But Machon was unmoved: "Not on boxing!" Finally I suggested that I would start training on my own; as soon as I felt myself to be in shape I would let him decide whether I should climb back into the ring or not.

Three days later I drove to Friedrichsruh in Sachsenwald. I trained harder than I ever had before. It was clear to me that everything depended on my legs. I had never logged so many miles as I did in those weeks. I ran until the sweat poured off me in rivers; and one day I knew that my legs were back. When I had reached my old fighting weight I called Machon in Berlin: "Machon, you can come now!"

Machon came and put me to a demanding test. He checked me out running, working on the heavy bag and the speedbag. He was impressed by my conditioning, but remained skeptical. It took a lot of effort, but I finally convinced him to start training me again.

So that's where things stood after about a year. We lived a Spartan existence—just the essentials, no diversions. It was as if the old training-camp days out at Lanke had returned. Once again self-denial was the ruling principle, but now without the stimulating mix of hope, youth, passion, and impatience. My training was no longer driven by the burning ambition of the twenty-year-old, but rather by the bitter determination of the forty-year-old. Despite all the sacrifice, the days out at Lanke had been happy; these days were an ordeal.

The opponent that had been chosen for my first outing was Werner Vollmer. He was an eager, energetic boxer and sixteen years my junior. On September 28, 1947, my forty-second birthday, I stood facing him in Frankfurt's *Waldstadion* [Stadium in the Forest]. Forty thousand spectators, among them thousands of American GIs, greeted me with a singing of the traditional "Happy Birthday to You!" The last time I had stood in a ring to fight had been eight years before.

The fight was scheduled for ten rounds. Right from the opening bell Vollmer went on the attack, but his technical skills didn't match his strength and fighting spirit. Towards the end of the first round a hard right ripped him off his feet. From that moment on I knew that I still had my old weapon. Vollmer fought back desperately. In every round he came back at me, but I continued to penetrate his cover and drive him around the ring. He went down a total of seven times, but his toughness and endurance were exceptional. Badly marked up, his right eye swollen shut, bleeding from his nose and mouth, he continued to fight back with gutsy persistence until a hard right in the seventh round put him down for the count.

The ovation in the stadium reminded me of earlier, greater victories. Sitting at ringside were experts from around the world, some with considerable reservations, while others had seemed to be merely waiting for the debacle. But I was used to that from day one—the odds had been against me in a lot of fights. Now there was a change of heart. Now they were coming around to agree with Alfred Eggert, one of the leading boxing experts:

> Max Schmeling's comeback has succeeded, mostly because he learned everything he could from his 1927 loss to Gypsy Daniels and never looked back. He methodically wore down his opponent, and for all Vollmer's courage, he wouldn't have lasted beyond the second round if Schmeling had been motivated to go all out. But he wasn't. It was precisely the unexpected duration of seven rounds which demonstrated to the experts Schmeling's self-control and the wealth of skills that he still possesses. Now we know: Max still has endurance, his sharp eye, and fluidity of movement. What has improved is his left jab, which hit its mark consistently. Only Schmeling's successor to the heavyweight crown, Jack Sharkey, threw a jab that well. Vollmer could never escape that left, and the

right, still as effective as ever, completed the package. In this form, Schmeling will play an important role not only in the German boxing picture, but also in Europe, to the extent that he's given a chance. That chance would be fully justified by the international respect which Schmeling still enjoys.

The gamble had paid off, and even Max Machon was astonished. Perhaps I was the only one in the stadium who hadn't missed what was barely perceptible; yes, my legs had held up, my punching power was almost as good as in the old days, and my strategy had proven itself. But in the midst of Vollmer's attacks I had noticed that my reactions were delayed. It was only a matter of fractions of a second, but that was what determined a boxer's ability.

From this moment forward, even as applauding fans crowded around me, I knew—I could handle the boxers that Germany had to offer. But my time was past. I had beaten my opponent, but strictly for the purpose of winning back the second half of my life, which had started and been lost at Ponickel.

The next weeks and months brought, on a smaller scale, a repetition of former experiences. American officers invited me to hunt with them, spa owners offered me free vacations, journalists pursued me for interviews, industrialists threw parties for me. Suddenly, after years of obscurity, I was "in society" again, almost a "star." My comeback seemed to everyone to be a success. Only I knew better.

In the following months I climbed into the ring four more times. In December 1947 I beat Hans-Joachim Drägestein in a re-match, and finally lost on points to Richard Vogt. And each appearance was accompanied by a chorus of many voices: sometimes I was "the old Max Schmeling," other times I was "the too old Max Schmeling." I was alternately admired and pitied. Before the referee announced the decision in my fight against Richard Vogt, I decided on my retirement from boxing, this time for good.

I dreamed of ending my career in glory, but circumstances had prohibited that. Yet boxing had once again given me the chance to start a new life. For my last fight, right after the currency reform, I got 40,000 marks.

A few weeks later I bought a piece of land in Hollenstedt, on the edge of the Lüneburger Heide.* I had held on to my dream. I wouldn't be a gentleman farmer owning an estate, but rather a breeder, tobacco farmer, and hunter. I wouldn't realize my great dreams, but I would find happiness.

A Look Back

Thirty years have gone by since then. My new life has taken all my time and energy. But the past was always there. I had barely gotten back on my feet when I was drawn back to my second home, America. In early 1954 I flew to New York. My first path took me to a Jewish cemetary.

The caretaker, a small, bent-over man wearing a black yarmulke, asked me whom I was looking for. And when I told him, he said, "So you come from Germany?" Then he showed me the way. It was a beautiful spring day. Trotting on ahead, the caretaker led me through a maze of headstones.

He stopped in front of a simple grave marked only by a flat stone plaque. Then he began to speak—"Joe," he said bending way over as if he wanted the deceased to understand, "Joe, here is a friend of yours! It's Max Schmeling. He didn't forget you. He came from Germany and wants to visit you. His first stop, Joe, was to visit you."

As the little man spoke, I stood unmoving, looking at the weathered stone. I imagined Joe, how he used to gesticulate excitedly from my corner of the ring, pulling animatedly on the ropes, chattering away wildly at me in the locker room; and always with the cigar in his mouth, which he really didn't smoke but rather chewed, literally eating the cigar from one end to another.

We had met, and the high point of one life became that of the other. When events finally separated us, both of our times were past. After the [second] Hamas fight I brought him to Hamburg's harbor, and we spoke of new plans. But really we both knew that they would forever remain only plans.

The old man brought me out of my thoughts. "Friends always die too soon," he said, "no matter how old they live to be. But Joe here, he died much too soon."

Then, still hunched over, he walked away.

~~~

Two days later I was in Chicago. The ostensible reason for my American trip had been an invitation to referee at a boxing show in Milwaukee. But my real goal was to see Joe Louis again. During the war and into the postwar years as well, journalists had sought repeatedly to play us off against each other, forever trying to put hateful or insulting words in our mouths.

Friends had driven me to Chicago. And one day, without calling ahead, I found myself standing at Joe Louis's door. A woman answered the door, seemed startled for a moment, and then said in surprise, "Oh, Mr. Schmeling! Please come in!"

She told me that Joe was unfortunately not at home but out playing golf, and that she would call him right away. But Joe was already on his way home. I had only waited a few minutes when the front door opened. I heard her speak to him and then he was standing before me. For a few moments he stood there as if he had grown roots. Then he dropped his golf bag and rushed over to me. "Max! How good to see you again!"

As we sat over coffee a little later I brought up how people had, since our first meeting, tried to turn opponents into enemies. "I just want you to know . . . ," I began, but he cut me off immediately: "Forget all that stuff!" he said. "For a long time people tried the same thing with me. There were times when I believed what they wrote. But today I know better." I sensed that he wasn't just saying that.

We sat there together for hours, until late in the evening, talking about the great fights and the old friends. And it was only then that I realized how much it had bothered me over the years that the hatreds of the times had managed to separate us. A short time later, Joe Louis visited me in Hamburg.

So I kept trying to repair the broken threads. Circumstances had scattered one-time friends to the four winds. In some cases, people were lost without a trace. Carola Neher had emigrated to the Soviet Union and dropped out of sight. Ernesto de Fiori's trail was lost somewhere in South America in 1945; Ernst Lubitsch* did not live to experience a German homecoming; Eric Hanussen was killed by the Nazis, and Heinrich George* died in a Russian prison camp. Alfred Flechtheim* was also dead.

Some came back. Overjoyed or deeply moved, we embraced. Fritz Kortner was pleased that I could still describe the apartment where I had given him boxing lessons in the mid-twenties. Ernst Deutsch remembered every one of my fights that he had attended. Together we visited Heinz Ditgens, who had opened his old Roxy Bar again. I laughed with Paul Damski in his New York jewelry store about how he had paid court to Anny on my behalf; and with Siegfried Arno I thought of that evening in Scheveningen and how we were the only ones of that circle of friends who had survived.

However diverse our paths may have been—in the old Berlin we had all come together to form a world, a network of fondness for one another, shared interests, dependencies, and friendships. Now it was only chance meetings between isolated individuals who reminisced about the days past and who began almost every conversation with the phrase, "Do you know what happened to . . . ?"

But time didn't repair every rupture. One day I met Frau Thorak again. She had come through the past years in England and had been employed as a teacher at a college in Bristol. And for a moment it had appeared that she would be able to take up her life where it had been torn apart.

As a favorite of the Hitler regime, Josef Thorak hadn't fared too well since its collapse, and he sought forgiveness and reconciliation from his wife. He had wanted statements from her for the allied authorities, saying that he had never wanted to separate from her or go along with the Nazi regime but had only done so under pressure.

Frau Thorak fought for her husband. She had written letters, petitioned, made every declaration that Thorak had asked of her. And in the end Josef Thorak was exonerated. But when she came to his studio in Baldham —proud of her victory and running exuberantly to embrace her man—he turned away from her in embarassment. Sensing the possibility of a revived career, he had gone and married an influential American woman.

I also received some bitter satisfaction in those years. During a trip through Spain some friends drew my attention to a series of articles appearing in the boxing daily *Marca*. The author was Mike Jacobs, my old acquaintance from the Twentieth-Century Sporting Club.

In all candor he confirmed that a well-planned intrigue had in 1937 intentionally deprived me of the chance to fight the then-champion Jimmy Braddock for the title. Everything had been played out as I had suspected. It was small consolation that Mike Jacobs wrote: "Everyone who knew Max Schmeling as a man and as a sportsman was sorry."

Not without regret did I think back on all my hopes and all my desperate attempts to get the fight—and the disappointment that hadn't let go of me for so long. But really, I had moved beyond all that by then.

But the past also came back to help me as well. [Jim] Farley, the one-time president of the New York Boxing Commission, had in the meantime become a successful businessman and had some years earlier taken over the leadership of Coca-Cola. Now he was suggesting to me that I get in on the ground floor of the Coca-Cola Corporation as it entered the German market. After some brief negotiations we came to an agreement. My boxing career had, excluding the war years, lasted about twenty years. Since then I have had a career in business lasting over two decades,[1] which my boxing career made possible.

I still spend many a pre-dawn hour in the forest or afield in the hunter's blind. And when the first pale light of dawn breaks, I often find myself lost in my memories—thoughts that have been with me for a lifetime. But then I catch myself. Certainly boxing reflects life in its most elemental form. But when a wild animal emerges from a thicket or a flock of birds flies noisily from the underbrush, then I think that I'm still close to life in its elemental form—that which I sought in boxing is still with me in this wild environment. I no longer need the fights, the hoopla, the notariety to bring me into harmony with life and with myself.

The only one who understands this about me is my wife, Anny. On my seventieth birthday—amidst all the chaos of well-wishers, guests, and the merely curious—she sent me off to hunt. "Go on," she said, "that's where you're happy."

---

[1] Max Schmeling's successful representation of Coca-Cola in the Hamburg area has continued to the present.

∽∾∿

Epilogue
Reflections from the Distance of Time

At the end of May 1928, exactly seventy years ago, I arrived as a twenty-two-year-old for the first time in New York. Since that time America has become, as I have often said and written, my second home—a home in the truest sense, where I have experienced everything possible, the very best as well as the worst. But it was all an adventure that I look back on with gratitude and pride: gratitude, because I had chances of which I could scarcely have dreamed as a boy growing up in Hamburg, and pride, because I used these chances and never ducked the challenge that they presented.

With this English translation of my autobiography I have, in a sense, undertaken what will probably be my last trip to America—a pleasant journey during which I would like to tell my story to the American people. I hope that my English-speaking friends, wherever they might be, enjoy this account of my life.

My time in America, which is covered in this book—the America of Jack Dempsey, Gene Tunney, Joe Louis, Young Stribling, and Al Capone—is already history for most readers. But I was there, both experiencing and playing a part in that long-ago era. American friends such as Joe Louis and Joe Jacobs have long since departed this earth, but they are still alive in my heart; and they will live on forever in the history of boxing and in the history of twentieth-century America. It is my great honor to have stood side by side with them.

The story of my life as I wrote it for this autobiography is also the story of a German life in the twentieth century. As a German living during this time I have experienced and survived a great deal in this most turbulent century in all of German history. I was born in 1905 in the Kaiser's Imperial Reich; that was the *Second* Reich, which came into being in 1871 after the Franco-Prussian War, brought to life by Kaiser Wilhelm I and the "Iron Chancellor"

⌒⌒⌒

Otto von Bismarck. The memoirs that you have read begin in 1919 during the first days of the Weimar Republic, a period that could be characterized in the words of Charles Dickens: "It was the best of times, it was the worst of times."

In that time an inexperienced young man of humble beginnings came of age during the "Golden Twenties" (as they were called in Germany) in *the* world city of that era: BERLIN. There my athletic ability brought me into a world that I otherwise would probably never have known. And it was in this world that I met my wife, my Anny, the love of my life.

I have also experienced a divided Germany, from the "Stunde Null" ["Zero Hour"] of the difficult postwar years—in which Anny and I found that we had lost everything—to the "Wirtschaftswunder" ["Economic Miracle"] of the German Federal Republic. I have lived through a Cold War in a divided land as well as the European Union in a Germany reunited since 1989.

I was always there—I'm still there. My life is that of a German in the twentieth century; or perhaps more precisely, it was a German-American life, a tie made even stronger through my association with Coca-Cola of Hamburg. It was, in any case, a fulfilled life which was never boring and of which, I must admit, I am somewhat proud.

Glossary

Adenauer, Konrad (1876-1967)—*Oberbürgermeister* of Cologne from 1917 until removed by the Nazis in 1933; first *Bundeskanzler* of the Federal Republic of Germany, 1949-1963.

Albers, Hans (1891-1960)—extremely popular stage and film actor.

Archipenko, Alexander (1887-1964)—Russian abstract sculptor; worked in Berlin 1921-23; lived in the USA from 1923 on.

Avus—a roadway built 1913-21 in Berlin; its stretch of 19.6 km. was the site of auto races and the fastest speedway of its time; its north curve was known to be particularly dangerous.

Barlach, Ernst (1870-1938)—sculptor in wood and bronze, graphic artist, poet; Expressionist of pacifist, social-activist orientation; considered "decadent" by the Nazis.

Bassermann, Albert (1867-1952)—stage actor, especially in Max Reinhardt's Deutsches Theater; lived in the USA 1933-1946.

Beckmann, Max (1884-1950)—Expressionist painter; emigrated in 1937 to Amsterdam and then to New York.

Belling, Rudolf (1886-1972)—sculptor; particularly abstract Expressionism (e.g., *Dreiklang* [*Triad*], 1919).

Benn, Gottfried (1886-1956)—a leading Expressionist poet.

Bergner, Elisabeth (1897-1986)—stage and film actress who came to Berlin in 1922; from 1933 on she lived in London and America.

Bergner, Ludwig (1892-1969)—theater and film director.

Bohnen, [Franz] Michael (1887-1965)—opera singer (bass baritone) in Berlin and at the Metropolitan Opera in New York; best known for roles in Wagner operas.

Bois, Curt (1901-1991)—Berlin actor in the twenties; lived in the USA 1933-1950.

Bouhler, Philipp (1899-1945)—a member of the Nazi party since its inception in the early 1920s; participated in Hitler's 1923 putsch attempt in Munich; was Hitler's chief of staff in the Reich Chancellory; committed suicide with the fall of the Third Reich.

Blue Rider—prominent Expressionist group dedicated primarily to painting, but also to other art forms; began 1912 in Münich under the leadership of Franz Marc; included Paul Klee and Wassily Kandinsky.

Brancusi, Constantin (1876-1957)—Romanian abstract sculptor.

Brecht, Bertolt (1898-1956)—one of the most prominent German dramatists and poets of the modern era; outspoken social/political critic who left Germany with the onset of the Third Reich; lived in California, but after World War II opted to finish his work and life in East Berlin; works such as *The Three Penny Opera* and *Mother Courage* have been widely translated and performed internationally.

Breker, Arno (1900-1991)—sculptor of massive neo-classical figures; a favorite of Hitler, his works filled the *Haus der deutschen Kunst* [House of German Art] in Munich.

Bruckner, Ferdinand (1891-1958)—prominent writer/dramatist in 1920s Berlin; emigrated in 1933 and lived in the USA until 1950.

Brüning, Heinrich (1885-1970)—Chancellor during the Weimar Republic (1930-32) whose termination in that office signalled the end of the Weimar Republic and the onset of the Third Reich; emigrated to the USA in 1934, where he taught at Harvard University.

⤳⤳⤳

The Cabinet of Dr. Caligari—extremely successful Expressionist silent film (1919), a mix of avant-garde aesthetics, horror, and political message.

Carow, Erich (1893-1956)—cabaret comic popular in Berlin's "Golden Twenties."

Cramm, Gottfried von (1909-1976)—foremost German tennis player in the thirties and forties.

Dagover, Lil (1897-1980)—theater and film actress; in *The Cabinet of Dr. Caligari.*

de Kowa, Victor (1904-1973)—film and theater actor in Berlin, later a director.

Deutsch, Ernst (1890-1969)—classical stage actor; emigrated to the USA in 1933.

Dietrich, Marlene (1901-1992)—Berlin-born film actress and singer; early career in Berlin; first major role in Josef von Sternberg's *Blue Angel* (1930); emigrated to the USA where she became a citizen in 1937 and continued to have a successful film career.

Döblin, Alfred (1878-1957)—a physician and leading author during the Weimar Republic; emigrated 1933 to Paris and 1940 to the USA; his best-known work is the novel *Berlin Alexanderplatz.*

Edschmidt, Kasimir (1890-1966)—Expressionist author known primarily for his prose works.

Expressionism—the radically modern and increasingly abstract cultural movement that spread throughout the western world in the early twentieth century; Germany was a leader in this movement, which extended to all art forms (art, design, sculpture, literature, music, theater, film); the Nazis were violently opposed to Expressionism (called "degenerate art") and sought to eradicate all traces of it during the Third Reich.

Flechtheim, Alfred (1878-1937)—art collector and dealer, publisher of the avant-garde journal *Querschnitt;* emigrated to London with onset of the Third Reich.

Freisler, Roland (1893–1945)—president of the notorious National Socialist *Volksgerichtshof* [People's Court]; was a symbol of "legalized" Nazi terror; killed in an air raid.

Frick, Wilhelm (1877–1946)—Minister of the Interior during the Third Reich; played a major role in the formulation of the anti-Semitic Nuremberg Laws; found guilty of war crimes at Nuremberg trials and executed.

Fritsch, Willi (1901–1973)—film actor, often paired in comedies with Lillian Harvey (e.g., *The Gas Station Three*).

George, Heinrich (1893–1946)—stage and film actor, theater director; especially involved in proletarian and activist theater during the Weimar Republic; appeared in the films *Metropolis* and *Berlin Alexanderplatz;* arrested by Soviet troops in 1945 and died in the military occupation prison of Sachsenhausen.

Grosz, George (1893–1959)—artist best known for bitter political satire and critique of reactionary and conservative elements in the Weimar Republic and his courageous defiance of the Nazis; emigrated to the USA in 1938.

HAPAG—Hamburg-based shipping firm (Hamburg-Amerika Linie); Hapag-Lloyd since 1970.

Harvey, Lillian (1907–1968)—British film actress who appeared in popular German films, particularly the comedy series *Die Drei von der Tankstelle* (*The Gas Station Three*)

Helldorf, Count (1896–1944)—former Nazi who became part of the largely monarchist resistance movement, which failed in its attempt to assassinate Hitler on July 7, 1944; arrested and executed.

Hesse, Hermann (1877–1962)—German-Swiss writer whose somewhat mystical works enjoyed tremendous popularity in America of the 1960s and 70s.

Hindenburg, Paul von (1847–1934)—top German military official in World War One; descended from Prussian aristocracy; *Reichspräsident* during the Weimar Republic from 1925 on; continued as president after Hitler became chancellor on January 30, 1933, yet he wasn't a National Socialist and did not like Hitler ("the Bohemian corporal"); upon Hindenburg's death, Hitler consolidated the offices of *Reichskanzler* and *Reichspräsident* into one office —*der Führer.*

Hollaender, Friedrich (1896-1976)—cabaret composer/writer; worked in the USA from 1935 to 1955 as a composer for films.

Homolka, Oskar (1898-1978)—stage and film actor; emigrated to England in 1935 and to the USA in 1937, where he had a long career as a character actor in films and television.

Ihering, Herbert (1888-1977)—extremely influential Berlin theater critic.

Jahn, Friedrich Ludwig (1778-1852)—known as "der Turnvater," the father of the *Turnbewegung* [exercise or gymnastics movement]; his *Turnbewegung* appealed to the youth as both a sports movement and as a nationalist political movement.

Jannings, Emil (1884-1950)—film and stage actor, known especially for his role in *The Blue Angel* (1930) with Marlene Dietrich; tried American film, 1926-1929, but returned to Germany.

Jessner, Leopold (1878-1945)—classical and Expressionist theater director; emigrated to the USA in 1933.

Kaiser, Georg (1878-1945)—extremely successful Expressionist playwright.

Kerr, Alfred (1867-1968)—writer/essayist/theater critic; emigrated to London in 1933.

Kisch, Egon Edwin (1885-1948)—originally Czech, was a writer/journalist in Berlin of leftist-activist political orientation.

Klabund (1890-1928)—tubercular Expressionist poet.

Kortner, Fritz (1892-1970)—Austrian actor/director, known especially for Expressionist theater in Weimar-era Berlin.

Kolbe, George (1877-1947)—a leading Berlin sculptor.

Kollo, Walter (1878-1940)—Berlin opera composer.

Krauss, Werner (1884-1959)—stage and film actor; in *The Cabinet of Dr. Caligari* (1919).

Krenek, Ernst (1900-1991)—radically modern composer best known for his jazz opera *Johnny Spielt Auf* (1927); emigrated to the USA in 1938.

Kurfürstendamm—known to Berliners as the "Ku'damm," it was and still is the fashionable 3.5-kilometer main thoroughfare of western Berlin.

Lang, Fritz (1890-1976)—foremost Expressionist film director (e.g., *Metropolis*); emigrated to the USA in 1933 where he continued his career as a successful film director.

Lasker-Schüler, Else (1869-1945)—a leading Expressionist writer; collaborated with Herwarth Walden on the avant-garde literary journal *Der Sturm*.

Lessing, Gotthold Ephraim (1729-1781)—foremost dramatist of the German Enlightenment; *Nathan the Wise* was one of his best-known works.

Liebermann, Max (1847-1935)—a leading German Impressionist painter whose works were banned by the Nazis.

Liedtka, Harry (1880-1945)—actor on stage and in silent films.

Lubitsch, Ernst (1892-1947)—film director who emigrated from Berlin to Hollywood in 1922; one of his best-known American films was *To Be or Not To Be* (1942) with Jack Benny.

Luckner, Graf Felix von (1881-1966)—as a *Hilfskreuzer* in World War One, his *Seeadler* [*Sea Devil*] was a kind of a free-lance support vessel for the German navy, running the British blockade when needed and capturing Allied shipping; also wrote adventure stories based on his exploits.

Lüneburger Heide—part of the flat lowland plain in northwest Germany in the Federal State of Niedersachsen.

Mann, Heinrich (1871-1950)—author and older brother of Thomas Mann; his novel *Professor Unrat* was filmed as *The Blue Angel;* emigrated to the USA in 1940.

Mann, Thomas (1875-1955)—author, essayist; considered by many to be the greatest modern German writer; works include *Death in Venice* and *The Magic Mountain;* emigrated to the USA in 1933.

〜〜〜

Massary, Fritzi (1882-1969)—Austrian singer and actress popular in 1920s Berlin.

Minetti, Bernhard (1905-)—Extremely popular Berlin stage, screen, and television actor; was the lead actor of the Berlin *Staatstheater* from 1930 to 1945; still professionally active in his nineties.

Mistinguette (1875-1956)—French actress and singer, best known as a cabaret performer.

Negri, Pola (1897-1987)—popular silent-screen actress for UFA in Berlin; came to Hollywood in 1923 along with Ernst Lubitsch, where she continued to live and work.

Nikolaus, Paul (1894-1933)—cabaretist known especially for political satire in twenties Berlin; committed suicide in Switzerland.

Orlik, Emil (1870-1932)—graphic artist and sculptor in wood, as well as a leading set designer for theatrical productions.

Ossietsky, Carl von (1889-1938)—leftist-pacifist who published the activist journal *Weltbühne;* sent to concentration camp in 1934; won the Nobel Prize in 1935; finally released from concentration camp as a result of international protest, but died from the effects of mistreatment.

Pallenberg, Max (1877-1934)—Austrian actor popular in 1920s Berlin.

Papen, Franz von (1879-1969)—Chancellor under von Hindenburg before helping broker Hitler's appointment as *Reichskanzler;* member of Hitler's first cabinet.

Pinthus, Kurt (1886-1975)—writer, critic (theater, film, literature); emigrated to the USA in 1937 where he remained as a theater critic.

Piscator, Erwin (1893-1966)—leading theatrical producer/director in twenties Berlin; founder of the Proletarian Theater and the Volkstheater; especially known for proleatrian/socialist and Expressionist theater productions.

Pomerania—formerly a northeastern province of the German Reich, part of the North German Lowland Plain; today the section west of the Oder River falls in the German Federal Republic state of Mecklenburg-Vorpommern, while the section east of the Oder has been part of Poland since 1945.

Rathenau, Walter (1867-1922)—industrialist and cabinet minister early in the Weimar Republic; assassinated by right-wing anti-Semites.

Reinhardt, Max (1873-1943)—innovative actor and director in Expressionist and classical theater; director of the Deutsches Theater in Berlin; emigrated to the USA in 1937.

Schaeffers, Willi (1884-1962)—Berlin cabaretist and actor.

Schirach, Baldur von (1907-1974)—youth leader in the Third Reich, head of the Hitler Youth; sentenced at the Nuremberg War Crimes Trial to twenty years in Spandau Prison.

Schlusnus, Heinrich (1888-1952)—concert and opera singer (baritone).

Schünzel, Reinhold (1888-1954)—stage and film actor/director; emigrated to the USA in 1937; acted and directed in Hollywood until 1949.

Sintenis, Renée (1888-1965)—sculptress, best known for abstract Expressionism; her works were largely confiscated and destroyed by the Nazis.

Slevogt, Max (1868-1932)—painter at the forefront of German Impressionism.

Speer, Albert (1905-1981)—Hitler's leading architect and Building Inspector General for Berlin during the Third Reich; one of the few Nazis who admitted guilt during the Nuremberg War Crimes Trials; served twenty years in Spandau Prison; wrote the widely-translated bestseller *Inside the Third Reich* (1969).

Springer, Axel (1912-1985)—headed the German and then international publishing giant, the Springer Press.

Steinrück, Albert (1872-1929)—Berlin stage actor; known for his work in abstract minimalist productions.

Sternberg, Josef von (1894-1969)—film director, discoverer of Marlene Dietrich, whom he directed in *The Blue Angel* (1930); emigrated to Hollywood where he continued his work in film.

Stresemann, Gustav (1878-1929)—the most talented and effective statesman of the Weimar Republic, served as both Reich Chancellor and Foreign Minister; responsible for the 1923 currency reform, which put an end to rampant inflation; won the Nobel Prize in 1926; his death was a blow from which the Weimar Republic did not recover.

Tauber, Richard (1891-1948)—Austrian opera singer (tenor); emigrated to London in 1938.

Thorak, Josef (1889-1952)—Austrian sculptor whose work was popular in the Third Reich.

Tucholsky, Kurt (1890-1935)—author, journalist, satirist; his works were burned and banned by the Nazis in 1933; committed suicide in Sweden.

Uckermark—area in northeastern region of present-day Germany, covering parts of Brandenburg and Mecklenburg-Vorpommern.

UFA (Universum Film Aktiengesellschaft)—first and most prominent German film corporation, founded in 1917 in Berlin.

Unruh, Fritz von (1885-1970)—Expressionist author/dramatist; emigrated in 1932, eventually to the USA.

Unter den Linden—the main thoroughfare of the traditional heart Berlin, running from the Brandenburg Gate, across Friedrichstrasse, up to Alexanderplatz.

Veidt, Conrad (1893-1943)—actor; emigrated to England 1932-40 and to the USA in 1940; in *The Cabinet of Dr. Caligari* (1919).

Walden, Herwarth (1878-1941)—writer and critic, his journal *Der Sturm* (1910-1932) was a highly influential Expressionist publication; emigrated to the Soviet Union with the onset of the Third Reich; victim of Stalinist pogrom, he died in the Saratov labor camp.

Wedekind, Frank (1864-1918)—dramatist whose work greatly influenced the Expressionist movement, especially through his play *Spring's Awakening*.

Weill, Kurt (1900-1950)—composer whose most famous work was the musical score of Brecht's *Three Penny Opera* (1928); emigrated to the USA in 1935 where he continued to compose musicals and popular music.

Wilder, Billy (1906-)—film director who emigrated to the USA in 1933 where he enjoyed an extremely successful career.

Zille, Heinrich (1858-1929)—artist whose sketches documented and satirized German urban (especially working-class) life of the late nineteenth and early twentieth century.

Zuckmayer, Carl (1896-1977)—dramatist and novelist; emigrated to Switzerland in 1938 and the USA in 1939.

Zweig, Stefan (1881-1942)—novelist/dramatist; emigrated to England in 1934, briefly to the USA in 1940, and finally to Brazil; in despair over their forced exile, he and his wife committed suicide.

Max Schmeling's Professional Ring Record

1924

Aug. 2	Düsseldorf	Kurt Czapp (Düsseldorf)	W TKO—6
Sept. 19	Cologne	Willi van der Vyver (Belgium)	W KO—3
Sept. 20	Bochum	Fred Louis (Duisburg)	W KO—1
Oct. 4	Cologne	Rocky Knight (USA)	W Dec.—8
Oct. 10	Berlin	Max Dieckmann (Berlin)	L TKO—4 (cut)
Oct. 31	Cologne	Fred Hammer (Godesberg)	W KO—5
Dec. 4	Cologne	Hans Breuer (Aachen)	W KO—2
Dec. 7	Düsseldorf	Battling Mathar (France)	W KO—3
Dec. 17	Berlin	Helmuth Hartig (Potsdam)	W KO—1
Dec. 26	Cologne	Jimmy Lygget (USA)	W Disqual.—2

1925

Jan. 14	Berlin	Joe Mehling (Würzburg)	W Dec.—6
Jan. 18	Cologne	Jan Clouts (Belgium)	W KO—2
Mar. 1	Cologne	Leon Randell (Belgium)	W KO—4
Mar. 5	Cologne	Alf Baker (USA)	W Dec.—8
Apr. 3	Berlin	Jimmy Lygget (USA)	Draw—8
Apr. 23	Bonn	Fred Hammer (Godesberg)	W Dec.—8
May 9	Cologne	Jack Taylor (USA)	L Dec.—10
Jun. 14	Brussels	Leon Randell (Belgium)	Draw—10
Aug. 28	Cologne	Larry Gains (Canada)	L TKO—2 (cut)
Nov. 8	Cologne	René Gompero (France)	W Dec.—3

1926

Feb. 12	Berlin	Max Dieckmann (Berlin)	Draw—8
Mar. 19	Cologne	Willy Louis (Duisburg)	W KO—1

Jul. 13.	Berlin	August Vongehr (Berlin)	W TKO—1
Aug. 24	Berlin	Max Dieckmann (Berlin)	W KO—1 (wins German light-heavyweight title)
Oct. 1	Berlin	Hermann van't Hof (Holland)	W disqual.—8

1927

Jan. 7	Berlin	Jack Stanley (England)	W KO—8
Jan. 23	Breslau	Lode Wilms (Belgium)	W TKO—8
Feb. 4	Dresden	Joe Mehling (Würzburg)	W TKO—3
Mar. 12	Dortmund	Léon Sebrilla (France)	W KO—2
Apr. 8	Berlin	Francis Charles (France)	W KO—8
Apr. 26	Hamburg	Stanley Glen (England)	W KO—1
May 8	Frankfurt	Robert Larsen (Denmark)	W Dec.—10
May 17	Hamburg	Raymond Paillaux (France)	W KO—3
Jun. 19	Dortmund	Fernand Delarge (Belgium)	W TKO—14 (wins European light-heavyweight title)
Jul. 31	Hamburg	Jack Taylor (USA)	W Dec.—10
Aug. 7	Essen	Willem Westbrook (Holland)	W KO—1
Sept. 2	Berlin	Robert Larsen (Denmark)	W TKO—4
Oct. 2	Dortmund	Louis Clement (Switzerland)	W TKO—6
Nov. 8	Leipzig	Hein Domgörgen (Cologne)	W KO—7 (retains European light-heavyweight title)
Dec. 12	Berlin	Gypsy Daniels (England)	W Dec.—10

1928

Jan. 6	Berlin	Michele Bonaglia (Italy)	W KO—1 (retains European light-heavyweight title)
Feb. 26	Frankfurt	Gypsy Daniels (England)	L KO—1
Mar. 10	Dortmund	Ted Moore (England)	W Dec.—10
Apr. 4	Berlin	Franz Diener (Berlin)	W Dec.—15 (wins German heavyweight title)
November		Schmeling relinquishes his German heavyweight title	
Nov. 24	New York	Joe Monte (USA)	W KO—8

1929

| Jan. 4 | New York | Joe Sykra (USA) | W Dec.—10 |
| Jan. 22 | New York | Pietro Corri (USA) | W KO—1 |

Feb. 1	New York	Johnny Risco (USA)	W TKO—9
Jun. 27	New York	Paolino Uzcudun (Spain)	W Dec.—15

1930

Jun. 6	New York	Jack Sharkey (USA)	W disqual.—4 (wins world heavyweight title)

1931

Jul. 3	Cleveland	Young Stribling (USA)	W TKO—15

1932

Jun. 21	New York	Jack Sharkey (USA)	L Dec.—15 (loses heavyweight title)
Sept. 9	New York	Mickey Walker (USA)	W TKO—8

1933

Jun. 8	New York	Max Baer (USA)	L KO—10

1934

Feb. 13	Philadelphia	Steve Hamas (USA)	L Dec.—12
Jun. 13	Barcelona	Paolino Uzcudun (Spain)	Draw—12
Aug. 26	Hamburg	Walter Neusel (Bochum)	W TKO—9

1935

Mar. 10	Hamburg	Steve Hamas (USA)	W TKO—9
Jul. 7	Berlin	Paolino Uzcudun (Spain)	W Dec.—12

1936

Aug. 19	New York	Joe Louis (USA)	W KO—12

1937

Dec. 16	New York	Harry Thomas (USA)	W KO—8

1938

Jan. 1	Hamburg	Ben Foord (South Africa)	W Dec.—12
Apr. 16	Hamburg	Steve Dudas (USA)	W KO—6
Jun. 22	New York	Joe Louis (USA)	L KO—1

1939

July 2	Stuttgart	Adolf Heuser (Bonn)	W KO—1 (wins European heavyweight title)

1947

| Sept. 28 | Frankfurt | Werner Vollmer (Magdeburg) | W KO—7 |
| Dec. 12 | Hamburg | Hans-Joachim Drägestein (Berlin) | W KO—10 |

1948

May 29	Hamburg	Walter Neusel (Bochum)	L Dec.—10
Oct. 2	Kiel	Hans-Joachim Drägestein (Berlin)	W KO—8
Oct. 31	Berlin	Richard Vogt (Hamburg)	L Dec.—10

Index

∽∼∾

❦